PIECING TOGETHER

Memoirs of an Archaeologist

Piecing Together
Memoirs of an Archaeologist

B.B. Lal

Aryan Books International
New Delhi

Piecing Together:
Memoirs of an Archaeologist

ISBN: 978-81-7305-417-4 (HB)
978-81-7305-418-1 (PB)

Published in **2011** by
ARYAN BOOKS INTERNATIONAL
Pooja Apartments, 4B, Ansari Road, New Delhi-110 002 (India)
Tel.: 23287589, 23255799; Fax: 91-11-23270385
E-mail: aryanbooks@gmail.com
www.aryanbooks.co.in

Printed in India at Mudrak, Delhi-110091

Tvadīyam Vastu Govinda !
Tubhyameva Samarpaye

Unto thee, Oh Lord, is dedicated
What thou hast given me

The Second Preface

I am sure you must be wondering at the above title. And you have every reason to do so. Why is the word 'Second' there? There is a tale behind it.

The first Preface was written in February 2009. Along with it three chapters of the book itself were also completed, as well as the Epilogue. Don't ask me why the Epilogue was written before the completion of the book. An urge was felt to write it and it was written. No other explanation, please.

In March 2009 the hard disk of my computer on which I was then working crashed. The computer was sent to an expert in Nehru Place (New Delhi), requesting him to recover the data. A week's waiting. Nothing happened. No recovery. Thus, I had to have a new hard disk installed into that computer and thereafter I started once again on the theme – undaunted.

In May 2009, my eldest son, daughter-in-law, wife and I reached Los Angeles to spend a couple of months with our two other sons and their families. During that period my second son presented me a new computer and I restarted working on this book. The work has been done in a most leisurely manner, as and when I could get some spare time. Otherwise, I was busy completing the report on my excavations at Bharadvāja Āśrama, which is now almost press-ready.

The book is supposed to be an autobiography, but it is not really so. To me my life itself has been a book, which, read objectively, has revealed the eternal truth that is reflected in the Epilogue. All the chapters in between this Preface and the Epilogue are nothing but mere examples of that truth.

New Delhi
June 30, 2010

B.B. Lal

Contents

Acknowledgements

As in the case of the previous books, my son, Air Vice Marshal (Retd.) Rajesh Lal, has kindly gone through the type-script and made some valuable suggestions. He has also helped me in proof-reading. Likewise, my wife, Kusum, has also helped me in a number of ways.

Ouside the family, Shri S. K. Sharma and Shri Vishnu Kant have helped me in the preparation of the illustrations. The latter has also read the proofs. The publisher, Shri Vikas Arya, has always been very co-operative.

To all the persons mentioned above my grateful thanks are due.

List of Illustrations

FIGURES

PLATES

XXXIX. Parents of Professor Lal: Shri Ramcharan Lal and Shrimati Sarayu Devi.

XL. Professor Lal with Shrimati Indira Gandhi, the then Prime Minister of India, who released the book, *Frontiers of the Indus Civilization,* edited by Professor Lal and others.

XLI. London, 1973. Participants in an International Symposium on Undeciphered Languages. Sir Mortimer Wheeler (middle row, extreme left), Professor B.B. Lal (on the left of Sir Mortimer), Sir Max Mallowan (middle row, center), Sir Harold Bailey (Chairman, front row, middle).

XLII. Professor B.B. Lal, taking down notes, in the Tank at Śṛiṅgaverapura.

XLIII. The taught and the teacher: Professor B.B. Lal and Sir Mortimer Wheeler, on the occasion of the latter's visit to the excavations at Purana Qila, New Delhi.

XLIV. Nubia (Egypt), 1961: Above, our boat on the Nile. Below, from right, Professor B.B. Lal, Shri Azim Hussain (India's Ambassador to Egypt) and his wife and Shrimati Kusum Lal. (Courtesy ASI)

1

The Tale of My Straying into Archaeology

In 1939, after passing the Intermediate in Arts examination from Government College, Jhansi (my home town), I moved on to join the Allahabad University. I offered the following three subjects for the Bachelor of Arts degree: Mathematics, English Literature and Sanskrit. Mathematics was my first love and I had a burning desire to complete my Masters in Mathematics.

For having obtained a very high position at the Intermediate examination of the UP Board, I was awarded a scholarship of Rs. 20 per month. But this was not sufficient to meet my expenses at the university, which were estimated to be about Rs. 50 per month. Since my father, too, was not in a position to finance me, I had no choice but to privately coach High School level students in the neighborhood and thereby earn some money to square off the expenditure. One tuition was given in the morning before I left for the university and another after sunset. I was also a member of the college hockey and volley ball teams, which kept my evenings occupied. The nights, of course, were spent finishing studies.

The first year passed, as also a major part of the second. But towards the end of the second year, the enormous strain that I was undergoing began to tell upon my health. I developed fever, cold and cough. I struggled to keep up the aforesaid routine, but finally came the collapse. I was completely bed-ridden, with high fever and severe bouts of cough. The Resident Tutor of the College Hostel, Babu Jamuna Prasad, arranged for my medical treatment and personally took good care of me but all this was of no avail. My condition kept on deteriorating. I could not do any studies myself. A very dear friend of mine, Shiv Govind Dube, who was senior to me by a year and was studying for his Master of Science degree in Mathematics, used to sit by my bed-side in the evening, trying to teach me mathematics. But nothing would work, since owing to prolonged illness I could hardly grasp anything.

The D-day was drawing nigh. Only a month was left for the examination to commence. In such a situation a debate cropped up. Some of my well-wishers advised me not to take up the examination since that would definitely mean my losing the first division which I have had at all the previous examinations. I was on the horns of dilemma. My main problem was financial. If I did not appear at the examination, it would mean my studying for another year for the same B.A. degree without any scholarship, which I could ill afford; and if I did appear, it was almost certain that I wouldn't get a high position so as to get a scholarship for pursuing my Master's degree. Finally, I decided to jump into the fray. The then Vice Chancellor of the University, Dr. Amaranatha Jha, on knowing about my illness, very generously offered to provide me a scribe who would take dictation from me and write the answers. This would have worked for subjects like English and even Sanskrit but not for Mathematics. Thus, I did not accept the kind offer. I summed up all my energy and decided to face the situation as it was.

The result was a foregone conclusion. I lost the first division. But, as chance would have it, I scored the highest marks in Sanskrit. This opened a hitherto unexpected vista. I was offered the Tirthanatha Jha Scholarship in case I chose to do my M.A. in Sanskrit. I was, again, in a fix: Sanskrit with a scholarship or Mathematics without any scholarship. Taking financial considerations in view, the scale turned in favor of Sanskrit.

For the Master's degree in Sanskrit, there was a common course for the first year, which included *Sāhitya, Vyākaraṇa, Darśana*, etc. But for the final year, one had the option of choosing any one of the above subjects or there was also another section under which were taught Ancient Epigraphy, Art, Architecture, Culture, etc. I opted for the latter and that became the turning point of my career.

Since I secured a first class first at the M.A. examination, I was offered a scholarship for pursuing a research program. I planned to do my Ph. D. on a topic related to early historical archaeology of the Gaṅgā Valley. A few months later, a part-time lectureship also became available. I took seriously to my new pursuits. But something unexpected came my way.

But before I move on to that 'something unexpected', I would like to narrate an incident and an event that took place while I was still a student of the Master's course in Sanskrit at the university.

Towards the close of the academic session, we the first year M.A. students, following the usual practice, decided to give a farewell party to the final year students. Our building was a combined one, which housed besides the Sanskrit Department those of Persian and Arabic as well. In front of the building there was a lawn which we chose as the venue for the party. We needed quite a few tables to spread the various dishes on. Thus, we took the tables out from the rooms of all the teachers of our Department. After the party was over, we asked the peons, who included those from the Arabic and Persian Departments as well (we had invited them all to have a cup of tea with us), to clean up the tables and put them back in the respective rooms.

Next morning, on entering his room Dr Umesh Mishra, who used to teach us *Darśana Śāstra* (Indian Philosophy), found his table somewhat wrongly placed. He enquired the reason for it. With apologies, we told him that we had taken out his table, as those of the other teachers, the previous evening for the farewell party and, after getting them thoroughly cleaned, had placed them back in the respective rooms. Dr. Mishra was furious with us, not because we had used his table out without his permission, but because we got it cleaned by the peons who included some Muslims.

He asked his own peon to take the table out, clean it once again and then place it back in his room. We asked him, "Sir, why is this re-washing necessary?" Shouting loudly at us, he replied, "How can I use a table cleaned by a Muslim? Hence the need to get it re-washed." At this I could not contain myself. "Sir," I told him, "You are a Hindu and also a great scholar of Indian Philosophy. On both these counts you believe in re-birth. Don't you? Thus, where is the guarantee that a Hindu (I avoided saying 'you') may not be born as a Muslim or Christian in his next birth?" Dr. Mishra flared up once again. We thought that the best course for us was to quietly leave the room. So we did. Yet, I remember to this day this philosophical encounter!

Now to the 'event'. In my final year, as already stated earlier, I had opted for a course which included Ancient Epigraphy, Art and Architecture. My teacher was Professor P.K. Acharya. He was fond of organizing extra-curricular activities. Thus, he decided to stage the *Abhijñāna Śākuntalam* of Kālidāsa at the annual show and asked the Sanskrit Department to prepare for it.

For the casts, he chose one Ganguly to act as Duṣyanta and a girl named Madhuri to be the heroine, Śakuntalā. For about a week the rehearsal continued, but suddenly Madhuri backed out without assigning any reason. Naturally, this completely upset Professor Acharya; and we noticed him downcast. All of a sudden, it occurred to me that I could bail him out and I offered to him that if Madhuri had refused to act as Śakuntalā, I was willing to take up the challenge. Professor Acharya was taken aback for he never imagined that I, a male, could act like a female. Anyway, he had no choice but to make the best of a bad situation. And there I was – Kālidāsa's Śakuntalā!

I had a close friend in a class fellow, Barada Charan Bhattacharya. He gave me a great deal of logistic support. He and I went to Chowk, the shopping mall of those days. We hunted out a traditional *rangareza* (cloth-dyer) and requested him to dye a couple of *sārīs* befitting the role of Śakuntalā. One of these, I distinctly remember, was *bāghāmbarī*, which went very well with the forest set-up of Śakuntalā's habitat.

On the scheduled night, the show began in the auditorium of the university. The hall was packed to capacity. Even though most of the members of the audience did not understand Sanskrit, would you believe that the show was so much appreciated that there was an immediate demand for it to be continued for another night? In fact, the show had finally to be staged for three consecutive nights. Unprecedented success for a Sanskrit drama! Isn't it?

There is another side-light of this show, which is very personal. In 1946 my marriage was settled with Kusum, the niece of Shri H.L. Srivastava, the then Joint Director General of the Archaeological Survey of India. Those days I was living in a temporary, tented accommodation on the premises of the Central Asian Antiquities Museum, New Delhi. Shri Srivastava was living in Flat 9, Sujan Singh Park. One evening he invited me to a cup of tea at his residence. I gratefully accepted the invitation and reached his flat. No sooner than I took my seat in his drawing room, the members of the family came and joined me. Hardly a couple of minutes had passed with preliminary greetings, a lady from amongst the hosts shot at me: "I believe this is Śakuntalā of the famous Sanskrit drama that I saw at my university." She waited a while, as if wanting me to confirm her observation. I had no choice but to nod my head in affirmation. This grand lady (Shrimati Sarala Prasad), it turned out, was the maternal aunt of my would-be wife. The aunt revealed that she was studying for her M.A. in Philosophy at Allahabad University during those very years when I was doing my M.A. in Sanskrit.

I do not know if her remarks were in appreciation of my performance as Śakuntalā or a veiled comment on my ..... .

To revert to that 'something unexpected'. This is, in fact, closely related to the state of affairs those days in the Archaeological Survey of India. The Government of India felt that the Survey needed a haul-up. Sir Leonard Woolley was asked to review the situation. One amongst his recommendations was that an expert from outside (read England) be brought in to head the Survey. The result was the appointment of Dr. Mortimer Wheeler (later knighted) as its Director General in 1944.

Wheeler's basic approach was that new blood should be infused into the Survey. To this end, he toured the entire country, met with the Vice Chancellors of various universities and heads of institutes teaching archaeology and allied subjects, and requested them to recommend young students who could be trained as archaeologists. He visited my university as well, and my VC and senior faculty members unanimously recommended my name for the training.

The training camp was set up at Taxila in Punjab, now in Pakistan. Over there, long back, Sir John Marshall had excavated three successive early historical sites, namely, Bhir Mound, Sirkap and Sirsukh. He had also set up a nice site-museum and other associated establishments, including a well-furnished guest house. Wheeler stayed in that guest house while for the other members of the Survey and trainees, tented accommodation was provided.

On receiving intimation that I could go over for the training, I left Allahabad in the morning by Kalka Mail, reaching Delhi in the evening. With a night's halt in Delhi, I left for Taxila next day by the Frontier Mail. Early next morning, before sun-rise, the train steamed into Taxila railway station. Someone from the Survey's staff was already there to receive me. We reached the camp and I was put up in a tent, with accommodation for four trainees. Since I was completed exhausted with the long journey from Allahabad to Taxila and it was still some time for the sun to rise, I unfolded my bedding and slipped into it. Though it was only early November, yet it was far too cold for a UPite.

When I woke up around 8 o'clock, I heard in the neighborhood of my tent a female voice chuckling and saying something of which I could hardly make out anything. But sure enough, it was a female voice. This made me certain that the trainees included some girls as well – a cause for some satisfaction! After a little bit of rolling around in the bed, I got up and moved out of the tent. At a distance of about 40 meters I saw the back of a person with the hair hanging down all the way. I was now fully convinced that the trainees did include some girls. As I moved on to the place where this long-hair 'girl' was sitting along with others, I got the first shock of my stay at Taxila. This 'lady' was none other than Sardar Raghbir Singh, a senior draftsman in the Survey. The Sardars, as is well known, do not cut their hair, and have therefore to clean the same thoroughly as and when an opportunity offers itself. It was a Sunday and the sun was kind and bright. So Sardar Raghbir Singh did his hair-dressing. And the next shock came when one trainee barged in, asking Sardarji, "Ki khobor, apni bhalo achhen to?" in the same female voice which I had heard an hour ago. This one was Debo Prosad Guha from Calcutta (now renamed as Kolkata). I was completely de-mystified and almost felt heart-broken!

That very evening I got a message that I had to meet the great boss, Wheeler. I reached his office in the Guest House at the appointed time. Hardly had I greeted him with a "Good evening, Sir", he started, "From the records I find that you have been a student of Sanskrit and have no background of archaeology. Have you come here to recite the Vedas?" "I have some knowledge of ancient epigraphy and architecture," I replied. "But that is not field-archaeology," he added. I summed up courage and finally told him, "Sir, it is true that I have no experience of field-archaeology, but I can fully assure you that whatever is written on my blank slate will be duly retained. You need have no fears on that count." With these exchanges, the interview was over and I moved from there to the dining tent on the premises.

Next morning I reported on the field at Bhir Mound where some trainees, who had joined the camp in October, were already there. The trenches had been laid out in the Square system and I was asked to join an October-batch student as an under-trainee. After about a week I was given independent charge of one of the Squares. I began to learn 'Layerology' as we the students nick-named the technique. I also learnt how to take down notes in the Site Note Book, making sketches as and when necessary.

The basic difference between the method of digging followed by the Survey at that time and the new technique introduced by Wheeler was in brief as follows. In the previous system, the provenance of artifacts found and structures met with in the excavation was recorded in terms of their depths below a datum fixed somewhere at the site and all the inter-relationship of the objects amongst themselves and with the excavated structures was determined on the basis of their depths below that fixed datum-point. In the Wheelerian method, the basis was the soil-deposits that got accumulated at the site during the course of its occupation. These deposits could behave in many different ways. These could slope down or could be cut for the foundation-trenches of the walls concerned. Thus, it was obligatory to make a close study of these deposits. For example, an object found in a given layer at a depth of X meters below the datum-line and a wall met with at the same X depth need not necessarily be contemporary, if the layer had been cut for a foundation-trench for the wall in question. The wall would obviously be later than the layer concerned, since the latter was already there before the construction of the wall. The existence of pits could play a greater havoc. Thus, if a pit had been cut into a layer and went to a depth of 2 meters below that layer, an object found in that pit, though found 2 metres below that layer, would be later than an object found in that layer itself. Thus, the new method required a very minute observation and recording of the soil-stratigraphy of the site.

A fortnight passed. One evening, after the day's field-work was over, I was leaving the site. Just then I saw the boss down below in one of the trenches, drawing on a graph-sheet the section of the trench. I stopped to have a look at what he was drawing. The boss was an excellent draftsman. But, somehow, I felt that while the drawing was technically superb, it did not do justice to the interpretative part of the layers. There was a very large pit on the floor, the section of which was also seen in elevation part of the trench. On one side of the pit, overlying the ground-level into which it had anciently been cut, there were three successive soil-deposits which somehow did not appear on the other side of the pit. These deposits were exactly in the reverse order of what they were inside the pit. To make the point clearer, if I said that the sequence of these deposits within the pit was A, B and C from bottom upwards, in the deposits that lay on the side of the pit it was exactly in the reverse order, namely, C underlying B and B underlying A. To me the interpretation was very simple, namely, when the pit had been dug, its soil was removed step-by-step and re-deposited **only** on one side of the pit. That is why it did not appear on the other side of the pit.

The boss's drawing did not bring out the above-mentioned aspect clearly. Summing up all my courage, I told the boss what I thought about these deposits. He raised his head upwards, looked at me and bluntly told me that my experience in stratigraphy was too short to make any sense to him. I could do no better than to leave the scene and move on to the camp.

But would you believe that the next morning just when the work was resumed, the boss came running to my trench and told me in unequivocal terms that my interpretation of the stratigraphy of the trench was perfectly correct.

There was yet another confrontation with the boss within a month. This time it related to the inter-relationship between two of the excavated structures, say X and Y. The layers between these structures had anciently been disturbed. Thus, it was not possible to establish their relationship stratigraphically. The boss thought that Structure X was earlier than Y, whereas I thought that it was the other way round. To begin with, he did not agree with me but when I pointed out that some of the stones constituting Structure Y underlay those of Structure X, the boss had no option but to agree with me. There was no resentment on his face; on the other hand, I could see a mild smile of approval.

The training course at Taxila included, besides excavation, practical lessons in surveying, photography and pottery-drawing. There also was a little bit of archaeological chemistry. There were individual officers who taught us these subjects. But the boss used to peep in every now and then in order to check up how these topics were being taught. Once when I was undergoing training in surveying, he appeared on the scene and had a look at the contour map that I had prepared. He appeared to like it. Next day he asked me to go to Sirkap, an adjacent site in Taxila, and prepare a drawing of a specific part of the fortification-wall over there. I did the needful and the boss greatly appreciated the plan I had prepared.

A mess was being run for the trainees and Shri Mangat Rai was in-charge of it. He, being a Punjabi, gave preference to Punjabi food, little bothering about the taste of students from other parts of the country. The Bengalis termed his *chapātī*s (breads) as 'card-board cakes', while the South Indian students very much missed their *iḍalī*s, *barā*s and *sāmbhar*. They had, however, no option but to accept what was being offered to them. Poor things!

Referring to the trainees from South India, I am reminded of a very interesting episode. Taxila is usually cold and surely cold enough for persons hailing from South

India. To cap it all, in January it became exceedingly cold to the extent that one night it even snowed. (Such a thing, we were told, had not happened for the past three-four decades.) Next morning we found the excavated trenches full of snow and thus it was almost impossible to work. Amongst the trainees there was Shri Anujan Achan, a member of the Archaeological Department in Kerala. Having never seen a snow-fall, he was so much excited about it that he collected a handful of snow and put it in the pocket of his overcoat. Just then the boss happened to come there. Noting what Achan was doing, the boss told him to make a parcel of the snow that he had put in his pocket and send it to his home for the family to have a look at it. Was it sarcasm or just a piece of innocent humor, I couldn't understand then.

Dr. Mortimer Wheeler's next venue of action was Arikamedu, in the then French territory of Pondicherry. From this site a typical Roman ware, called the Arretine and datable to the 1st century CE, had been collected some time earlier. By carrying out a stratigraphically controlled excavation over here, Wheeler wanted to check up its horizon and thereby to provide a somewhat firmer dating to the associated Indian pottery – something which had not been attempted earlier.

A few students from the Taxila training camp were selected by Wheeler to act as Supervisors at this site, and Shri B. K. Thapar and I were amongst them. Besides, about twenty students, particularly from South India, were taken in as fresh trainees. The work continued for about three months, during which the above-mentioned objective of providing a chronological horizon to the pottery used in South India was duly achieved. Besides, some noteworthy structures were also discovered, amongst which particular mention must be made of a dockyard very close to the sea-shore.

There are a few memories (good, bad and indifferent) of this camp that I can still recall. As a Hindu, I used to have a *choṭī* (a thin tuft) amidst the hair on the hind part of my head. Some of my colleagues used to make fun of it. Thus, once when we went site-seeing in a bus, a student who was known to be very mischievous took a seat right behind me, quietly took out a pair of scissors from his pocket and chopped off my *choṭī*. Evidently, he had pre-planned the whole operation. I was greatly annoyed but there was little that I could do.

Thapar and I shared a small tent for living. At the beginning, no cots were available. Thus, we had to sleep on the floor which, however, was covered with a *durrie*. We had to spread our own beddings. One morning, on waking up I saw a large, black snake lying between our beddings. I was terrified at the sight and shouted out, waking Thapar from his slumber. We almost ran out of the tent and asked the neighbors to help us in driving away the snake. The area we were camping in was full of snakes of all descriptions. One day we saw a thin, greenish snake on a tree in the process of moving to an adjacent one. Never before had I seen a snake inhabiting a tree and was thus greatly astonished at the sight.

There were an improvised Field Laboratory and an Antiquities Section in the camp. One Shri Sheetal Banerji was in-charge of the antiquities recovered from the excavation. He was a sincere worker, but was hard of hearing. One day the boss, while walking around the trenches, learnt that a special kind of bead had been found the previous day. It was somewhat flattish in shape and had an extension at each end. In technical parlance it is known as a 'collared bead'. Realizing its significance, the boss lost no time and rushed to the Antiquities Section to have a look at it. He asked Sheetal Banerji to take out and show him the bead. Banerji couldn't follow him. The boss then held the collar of his shirt and told Banerji that it was a 'collared bead'. Even then Banerji did not follow him. Enraged at this, the boss shouted out 'you idiot' and was about to leave the place. Just then Banerji told him, 'Sir, say it again, I cannot properly hear you.' An amused boss finally left the Section without seeing the bead.

Amongst the members in the camp, there was Shri V.D. Krishnaswami who was already an employee of the Survey, working on megalithic sites in South India. Wheeler thought that Krishnaswami, too, should be inducted into the new techniques of excavation and thus asked him to join the camp. Once, in an effort to please Wheeler, Krishnaswami organized a dance-show by local artists. He, along with the artistes, profusely garlanded the boss and made the singers sing his praise. Unfortunately, all this had no effect on the boss and poor Krishnaswami was greatly disappointed.

At Pondicherry was located the *āśrama* of Shri Aurobindo and it was only on rare occasions that the general public could have his *darśana.* On one such occasion, I wanted to visit Shri Aurobindo's *āśrama* and pay my obeisance to him. I requested the boss to grant me half-day leave so that I could go to Pondicherry. He flatly turned down my request. When I repeatedly pleaded for a reconsideration of his decision, he very reluctantly agreed to let me go. To Wheeler, work alone seemed to be worship. The spiritual side of life had, perhaps, no meaning for him. Anyway, I got my half-day off and got the satisfaction of having seen the great saint in flesh and blood.

After the excavation at Arikamedu was over, I went back to Allahabad and started preparing myself for a likely interview for the posts of officers in the Survey, which, I gathered informally, were soon to be advertised in the newspapers. The day came, but I was shocked to find in the advertisement that the minimum age of the applicants should be 25 years. I immediately wrote to the boss: "I am sure you must have seen the advertisement inviting applications for the posts of Assistant Superintendents. The lower age-limit is twenty-five, whereas I am only twenty-three. Evidently, therefore, I cannot apply for the post. I must, however, let you know that you have wasted your time and my time, your energy and my energy in training me. But before I lay down my arms, I would like you to answer a simple question: Do you think I will put more brains in myself after two years?"

At that point of time the boss was out on a tour, in Bombay. His Personal Assistant, Shri Bishu Babu, when he met me later, told me that on receipt of my letter the boss was very much upset, but took a flash decision to send me a telegram, 'Suggest apply irrespective of age.' On return to Shimla, the then headquarters of the Survey, the boss phoned the Secretary, Ministry of Education, Health and Land (as it was then called) in Delhi, apprising the latter of the situation and requesting him to lower the age-limit to twenty-three. The Secretary, a seasoned bureaucrat, gave a reply in the negative. Thereupon the boss told the Secretary that he (Wheeler) had specially been invited by the then Viceroy to set the Survey right and if he failed to recruit the right persons for the job, he would prefer to leave. The threat seems to have worked since the lower age-limit was relaxed to twenty-three!

Thus, I was called for the interview which too was held at Shimla, the then headquarters of the Union Public Service Commission. At the interview I was placed first in order of merit out of all the candidates selected for the posts. This gave me an immense advantage in going up the ladder in the Survey.

The foregoing is in brief the story of my straying into archaeology and even gate-crashing into the Archaeological Survey of India.

2

Baḍe Hakim Ji of Datia

The illness that had overtaken me in Allahabad prior to my B.A. examination did not leave me. It continued even after my return to Jhansi. Over there the doctors at the Civil Hospital were consulted and they all thought that it was a case of pulmonary tuberculosis. Besides fever and cough, there were regular night-sweats, which were regarded as sure signs of TB. The doctors advised that I should be admitted to Bhowali Sanitarium and necessary reservations were made.

Meanwhile, some friends of the family, who were known to the Baḍe Hakimji of Datia, a State capital hardly 30 kilometers from Jhansi, suggested that before going to Bhowali we should go to Datia and consult the Hakimji. A drowning person attempts to catch every straw that comes his way. So we went to Datia. There was no logistic problem since my maternal uncles used to live there. However, on reaching Datia, we discovered that the Hakimji had accompanied the Maharaja Saheb to Seondha and would not be back before a fortnight. We had no option but to wait, though the wait was full of agony.

Finally, when the Hakimji returned to Datia, my father, one of the maternal uncles and I called on him. The maternal uncle, who already knew the Hakimji, introduced us to him. Hakimji asked us to see him the next morning, bringing with us a sample of my urine. We did that. The Hakimji asked me to shake the bottle of the urine in which he observed certain particles. What these were I wouldn't know. Anyway, he prescribed the *arqa-gaza*, a liquid essence of a bush that grows on the banks of rivers. Would you believe that there was no temperature in the evening and no sweats in the night? An unbelievable miracle, indeed! Later on, the Hakimji prescribed a tonic called *motī-mahalūl* (a tonic based on pearls), which helped me to fully recover within a fortnight.

After staying for a week more in Datia, just to ensure that the symptoms of the illness did not return, we planned to go back to Jhansi. Thus, one morning my father and I went to Hakimji's place to take our leave of him. My father offered a sum of Rs. 100 to the Hakimji towards his fees for the treatment. The Hakimji refused to accept it. Thinking that the amount may be less for the status of the Maharaja Shaeb's Baḍe Hakimji, my father doubled it up and offered him Rs. 200. At this the Hakimji became rather angry and told my father, *"amān, ina rupayon se laḍake ko achchhī gizā khilāo to waha jaldī tagaḍā ho jāyagā, mujhe yaha rupaye kyon bekāra men dete ho?"* (Dear one, spend this money on providing good diet to your son so that he may recover soon. Why are you giving it to me?) So very generous was the Hakimji. He was content with what the State Exchequer gave him as his monthly salary and never took any money from the patients.

The Hakimji was really not very well-off financially. I never saw him in fine clothes except when he visited the Maharaja Saheb. His food-habits were not at all lavish and an aura of simplicity always surrounded him. He would go the market and do his own shopping. Once I saw him standing in front of a grocer's shop with a basket in his left hand. He was ordering various items – from wheat flour and *dāla* (lintel) to *ghee* (clarified butter), since that evening he had to feed about fifty destitutes from the neighborhood. I have never come across any other highly qualified physician, so much self-negating and affectionate as the Baḍe Hakimji of Datia.

3

The 1942 'Quit India' Movement

Way back, around 1931, when I was a student of Class V, a teacher used to come home to coach me in mathematics – a subject which very much fascinated me and which I wanted to pursue later on. (Unfortunately, I couldn't, as mentioned in an earlier chapter.) One day, after the coaching was over, the teacher told me that he would not be able to come with effect from the following day. I asked him the reason. He simply told me that he had plans to resign from his post in the school and was going to join the 'Non-Cooperation Movement' for which a call had been given by Mahatma Gandhi. I couldn't make out anything of what he said then. He then explained to me that Gandhiji had launched this Movement in order to demand freedom from the British rule over the country. At that age – I was only ten, I did not know much about the British rule but felt excited over the idea that foreigners had no right to rule us and they should leave us to ourselves.

On August 9, 1942, Gandhiji gave the clarion call, asking the British Government to 'Quit India'. The message spread like a wild fire which engulfed the entire country. Besides the other sections of the society, teachers and student community came to the fore. That year I was studying for my M.A. First Year at the Allahabad University. Along with thousands of us, I too left the classroom to join the movement. To begin with, we marched in a procession to the District Magistrate's office and staged a *dharanā* in front of it. We also shouted slogans like *'Angrezo! Bhārata Chhoḍo'*. The police charged us with batons, asking us to disperse. When we refused to comply, the police force got aggressive and finally started firing at us with their guns. Some of us got injured and one of our colleagues succumbed to the police bullets. The agitation continued for days together, but there was little response from the Government.

After about a fortnight the students decided to spread out to rural areas and carry on the mission of awakening the *janatā* (masses) against the British rule. I had a very close friend at the University, named Swami Saran. He and I decided to work together. We left for Banda, where I had a near relation of mine and thus found it convenient to operate from there. In different parts of the town and its neighborhood, we delivered lectures and distributed pamphlets. After about a week we decided to go to our respective places. He went to Gwalior and I to Jhansi.

In Jhansi I met a school friend, Ram Babu, who was serving in the local Municipal Office. Being in government service, he could not come out in the open and deliver lectures. Thus, we decided to go with pamphlets only. We used to prepare the pamphlets at his house during the night and I alone would go round the city and neighboring villages to distribute them. This went on for about a week, when a young Muslim boy, who was known to Ram Babu, offered to join us. We did not know that this boy had been hired by the local police to keep a watch over our activities.

Thus, within a few days of his joining us, a police squad raided the house of Ram Babu and recovered the anti-British pamphlets that had been prepared by us. Poor Ram Babu was straightaway arrested and imprisoned.

That day, in the morning, I had left for Rakasa, a village close to Jhansi, with a view to distributing the literature. This was also the village where my sister's father-in-law lived. I went and stayed with them. The father-in-law was an influential person in the village and even the village policemen knew and respected him. After the arrest of Ram Babu, the Jhansi Police set out to collect information about me. On learning that I had gone to Rakasa, two of the Jhansi policemen left for that place and contacted the local police. My sister's father-in-law came to know what was going on in the local police station. He immediately made me burn the entire anti-British literature that I had carried with me. After about an hour, the police raided the house, but to their dismay found nothing 'incriminating'. Even then the Jhansi policemen arrested and handcuffed me and took me with them to Jhansi Police Headquarters, putting me behind the bars in the *Hawālāt*. In spite of using their usual third-degree methods of enquiry, they could not establish any charges against me. Hence, they let me off.

Meanwhile, my father who was at that time posted in Moth, a Tahsil Headquarters in District Jhansi, came to know about my arrest. He rushed to Jhansi and took me away to Moth in order to keep me under strict surveillance. Though my father, too, was a nationalist, he had to take such a step, since the government had warned him that if he did not keep his son under control, he would lose his job. I had no option but to abide by my father's wishes.

For about two months, I was practically under house-arrest. My friend, Ram Babu, however, was in the jail in Jhansi. I gathered information about the kind of food that was being served to him and decided to at least follow him in this regard. Thus, I ate only once a day and took two *chapātīs* and some *dāl*. I wish I could have been his companion in the jail, but that wasn't to be.

After about two months, the University re-opened and I went back to Allahabad for my studies, quite dissatisfied with my role in the 'Quit India Movement'.

4

Harappa 1946

On being selected as an Assistant Superintendent in the Survey, I was called upon to join Wheeler in his excavations at Harappa in Montgomery (now called Sahiwal) District of Punjab. This site had earlier been excavated by Pandit M.S. Vats, but Wheeler was in search of something altogether new. He was looking for a fortification-wall and he did find it around one of the mounds, called AB. A great achievement, indeed, but unfortunately thoroughly misinterpreted in terms of historical perspective.

As usual, students from different universities had been invited to Harappa for training in the new excavation techniques. The excavation also attracted a number of eminent scholars. It was our practice to request the visiting dignitaries to deliver lectures. On one such occasion, Dr. V.S. Agrawal was the guest lecturer. During the course of his talk, he referred to a Vedic verse in which Indra was described as *puraṁdara*, meaning 'destroyer of forts'. Wheeler was greatly attracted by this reference and at once came to the conclusion that the Vedic Aryans (represented by Indra in the given verse) were invaders who destroyed the Harappan Civilization (*Ancient India*, No. 3, 1947, p. 82). This postulation of Wheeler has since taken a thorough beating and no one any longer believes in the Aryan Invasion theory. Anyway, there is little doubt that Wheeler's excavation at Harappa did add new dimensions to our knowledge of the Harappan Civilization.

There were some episodes at Harappa which seem worth mentioning. Wheeler's wife, Margaret, was in-charge of a trench in which a circular brick-platform had been exposed. She was required, as a supervisor, also to draw its plan and a section across it. Wheeler had asked her to complete the drawings at the earliest. It was the month of June. The mercury had gone up to 118 degrees Fahrenheit. During this month, dust storms were also a usual feature. Mrs. Wheeler had started work on the drawings in all seriousness, but it had to be suspended that evening because of a very heavy dust-storm which blinded the eyes. As chance would have it, tearing the dust-storm Wheeler appeared on the scene. He found his wife sitting in a corner of the trench covering the eyes with her hands. Wheeler lost no time and started shouting at her for suspending the work. I happened to be in a nearby trench and, on hearing the boss's roar, rushed to Mrs. Wheeler's trench. I tried to plead on behalf of the lady by drawing the boss's attention to the blinding dust-storm. As was to be expected, he doubled up the pitch of his voice and shouted at me as well: "This is your weather. I have not brought it from England. If I can work in it, why can't you people?" I had no answer. After a while when Wheeler left the scene, the poor lady sobbingly spoke to me, "Look here Lal, this is the kind of husband I have to put up with." Again, I had no answer.

There is yet another episode, but more personal in nature. In that very month of June, I saw my father walking down to the camp, with his luggage placed on the back of a donkey. From the Harappa Road railway station, there was no regular vehicular transport and passengers had no option but to foot the distance – four miles or so. Had my father informed me of his visit in advance, I would have arranged a vehicle and gone to the railway station to receive him. But on purpose he hadn't, because had he written to me about the mission of his visit, for certain I would have advised him not to come. He had settled my marriage and had come to Harappa to request my boss to grant me a fortnight's leave so that I could go to my home town for the marriage. When he met Wheeler and, through me as an interpreter (my father did not know English enough to converse with Wheeler), conveyed to the latter his request to grant me leave, Wheeler jumped up and said, "How ridiculous. Don't you see that the excavation is in progress and your son is deeply involved in it. This work cannot wait. The marriage certainly can." When my father told him that according the pandit certain dates in June were most auspicious for the marriage, Wheeler retorted by saying, "There can't be anything more auspicious than one's duty." My father had no option but to return, highly disappointed.

5

Brahmagiri 1947

From Harappa the scene shifted to Brahmagiri. By now I was promoted as Superintendent in-charge of the Excavation Branch of the Survey. (At that point of time there was only one Excavation Branch, whereas there are about half-a-dozen now.) My Superintendentship notwithstanding, the overall direction of the excavation at Brahmagiri was that of Wheeler. The objective of the excavation was to determine the exact interrelationship between the three cultural entities that were expected to be encountered at the site, viz., the Southern Neolithic Culture, the Megalithic Culture and an early historical culture called the 'Andhra Culture'.

The excavations revealed that the Southern Neolithic Culture, characterized by polished stone axes, some microliths and a grey burnished pottery, well preceded the subsequent Megalithic Culture. We did not have in use at that point of time the Carbon-14 method of dating, hence no absolute or near-absolute dating was arrived at for the Neolithic Culture. However, it may be placed in the 1st millennium BCE, with a somewhat earlier beginning.

The Megalithic Culture, as the name suggests, had the megaliths as its distinctive identity. These included pit-circles and cists. The available evidence indicated that the former may have been used for a primary exposure of the dead body, from where selected bones and skulls were collected and interred into the cists. The cists had four vertical slabs, called orthostats, forming a kind of chamber in which the skeletal remains were placed. The chamber was covered with a large stone, named as 'capstone', over and around which stone-rubble was scattered, the entire complex being further surrounded by a ring of stone boulders. A great deal of pottery was also placed in these graves. It was a black-and-red ware – black inside and black-and-red on the exterior. The technique used for the firing of this kind of pottery is known as 'inverted firing', in which the pots are placed upside-down in the kiln.

The uppermost culture complex met with at this site was the 'Andhra Culture'. It is characterized by a russet-coated and painted red ware. In these levels was also found the 'Rouletted Ware' for which a firm chronological horizon in the 1st-2nd century CE had already been arrived at because of its association with the Roman Arretine Ware at Arikamedu.

Though I had been married a few months earlier (in January 1947), my wife did not travel with me to Brahmagiri. Her uncle and aunt, who had brought her up after her parents' death, perhaps thought that it would be too uncomfortable for her to be out in a camp. Anyway, my mother agreed to accompany me and look after me. We stayed in a tented accommodation and, though we had a help, she looked after the kitchen.

Joining us during the excavations were a French archaeologist, Jean-Mari Casal, and his wife. They were very nice persons and stayed in a tent next to ours. It is interesting that my mother met Mrs. Casal quite often and, though neither of them knew the other's language, they passed quite some time in the company of each other. It remained a mystery to me as how they managed to communicate their thoughts. The Casals became so friendly with us that during their future visits to Delhi, they came and stayed with us at our residence, D 127, Satya Marg, Chankyapuri. In fact, we used to have a very nice photograph (now misplaced) in which there are the Casals lighting the lamps and celebrating the Diwali at our place.

6

Śiśupālgarh 1948

The contract of Wheeler with the Government of India expired in 1948 and he left the Survey, handing over its charge to Dr. N.P. Chakravarti. After Wheeler's departure, I was placed in independent charge of excavation activities, even though I was only 27 then. My first field-work was at Śiśupālgarh, a site near Bhuvaneshvar, the capital of Orissa.

As one comes out of Bhuvaneshvar and moves in a south-easterly direction about three kilometers on the road to Puri, one notices on the left the massive fortifications surrounding Śiśupālgarh. Forming a rough square on plan and oriented along the cardinal directions, the fortification-walls rise approximately to a height of about 8-10 meters above the surrounding ground level. On plan, each arm measures a little over a kilometer and is marked out by two prominent, outward-projecting gateways. Circumscribing the fortifications is a moat which drew its water from a river flowing a little away on the east (Pl. I).

The setting of Śiśupālgarh is in an interesting historical environment. About 5 kilometers to the south-south-east

Pl. I. Air-view of Śiśupālgarh, 1948, showing the fortifications with two major gateways on each side. The zig-zag band around the fort is a streamlet, probably an ancient moat. (Courtesy ASI)

Pl. II. Bowl of Painted Grey Ware, Pānīpat. (Courtesy ASI)

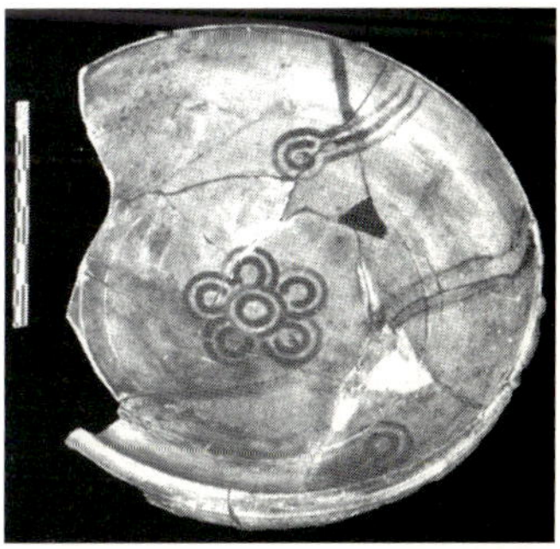

Pl. III. Dish of Painted Grey Ware, Ahichchhatrā. (Courtesy ASI)

Pl. IV. Hastināpura: The erosion-line (pointed out by the man) left by a flood that brought to an end the Painted Grey Ware settlement at the site. (Courtesy ASI)

Pl. VI. Kalibangan: An inscribed potsherd.The overlap of letters shows that the direction of writing in the Harappan script was from right to left. (Courtesy ASI)

Pl. V. Hastināpura: Boring in the river-bed adjacent to the mound. It brought to light potsherds of the PGW period, from a depth of about 15 meters. (Courtesy ASI)

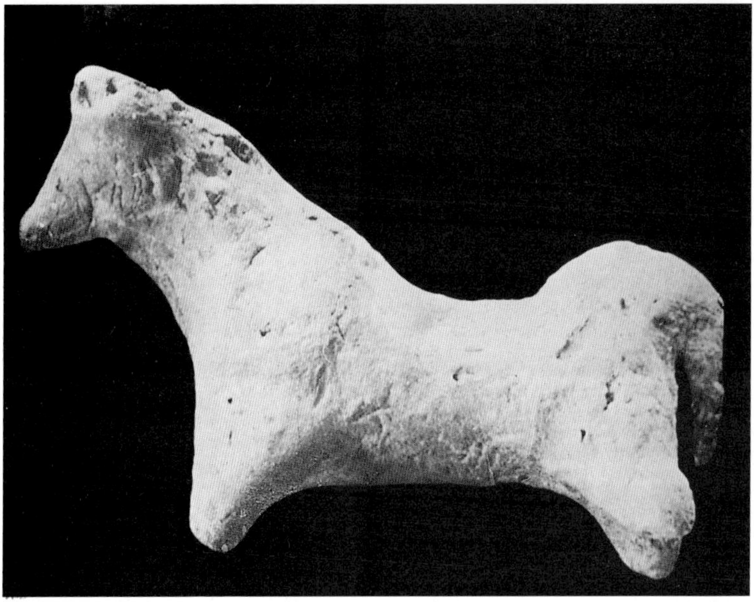

Pl. VII. Lothal: terracotta horse, Mature Harappan. (Courtesy ASI)

Pl. VIII. Kalibangan: Criss-cross furrows of an Early Harappan agricultural field. (Courtesy ASI)

Pl. IX. Kalibangan: Modern system of ploughing, which also has a criss-cross pattern. (Courtesy ASI)

Pl. X. Kalibangan: Modern field with mustard plants in the widely-distanced furrows and those of gram in the others. (Courtesy ASI)

Pl. XI. Kalibangan: A 'fire-altar' in a house in the Lower Town. (Courtesy ASI)

Pl. XII. Kalibangan: A row of seven 'fire-altars' on a platform in the southern half of the Citadel. (Courtesy ASI)

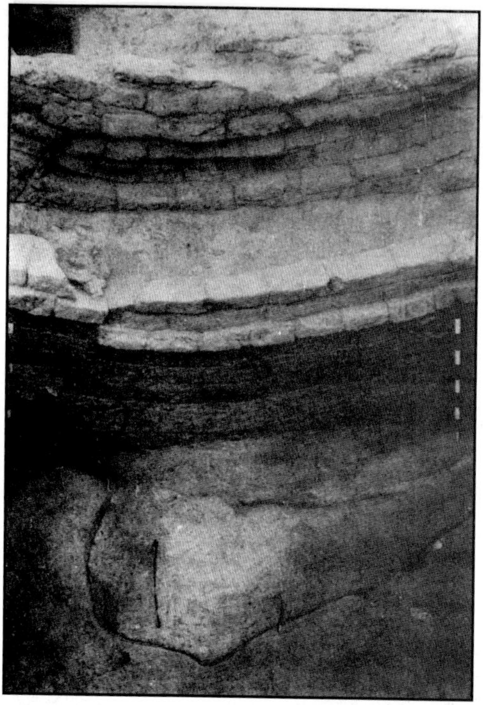

Pl. XIII. Kalibangan: Faulted walls of the Early Harappan Period, resulting from an earthquake. (Courtesy ASI)

Pl. XIV. Kalibangan: A street in the Lower Town. Mark that there was no encroachment on the street, although there were many phases of reconstruction of the walls. (Courtesy ASI)

Pl. XV. Bharadvāja Āśrama: A view of one of the trenches. In it two successive structures were met with in the Gupta levels. Lower down there were no structures, but only deposits of sandy loam in which there occurred stray potsherds of the Northern Black Polished Ware and lumps of clay with reed-marks, the latter indicative of wattle-and-daub huts. (Courtesy ASI)

Pl. XVI. Śṛiṅgaverapura: A view of Tank B. At the bottom may be seen one of the many wells which were dug down to the sub-soil water, so that during the summer, if need be, the underground water could supplement that of the tank. (Courtesy ASI)

Pl. XVII. Ayodhyā: View of a trench in the Janmabhūmi area, showing pillar-bases constructed of brick-bats with occasional use of stones. (Courtesy ASI)

Pl. XVIII. An archaeologist tries to deny the individual identity of the pillar-bases by drawing a black line along their right-hand edges and thereby calling them a 'wall'. (Mandal's 1994 book, Pl. III)

are the Dhauli hills where on a granite boulder are engraved the edicts of the great emperor Aśoka, addressed to the *mahāmātra*s of Tosali. About 10 kilometers in the north-north-westerly direction are the Khaṇḍagiri-Udayagiri hills where in one of the caves is the famous inscription of King Khāravela narrating the principal events of his life year by year. However, nothing was known about the antiquity of Śiśupālgarh itself until revealed by the excavations, a brief summary of which is given below.

The habitation deposits inside the fort accounted for a thickness of about 8 meters, without any break of occupation. At that time (1948) the technique of Carbon-14 dating was not available in India. Hence, the dating was done on the basis of the material obtained at the site itself. From a depth of about 6½ meters from the surface were found the earliest examples of the black-and-red ware, which could broadly be assigned to circa 4th-5th century BCE. (In the Report published in *Ancient India,* No. 5, pp. 62-105, the earliest occurrence of this ware was placed in late 3rd-early 2nd century BCE, as per the then prevailing date for it, which, in the light of the recent evidence, was far too conservative.) A few shards of the Rouletted Ware, datable to the 1st century CE, occurred around 3½ meters below the surface. In the strata adjacent to the defences and in other excavated areas were found Kushan as well as what are known as the 'Puri-Kushan' coins. Thus, the site can be placed broadly between the 5th century BCE and 4th century CE.

The layout of the township is, indeed, very interesting. As mentioned earlier, there were two major gateways on each side of the fortifications. Although only small segments of the site have been excavated (including the recent work by a joint team of Deccan College, Pune and the University of California, Los Angeles), indications are that the streets ran north-south and east-west, crossing one another at right angles. If further excavations are carried out, it will be found

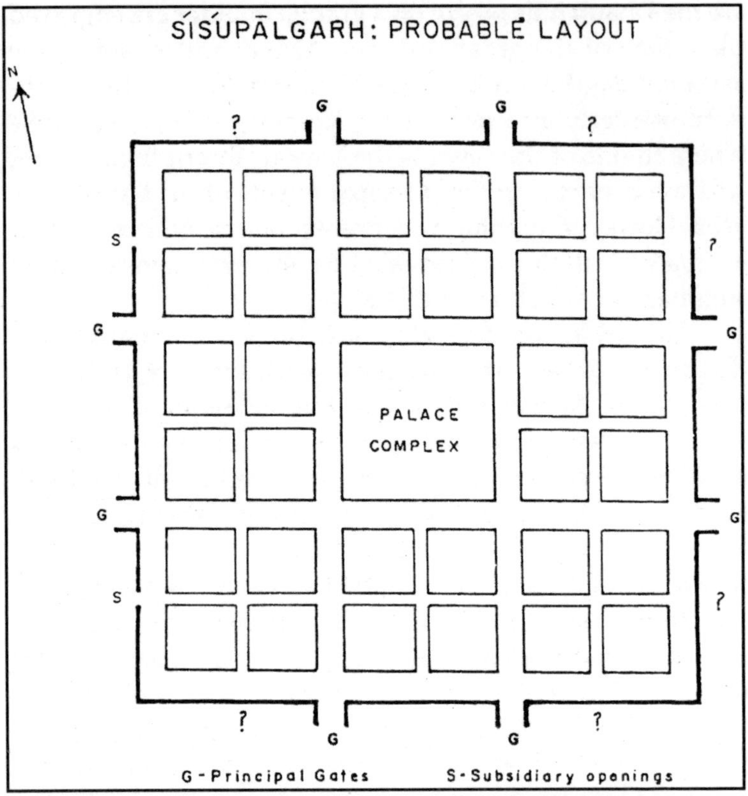

Fig. 1. Śiśupālgarh: Probable layout of the settlement.

that these streets ran all through the township, connecting the two gates on the north to their counterparts on the south. A similar pattern of streets will be found in the east-west direction (Fig. 1). In an area already excavated, an east-west street was found paved with stones and on each side of it there were houses. The stone used in all the constructions was laterite, which is found in abundance in the neighborhood. In the central part of the town there stand many pillars. Though this area was not excavated by me, a surmise was, nevertheless, made that these might belong to a palace-complex or some such edifice. The recent work just referred to above seems to confirm this guess.

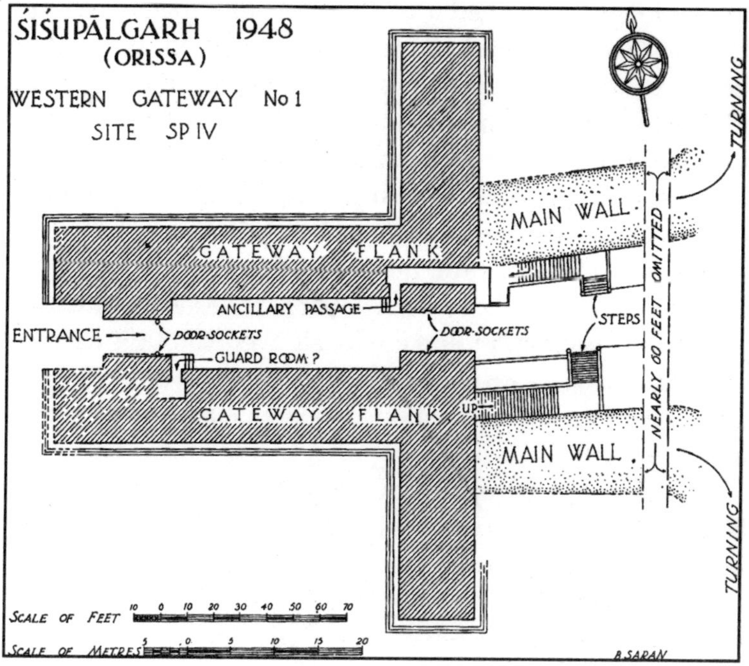

Fig. 2. Śiśupālgarh: Plan of the northern gateway on the western side. (Courtesy ASI)

A section cut across the fortification wall on the western side revealed that it consisted of a basal mud rampart over which there stood a superstructure with earthen core and veneer of kiln-fired bricks. The fortification did not come up right at the beginning, but a little later, as is indicated by the presence of some occupation deposit underneath it.

Of the eight gateways, the one on the western side, south of the north-west corner, was excavated (Fig. 2). It revealed a very interesting plan. Here the two ends of the fortification-wall turned westwards where each one was joined by a massive L-shaped structure made of large-sized laterite blocks. Juxtaposed to each of the shorter arms there were flights of steps which led to an upper storey, constructed of kiln-fired bricks. The passageway, flanked by the longer arms, had a width of about 8 meters. Within the passage deep cart-tracks were identified, indicating heavy in-and-out vehicular traffic. However, there was an elaborate arrangement for controlling entry into the township. Doors, as indicated by the presence of door-sockets, were provided at two points, one at the beginning of the passage on the western end and another a little over half-way up towards the interior. It appears that at some time in the night these doors were closed for vehicular traffic, but pedestrian entry was allowed through narrow ancillary passages provided through the body of the longer arms near the above-mentioned doors. What a thoughtful arrangement!

It may not be out of place to tell the reader that a Sanskrit text on polity, namely, the *Arthaśāstra* of Kauṭilya, ascribable to circa 4th century BCE, gives a detailed description of what a fort ought to be like (cf. the translation of the text by Shamasastry, 1960: 50-55). Some portions of it are quoted below:

> At a distance of four *daṇḍa*s (about 7.4 meters) from the ditch, a rampart, six *daṇḍa*s high and twice as much broad, shall be erected by heaping mud upwards. (The text uses the expression *khātādvapram kāryet*, implying that the earth obtained in the course of digging the moat is to be used for the construction of the rampart. .....)
>
> Above the rampart, parapets in odd or even numbers with an intermediate space of from 12 to 24 *hasta*s from each other shall be built of bricks and raised to a height of twice their breadth. ....
>
> Having made on both sides the rampart bulge out to extent of a *daṇḍa*-and-a-half, an entrance gate (to the fort) one-sixth as broad as the width of the street shall be fixed. ....
>
> A turret above the gates and starting from the top of the parapet shall be constructed up to three-fourths of its height. ....

> Demarcation of the ground inside the fort shall be made first by opening three royal roads from west to east and three from south to north. ....
>
> The fort shall contain twelve gates, provided with both a land and a water way and a secret passage. ....
>
> In the midst of the houses of the people of all the four castes and to the north of the center of the ground inside the fort, the king's palace, facing either the north or the east as described elsewhere (Chapter XX, Book I), be constructed occupying one-ninth of the whole site inside the fort.

These descriptions given in the *Arthaśāstra* tally by and large with the already excavated remains at Śiśupālgarh, except that, being not so large a fort as envisaged in the *Arthaśāstra,* it has only eight gateways. However, there is a lot more that has to be done at the site. The *Arthaśāstra* even indicates the areas to be occupied by the members of the different castes. Thus, for example, it goes on to say:

> On the eastern side (of the king's palace), merchants trading in scents, garlands, grains and liquids, together with expert artisans and people of Kṣatriya caste shall have their habitation.
>
> To the south, the superintendents of the city, of commerce, of manufactories and of the army as well as those who trade in cooked rice, liquor and flesh, besides prostitutes, musicians, and people of Vaiśya caste shall live.
>
> To the west, artisans manufacturing worsted threads, cotton threads, bamboo-mats, skins, armors, weapons and gloves, as well as the people of the Śūdra caste, shall have their dwellings.
>
> To the north, the royal tutelary deities of the city, ironsmiths, artisans working on precious stones, as well as Brāhmaṇas shall reside.

It might reasonably be asked, how does one identify the residences of the Brāhmaṇas, Kṣatriyas, Vaiśyas and

Śūdras? While, admittedly, there is no easy yardstick by which this can be determined, at the same time this need not necessarily pose an insurmountable difficulty. Perhaps the houses of the first three *varṇa*s would be larger than those of the Śūdras. Perhaps their plans would also be different. Besides, it is likely that in the houses of the Brahmaṇas *yajñaśālā*s and *havan-kuṇḍa*s may be discovered; those of the Kṣatriyas might yield evidence of bows, arrows, swords and shields; those of Vaiśyas may contain trading equipment and precious goods; while those of the Śūdras may perhaps be devoid of any noteworthy possessions. This is only a tentative supposition. Anyway, what is called for is that large-scale horizontal excavations should be carried out on all the four sides of the palace-complex to get a clear picture of the nature of the houses. The site must be thoroughly excavated and preserved. It is ideally suited for cultural tourism.

The interim report on the excavations at Śiśupālgarh (published in *Ancient India*, No. 5, 1949, pp. 62-105) drew the attention of scholars the world over. Commenting on it, the distinguished archaeologist of Edinburgh University, Professor Stuart Piggott, wrote in *Antiquity* (No. 9, September 1951) as follows:

> The interim report on Sisupalgarh is a model of its kind, admirably arranged and illustrated .... Several of us, the reviewer in particular, have been sharply critical of the fieldwork reports on oriental sites. The criticism has been prompted by the belief that the exacting standards built up in Europe on the basis of such traditions as of Pitt-Rivers or the German Lines Commission could perfectly well be applied east of the Suez if only the problem was approached in the right way. And it is now clear that with such work as that of Mr. Lal reviewed above, India is applying these standards and leading the way among the eastern nations in scientific examination of her past.

7

The Yawning Gap and I

While the excavations at Śiśupālgarh did no doubt give me immense satisfaction, there was still something that was haunting my mind and making me uneasy. This was a deep urge to enquire into what the archaeological scenario was after the gradual decline of the Harappan Civilization around 2000 BCE and before the well-known cultural assemblage associated with the Northern Black Polished Ware (NBPW) whose beginning was then adjudged to be around 600 BCE. This yawning gap of more than a millennium was something which I could not accept lying down, particularly since a good deal of the traditional history of the country appears to have belonged to this period.

Where then to look for such sites as might throw light on this 'dark' period was the next question. Sites ascribable to a devolutionary stage of the Harappan Civilization were known to exist in the area lying between the upper reaches of the Gaṅgā and Yamunā in north-western Uttar Pradesh. To the south-east of this area was a fairly heavy concentration of sites belonging to the NBPW. It was, thus, thought that somewhere here was the region which might provide the answer. And thus began the hunt. To begin with, about half-a-dozen sites were explored. The already-exposed sections at some of them showed that beneath the NBPW there lay a very specific kind of pottery distinguished by its grey fabric and painted designs in black color (called thereafter the Painted Grey Ware and abbreviated as PGW). This was very encouraging since at least one stage backwards from the NBPW had been identified.

The exploration work was intensified and within a couple of months more than a dozen sites of the PGW were put on the map. It was also noted that many of these sites were associated, either through literary evidence or local oral tradition, with the *Mahābhārata* story. While I shall deal with the culmination point of these explorations a little later, here I feel tempted to narrate the odd experiences – sometimes even harrowing – we had during the course of our operations.

I shall begin with Amin, a small town in Thaneshwar Tehsil of Karnal District of Panjab. Local tradition associates it with Abhimanyu, son of Arjuna of the *Mahābhārata* fame. The ancient mound, which is fairly large and rises to a height of about 15 meters above the surrounding plains, is heavily overloaded with recent houses. It was the month of July and we – Shri B. K. Thapar, at that time my Technical Assistant, myself and an attendant named Girja Ram – were moving all the way around the periphery of the mound looking for an exposed section which could possibly reveal the stratification of the site. Several hours of search yielded no result. We were thoroughly drenched in the July rains and when these stopped for a while, the bright sun took our toll. Foolishly, we had taken with us nothing to eat and whatever little water that we had carried had exhausted in no time. Those days we had no vehicle at our disposal and it was no easy job to go back to the base-camp which was several kilometers away. Finally, we decided to send Girja Ram on a food-hunt. There was not even a *dhābā* nearby and all that Girja Ram could bring back were *bhune chanā* (fried grams) and *gur* (jaggery). We had to be content with this. And for water, there was 'water, water everywhere but not a drop to drink'. Howsoever we were tempted to drink the rain-water, the fear that it might lead to infection prevented us from doing so.

We then decided to give up our hunt around the periphery and move up to the top where we could see some houses, hoping that some kind soul might give us some water to drink. We reached a well near the top of the mound where some people were engaged in taking mud out of it. The well had run dry and the only way to restore its water-supply was to de-silt it. All three of us sat down near the well and when we were about to request these people to give us some water to drink, our eyes fell on the silt that had been taken out of the well and dumped nearby. And lo and behold, there were stray pieces of the PGW in it. We forgot all about water and started turning the silt upside down. And the reward: at least a dozen pieces of the PGW. What an immense satisfaction! Of course, the kind villagers provided us not only with water but also something to eat. Like winning warriors we returned to our camp and celebrated the 'victory' by 'sacrificing' a *murgā* and having chicken curry and *tandoorī rotī* for dinner. (At that point of time I was a thorough non-vegetarian.)

I will now narrate another experience which was no less exacting and certainly more harrowing. The site concerned was Tilpat, ancient Tilprastha, which according to oral tradition was one of the five villages the Pāṇḍavas had demanded to be given to them by the Kauravas in order to avoid a war. The ancient mound, nearly 10 meters high above the surrounding ground level, lies a little away to the east of the Delhi-Mathura highway, about 20 kilometers south of Delhi. Madness knows no reasoning, and thus we decided right in the hottest part of the year – June – to do some trial-trenching at this site in order to ascertain if, like other Mahābhārata sites, this one too contained the Painted Grey Ware. Thapar and I decided to jump into the fray. With us was also a photographer, whose name I am unable to recollect right now. The Headquarters' Office generously placed at our disposal a military truck which was given to it after the end of the Second World War. It was as rickety as one could imagine, but beggars are not choosers and we thankfully accepted the offer. Thus began our attack on Tilpat.

We laid out two small-sized vertical trenches in different parts of the site in order to cross-check our findings. The site is heavily loaded, from the top downwards, with medieval, Gupta, Kushan and Śunga material. Piercing these strata we reached the NBPW levels. And underlying these were deposits yielding the 'hunt', viz., the Painted Grey Ware. There was no other cultural material below the PGW strata. The natural soil had been reached.

We worked at this site for nearly four weeks, drenched in sweat throughout the day. We carried our lunch-packets with us and consumed the same during mid-day break. There was no shade of a tree nearby, almost all the trees having been cut away by the villagers for procuring fire-wood. Hence, we were obliged to slip underneath the truck to have a little post-lunch siesta. One day when, lying down on our backs, we pushed ourselves beneath the truck we found a six-foot long, dark-complexioned guest waiting to greet us. He raised his hood and started hissing. Panic-stricken, we hurriedly pushed ourselves out. After a short while, the guest very kindly decided to leave, but so much shaken were we that that day we decided to forego our (little) rest. Anyway, our objective had been achieved and in a couple of days we wound up our show.

The discovery of the Painted Grey Ware was not confined to sites associated with the Mahābhārata story through literary data. Even sites associated with that epic through mere oral tradition also yielded that ware. And sometimes the oral tradition was quite funny. Thus, for example, there is a site called Saini, located between Meerut and Hastināpura. Local tradition has it that when Bhīma, one of the Pāṇḍava brothers, passing by this area dusted his shoes, this mound grew up. Surely, Bhīma's shoes had not accumulated that much dust so as to create such a high mound as that at Saini. All that the legend indicates is that the site was associated with Bhīma, one of the figures of the Mahābhārata story. An exploration of the already-exposed sections of the mound did reveal the Painted Grey Ware! Indeed, oral tradition should not be looked at with contempt, as some of us are prone to do. It should first be scientifically verified, and then accepted or rejected on the basis of the result so obtained.

8

1950-52: Excavation at Hastināpura and Historicity of the *Mahābhārata*

The discovery of the Painted Grey Ware at sites associated with the Mahābhārata story, through either literary data or oral tradition, goaded me to find out if that story had any historical basis or it was a mere figment of the imagination of someone called Vyāsa. This resulted in my undertaking excavation at the key site of Hastināpura, the capital of the Kauravas.

However, before I proceed to place before the reader the outcome of the excavation at Hastināpura, I would like to apprise him of the basic problem facing the historicity of this epic. Let us assume for a while, just for argument's sake, that Kṛiṣṇa, who figures prominently in the Mahābhārata story, was a historical figure. In that case, he is unlikely to have been later than Buddha, since the history of India is fairly well documented after the latter, i.e., from the sixth-fifth century BCE onwards and no one by the name of Kṛiṣṇa occurs therein. Thus, Kṛiṣṇa must have lived prior to the sixth century BCE. How much earlier is anybody's guess. On the other hand, the *Mahābhārata* text includes references not only to the *Yavanas*, i.e., Ionian Greeks and the *Romkas*, i.e., the Romans but also to the *Hūṇas* (White Huns) who are known to have appeared on the Indian horizon as late as the fourth century CE. There is, thus, a time-gap of at least a thousand years between the Mahābhārata event and the *Mahābhārata* text, as available to us now.

Further, the *Mahābhārata* is famous, or infamous (?), for the interpolations that it has witnessed. The present text comprises more than 100,000 verses. However, it is well known that at an earlier stage it had only 24,000 verses and was called the *Bhārata.* Still earlier, it was called the *Jaya* and had only 8,800 verses. One need not be surprised if there was yet another earlier version with a much smaller number of verses. Anyway, there is at least an eleven-time inflation from the earliest known text to the present one. All attempts to find out the nuclear text on linguistic basis have failed so far and hence one does not know what the original story must have been like.

Against such a gloomy background, one may hopefully look for some light that the excavation at Hastināpura has thrown on this complex issue. The excavation over here was carried out by me during 1950-52. The site is located on the right bank of the Gaṅgā, in Meerut District of Uttar Pradesh. The ancient mound stretches along the river for a little less than a kilometer and rises at places to a height of about 18 meters above the surrounding ground-level. Width-wise, it measures only one-fourth of its length, but this does not represent the original width of the settlement since, as would be seen later, a good bit of the river-side part of the mound had been washed away by a mighty flood in the river in ancient times.

Though the site was not subjected to large-scale horizontal excavations, quite a few trenches were laid out at different parts of the mound in order to ensure that a complete stratigraphic sequence was obtained. In fact, one of the trenches, named HST-1, was laid right across the mound to get a running story from one end to the other. Vertically, five periods of occupation were identified, with a break in between them all. The characteristic features of these, from bottom upwards, were briefly as follows.

Period I, the earliest, was distinguished by the occurrence of a pottery known to archaeologists as the Ochre Colour Ware. In the absence of any better name, this name was given to the pottery just because it left ocherous stains on the fingers, when handled. The evidence from a site named Saipai, in District Etawah, Uttar Pradesh, conclusively shows that this ware was associated with what are known as the Copper Hoards. Besides other simpler types of tools, these hoards include harpoons, antennae swords, spearheads and anthropomorphic figures. However, no such tool or, for that matter, any other antiquity was met with in the Ochre Colour Ware deposit at Hastināpura.

After an interval of time, the duration of which is difficult to determine but may have been anything up to half a millennium, the site was again occupied by a people who used a very distinctive pottery called the Painted Grey Ware, to which a brief reference has already been made earlier. As the name indicates, it was a ware with grey surface (and also a grey core), which was the result of its having been fired under reducing conditions in the kiln. On the surface, both inside and outside, there were designs painted in black color, which included, besides simple horizontal or oblique lines, svastikas, sigmas, chains of short spirals, concentric circles, etc. The more noteworthy shapes in this ware were dishes, bowls and globular drinking vessels (cf. Pls. II & III, PGW pots from Pānīpat and Ahichchhatrā). Though the associated culture-complex has since become known after this particular kind of pottery, as the Painted Grey Ware Culture, the fact remains that this pottery was only the de luxe ware and accounted for only 10 to 15 per cent of the total pottery. There were also some specimens of a black-slipped ware, but the majority was that of red ware, sometimes slipped.

As already mentioned, the excavations were not horizontal in nature. Hence, no large-scale plans of houses were encountered. However, walls of mud or mud-bricks were duly met with, so also a few examples of kiln-fired bricks. In order to give a better idea of the Painted Grey Ware Culture as a whole, we include here the data from other excavated sites of this culture-complex. Thus, the evidence from Bhagwanpura, a site in Haryana, would indicate that some of the houses could have as many as thirteen rooms, besides a large open courtyard. Bhagwanpura has also yielded evidence of substantial use of kiln-fired bricks.

In so far as the use of metal is concerned, it appears that there were two stages in the life of the Painted Grey Ware Culture, in the earlier of which only copper/bronze was used, but in the later it was iron as well. Thus, whereas some of the PGW sites in Panjab and Haryana belonged to the former stage, most of the sites in Uttar Pradesh have shown use of iron. The combined evidence from Hastināpura itself and from a site called Ataranjīkhera in District Aligarh, Uttar Pradesh, indicates that the iron objects included tools for domestic use such as nails, hooks, axes and tongs as also those that may have been used in warfare such as arrowheads, spearheads and daggers. The use of iron by the Painted Grey Ware people is in marked contrast to its total absence during the Harappan times. Another noteworthy technological aspect of the PGW Culture was the manufacture of a variety of glass objects.

Agriculture and cattle-breeding seem to have been the mainstay of these people. The principal crops cultivated by them were those of wheat, barley and rice. The domesticated animals included the cattle, buffalos, sheep, pigs and horse. Wild animals were also hunted for meat and so also fishing was done.

The small finds associated with the Painted Grey Ware Culture included stone-moulds for jewellery, beads of semiprecious stones, antimony rods and nail-cutters of copper, ivory combs, etc. Of particular interest was a potsherd on which intersecting circles had been engraved, with centers duly marked. This shows not only the knowledge of geometry but also suggests the existence of a divider-like instrument.

Amongst the games played by the Painted Grey Ware people, that of *chaupar* or *chausar* deserves special mention. The game continues even to this day. The board is usually made of cloth and has the form of a cross with all the four arms being of equal size. On each arm there are three rows of squares. The gamesmen, usually made of wood and colored, are plano-convex in shape, while the dice are square-sectioned oblong pieces, generally of ivory and marked on respective sides with blind holes numbering 1, 2, 3 and 4. It is obvious that one cannot expect the survival of the cloth-made board of the PGW times, because of the hot and humid climate of our country. However, the excavations at various sites have duly yielded the gamesmen of the aforesaid shape, though in terracotta, and the dice, usually made of bone and bearing the aforementioned kind of the numbering arrangement. In this context, it may incidentally be mentioned that it was at this game that the Kauravas defeated the Pāṇḍavas.

The Painted Grey Ware occupation at Hastināpura continued for quite some time as indicated by several structural levels, accounting for a thickness of about

2.5 meters. However, its end was sudden and sad. A huge flood in the Gaṅgā washed away a considerable portion of the settlement on the river-front, with the result that the site had to be abandoned. The evidence of this flood and of the severe damage it inflicted was duly discovered in the excavation. A huge scar left by the erosion was noted on the eastern face of the mound (Pl. IV). At the foot of this erosional scar there lay scattered a part of the washed-away material, overlain by layers of silt and sand. On finding this kind of evidence in the excavation, it just occurred to me that it was not unlikely that some of the washed-away material may still be lying buried deep in the river-bed, although most of it must have obviously been carried away by the floods. Accordingly, we bored four holes in the adjacent river-bed and, to our pleasant surprise, found in these bore-holes, at a depth of 15 metres below the bed-level (Pl. V), potsherds characteristic of the PGW Period.

As a result of this massive destruction, the site had to be abandoned. However, it once again came under occupation after a couple of centuries. By now the painted designs on the Painted Grey Ware had disappeared and the fabric, too, became coarser. But some of the shapes, particularly the dish, continued. However, another de luxe ware emerged. It is known to archaeologists as the Northern Black Polished Ware (NBPW). It had the same kind of fine grey core as that of the PGW, but the surface had a very fine lustrous slip in a variety of colors: black, indigo, silvery and golden. Shapes in the associated red ware also underwent some changes. On the whole, the cultural components of Periods II and III, while showing a change, did reflect a generic relationship.

There were many other noticeable changes between Periods II and III. Thus, in the latter period there was profuse use of kiln-fired bricks, though no doubt mud-bricks also continued to be used. With town-planning, a system of public drainage also came into being. For soakage of the sullage inside the houses, 'ring-wells' were used. That the economic level of the people had substantially risen is indicated by the introduction of systems of weights and coinage, both pointing to an augmentation in trade. Indeed, this was the time when the Sixteen States (*Ṣoḍaśa Mahājanapadas*) had come into being. It was also during this period that the two great religious figures, Buddha and Mahāvira, were born. Nobody is sure about the exact time when the Brāhmī script originated, but it was during the NBPW times that we do have its clear evidence in the form of inscriptions of the great emperor Aśoka.

The third occupation at Hastināpura, too, had a disastrous end. A large-scale fire engulfed the settlement, traces of which were noticed all over the area. As a result, the site was once more abandoned. However, this time too it was not long before the fourth occupation started. But there were some characteristic changes in the cultural equipment. For example, the Northern Black Polished Ware was completely given up and in the red ware also many new shapes made their appearance. There were new types of terracotta figurines, both male and female. The latter were distinguished by their round faces, elaborate hair-do and ornaments, and are generally known as belonging to the 'Śuṅga' style. In the lower levels of this period were found coins of the rulers of Mathurā (second century BCE), followed by those of the Yaudheyas (datable to around the beginning of the Common Era) in the middle levels, and imitation coins of the Kushan king Vāsudeva (about the middle of the third century CE) in the upper levels. There is no evidence to indicate how this fourth occupation was abandoned.

However, there was a long gap between the fourth and the fifth (final) occupation of the site. This time the history was laid right in the medieval period. The ceramics were totally different and included two typically distinct glazed wares, one with a whitish sandy core and the other with a red and sturdy one. The former of these is said to have been introduced into India by the incoming Muslim rulers, while the latter seems to have been a local imitation of the former. That the scene was really set in the medieval times is established by the occurrence of a coin of Balban (1266-87 CE) in a middle level. With this period the settlement at the mound came to an end, though there do exist some later Jain temples in the neighborhood. In fact, an altogether new settlement, planned by the Uttar Pradesh Government, has come up since we wound up our excavations in the middle of the last century.

We may now turn our attention to the chronological horizons of the various periods at Hastināpura. As per the details already given above, Period V is datable to circa eleventh-fifteenth century CE and Period IV to circa second century BCE-third century CE. Since there was a gap between Periods III and IV, the end of the former may reasonably be ascribed to the third century BCE. With its 2½-3-meter thick deposit, the beginning of Period III may well go back to sixth-seventh century BCE.

Since there was a break of occupation between Periods II and III, and there were also some major elements of cultural evolution from the former to the latter period, as mentioned earlier, the end of Period II is unlikely to have been later than circa 800 BCE. With this as the upper limit and with over 2-m thick regular occupation deposits, the site is likely to have been occupied by the Painted Grey Ware people some time in the 11th century BCE.

As already mentioned, there was not only a break of occupation between Periods I and II, but also a fundamental difference between their respective cultural assemblages. Thus, Period I, characterized by the Ochre Color Ware, must have well preceded 1200 BCE. On the basis of certain thermoluminescence dates for the OCP Ware at other sites, Period I at Hastināpura may be dated to somewhere between 2000 and 1500 BCE.

The above chronological assessment of the various periods was made prior to the introduction of the Carbon-14 method of dating in India. It is, however, interesting to note that even after the application of the C-14 method, the position has remained by and large the same.

Now to the crucial discussion relating to the historicity of the *Mahābhārata*. To recall, at Hastināpura five periods of occupation had been met with. Of these, the uppermost two (Periods V and IV) do not call for consideration in the context of the *Mahābhārata*, since these are very much later than the likely date of that episode. Even Period III will have to be ruled out, since its date ranges between circa 700 and 300 BCE. Buddha and Mahāvīra lived in the earlier part of this period and, as already stated, if the Mahābhārata episode had any basis in history, it has to be pre-Buddha and pre-Mahāvīra.

We are now left with only Periods I and II in the consideration zone. We would have opted in favor of Period I had there not been a very major snag. Of the large number of sites associated with the Mahābhārata story only two, viz., Hastināpura and Ahichchhatrā, have yielded the Ochre Color Ware. Thus, if the Mahābhārata scene is laid in the OCW period, sites like Mathurā, Indraprastha, Pāṇiprastha, Vṛikaprastha, Vāraṇāvata, Tilaprastha, Virāṭanagara, Kurukṣetra, Kāmpilya, etc. were not at all in existence at that point of time. Could the Mahābhārata episode have been enacted without these sites? Obviously not. Thus, the Ocher Color Ware occupation at Hastināpura cannot claim its association with the Mahābhārata episode.

In the final analysis of the archaeological evidence from Hastināpura, therefore, it is only the Painted Grey Ware

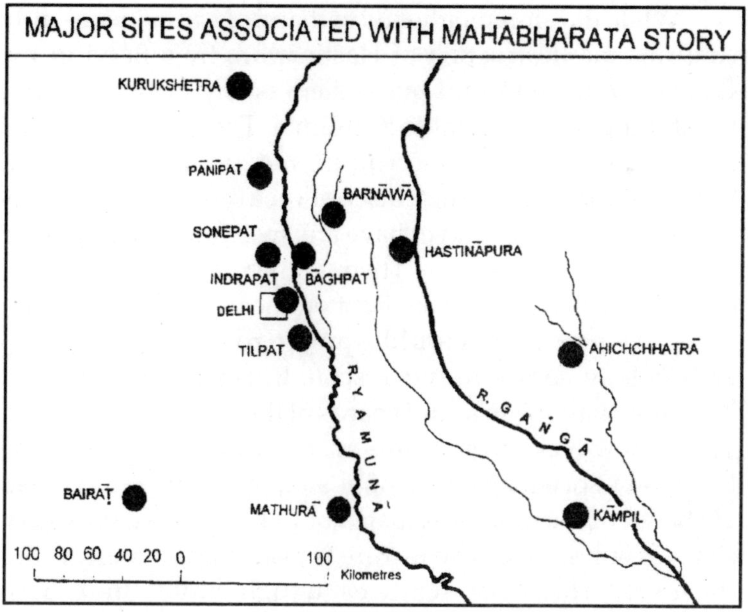

Fig. 3. Principal sites associated with the Mahābhārata story.

Period that qualifies for its association with the Mahābhārata times. In this context, it must also be emphasized that all the sites associated with the Mahābhārata story (Fig. 3) have invariably yielded the Painted Grey Ware – a fact which links them together.

Now we recall the most vital archaeological evidence. It is that of the destruction of the Painted Grey Ware settlement at Hastināpura by a flood in the Gaṅgā. In this context, the texts aver:

Gaṅgayāpahṛite tasmin nagare Nāgasāhvaye
Tyaktvā Nichkṣur nagaram Kauśāmbyām sa nivatsyati

i.e., 'When the city of Nāgasāhvya (Hastināpura) is carried away by the Gaṅgā, Nichakṣu will abandon it and dwell in Kauśāmbī.'

While the aforementioned archaeological evidence duly confirms the destruction of Hastināpura by a flood in the Gaṅgā, we have to find out if there is any evidence about the shifting of the capital to Kauśāmbī. This could best come from a contemporary inscription mentioning that event. But, alas! there is no such inscription available to us. As is well known, we do not yet have any inscription dating prior to the fourth century BCE. Then, is there any other kind of evidence which may throw light on the issue? The situation is not as bad as it would appear to be. Here, again, archaeology comes to our rescue. In the lowest levels of Kauśāmbī have been found shards of the Painted Grey Ware. These, however, do not present the ware at is peak. The Kauśāmbī specimens bear only simple linear designs and are bereft of the more variegated ones like sigmas, svastikas, chain of spirals, etc. The texture is also slightly coarser. But these are the very features which have their own significance. They represent the decadent stage of the ware and thus provide a significant link between the fag-end of Hastināpura and the beginning of Kauśāmbī.

The Kauśāmbī PGW levels are bereft of any NBPW, which appeared only later. Further, since the emergence of the NBPW in the Gaṅgā valley goes back to at least the seventh century BCE, the PGW levels at Kauśāmbī may well be dated to circa 800 BCE. Thus, put together, the archaeological evidence from Hastināpura and Kauśāmbī would show that the desertion of the former site and the establishment of a settlement at the latter can safely be placed around 800 BCE, if not somewhat earlier. It may be recalled that, according to literary evidence, the flood occurred during the reign of Nichakṣu. As per the genealogy given in the texts, he was the fifth ruler in succession from Parikṣhit; and the latter, in turn, ascended the throne of Hastināpura immediately after the Mahābhārata war. Thus, the war itself may be deemed to have taken place around 900 BCE or somewhat earlier.

The above-mentioned date of the Mahābhārata War, arrived at on archaeological grounds, may now be cross-checked with literary evidence. The texts say that after Nichakṣu there were nineteen rulers at Kauśāmbī before Udayana came to the throne. While skeptics may doubt the historicity of the earlier kings of Kauśāmbī, even they would not deny that there did exist a king called Udayana, since his contemporaneity with Buddha has never been questioned. It was he who invited Buddha to visit Kauśāmbī and the latter duly responded. Buddha passed away in 487 or 483 BCE. Thus, Udayana can well be taken to have ruled around 500 BCE.

Now comes the most baffling aspect of the issue: How many years did actually elapse between the time of Nichakṣu and that of Udayana? And the answer at once falls in the realm of subjectivity. There have been a number of estimates for the average reign per ruler. There are those who hold it to have been 33 years or even 37, but most sober scholars regard this to be an over-estimate. There are, however, other moderate estimates which deserve consideration. While A.L. Basham puts it at 19 years, Pargiter does it at 18. However, even while recommending the estimate of 18, Pargiter inserts a caveat: 'I have examined 14 series of dynasties from 20 to 30 kings in various eastern and western countries; the longest average just exceeded 24 years in one case, the shortest was about 12 and the average of all was 19; but the average was higher in western countries and lower in eastern countries. Hence the medium average for these contemporary eastern dynasties must be taken something less than 19 and 18 will be a fair, **even liberal** estimate.' (Emphasis added.)

Like Pargiter, I thought of doing my own exercise; and since the problem is related specifically to India, I thought of examining it in the light of Indian dynasties whose dates are already well known. Thus, to begin with, I took up the

Muslim rulers of Delhi. Qutbuddin Aibak was the first one to occupy the throne of Delhi after defeating Prithvi Raj Chauhan. The last Muslim ruler of Delhi was Bahadur Shah Zafar whom the British ousted. Altogether there were 47 rulers from the first to the last, and the total duration of their reigns was 652 years. This gives an average of 13.9 years per ruler. When this average was presented to scholars, they were not happy with it, arguing that since there were many coups and killings in the various Muslim dynasties, the average is bound to be low. But they forgot that while some of the kings may have ruled for only a couple of years, there were others like Akbar and Aurangzeb who ruled for a very long time. But this did not satisfy them. So I took up the ancient Hindu dynasties. Of these, the Guptas gave the highest average, which stood at 17.6 years. On the other hand, the Kaṇvas yielded an average of only 10.5 years and the Śuṅgas that of 11.2. The Mauryas stood in between. On piecing together the averages of all the Hindu dynasties whose reigns are well fixed, it was observed that their overall average was still a little less than 14 years per ruler. Thus, in the Indian context, whether medieval or ancient, the safe and reliable average would be around 14 years, which may at best be rounded off to 15 years.

Taking even this average of 15 years per ruler and multiplying it with the number of rulers that preceded Udayana back to the Mahābhārata War, viz., 24 (19 from Udayana to Nichakṣu and 5 further back to the War), the total period that elapsed would be 15 x 24 = 360 years. Since, as already stated, Udayana was ruling around 500 BCE, the date of the Mahābhārata War would work out to around 860 BCE. It would, however, be too presumptuous to stick to a precise figure like this, and all that one can say is that even the literary-cum-historical analysis supports the date of around 900 BCE for the war, arrived at on the basis of the combined archaeological evidence from Hastināpura and Kauśāmbī.

But a doubt lurks in my mind if such a late date would please the orthodox school of scholars, for to them the Mahābhārata war is very 'hoary', going back to 3102 BCE. The reason why they regard it to be so early is that an inscription at Aihole, dated to Śaka era 556, i.e., 634-35 CE, mentions that 3735 years had elapsed since the Mahābhārata war. In this context, it must be emphasized that there is no mention of this kind in any other inscription, earlier or later, and thus one wonders where the author of the Aihole inscription got his information from – suddenly 3735 years after the event. Added to this is the fact that, as the archaeological data indicate, in 3102 BCE the entire region where the Mahābhārata story was enacted was bereft of any habitational remains.

However, there are a few other dates which do call for consideration: for example, 1424 BCE (proposed by K.P. Jayaswal), 1400 BCE (A.S. Altekar), 950 BCE (F.E. Pargiter) and ninth century BCE (H.C. Raychaudhury). As regards the first two dates, it may be recalled that this was the time up to which the Copper Hoard-cum-Ochre Color Ware Culture may have persisted. But then, with the exception of Hastināpura and Ahichchhatrā, the remains of this culture have not been found at any of the other sites figuring in the Mahābhārata story. Also conversely, no other Copper Hoard-cum-Ochre Color Ware site, such as Nasirpur, Bahadarabad, Jhinjhana, Saipai, Bisauli, to name just a few, finds any mention in the *Mahābhārata*. How can then one correlate the two?

We are now left with 950 BCE (Pargiter) and ninth century BCE (Raychaudhury). Pargiter's dating is based on the average of 18 years per reign. However, he himself thought this average to be 'liberal', and, as shown earlier, a more reasonable average would be about 15 years.

Thus, even Pargiter's dating is a little off the mark. Raychaudhury's dating has an additional merit. He steers clear of the oft-debated Paurāṇic data and uses completely independent evidence, viz., that of the later Vedic texts. Thus, basing his arguments on the teacher-disciple sequence given in these texts, and working backwards from the known ones, he observes that the time of Parikṣit, who ascended the Hastināpura throne immediately on the conclusion of the Mahābhārata war, is likely to have been around the ninth century BCE. And this is more or less what our archaeological evidence suggests.

The upshot of all that has been discussed in the previous paragraphs is that the *Mahābhārata* was not a figment of the imagination. **It did have a basis in historical reality,** although the descriptions in it of elaborate palaces or of large armies (comprising several *akṣhauhṇī senā*s, each *akṣhauhiṇī* unit, according to the laid-down norms, consisting of 21,870 elephants, 21,870 chariots, 65,610 horses and 1,09,350 foot-soldiers) appear to have been highly exaggerated. Further, as already mentioned, the text had journeyed from a bare 8,800, or even less verses, to an eleven-time inflated 100,000 verses, which allowed for lots of interpolations. Finally, it must also be borne in mind that the *Mahābhārata* was not *itihāsa* (history) but a piece of *prabandha kāvya* (epic) whereby the poet had full right of letting his imagination fly.

Perhaps the reader might like to know how the scholarly community the world over reacted to my analysis of the data offered by the excavations at Hastināpura, particularly in respect of their bearing on the historicity of the *Mahābhārata*. As an example of this reaction, I will now give the review by Professor A.L. Basham, the then Professor of Indian History at the School of Oriental and African studies, University of London, published in the *Journal of Economic and Social History of Orient,* Vol. I, fasc. 3, Leiden, 1959.

The historian must thank Mr. Lal for his excavations, his well reasoned conclusions. We believe that the latter provide the most probable hypothesis at present available to us. It seems in fact that the remains of Period II do show us something of the way of life of the people remembered in the Epic (Mahābhārata) story. These, if we are to believe Mr. Lal's very reasonable hypothesis, are the people whose priests composed and orally transmitted the enormous later Vedic literature ....

9

Naughty (or Nasty?) Boy

I have been told that I was born in a village called Baidora, located at a distance of about 20 kilometers from Jhansi, a District headquarters in Uttar Pradesh. My grandfather, Shri Harcharan Lal, was a Lekhpal (a junior-level revenue official) over there. He also owned some farm-land in the neighborhood and was thus placed financially reasonably well. My father, Shri Ramcharan Lal, was in government service at the District headquarters in Jhansi.

There is some mix-up about the date of my birth. When I was a little over three-and-a-half years old, I am told, my grandfather took me for admission to a local school. The teacher insisted that I could be admitted only if I was four. So, grandpa told the teacher to write down my age as four. Thus, my official date of birth, viz. May 2, 1921, is about four months earlier than the real one which, according to the horoscope prepared at the time of my birth, works out to be September 18, 1921. Anyway, this difference is hardly of any consequence.

The earliest memory I have of my childhood is my having travelled, along with my father and others, in a *sikaram* (a bullock-cart specially designed to carry passengers) to a place called Pichhor for the marriage of my youngest uncle. I was around four years of age. But what I can vividly recall is that I was wearing a pair of silver *chūḍās* on my wrists and a pair of silver *toḍās* on my ankles. The children, today, no more wear such antiquated ornaments.

After the marriage was over, my father took me and my mother to Moth, a Tehsil headquarters in the same Jhansi District, whereto he had recently been transferred. Those days the *Rāma-Līlā* (the story of Lord Rāma) was being staged there and my father used to take me in the evenings to see some of the shows. I was greatly excited by these, particularly by the use of the bow and arrows by Lord Rāma. Thus, once when my father was leaving for a tour in connection with his official work, I requested him to get me a set of bow and arrows. He agreed to do so. As chance would have it, the day he returned, the doors of our house were closed from inside and I was away somewhere inside the house. When he knocked at the door, I went close to it and from inside enquired of him if he had brought the bow and arrows. The reply was in the negative. I did not open the door, saying that unless he brought the bow and arrows, the doors would not be opened. Poor father had no choice but to go back to the market, look around for a bow and arrows, buy the same and then return home. When he knocked once again at the door and I was convinced that he had brought what I had asked for, I opened the door and let him enter. My father did not admonish me for my obstinacy. On the other hand, he lifted me up, kissed me and gave me the bow-and-arrow set. What a father!

There is yet another incident of around the same period. We had a cow that used to give us milk. A cowherd used to take the cow out in the morning and bring her back in the evening. One evening, on returning home, the cow, being very thirsty, drank the entire water that was there in the *nāda* (a large-sized earthen trough). I watched her intently and was very much excited about it. When my father returned home from office that evening, I told him what I had seen and insisted that the cow should give the same amount of milk as the water she had drunk. My father was perplexed and did not know what to do. Anyway, he found a way out. While I was away from the scene, he filled the *nāda* with water, milked the cow and mixed whatever milk had been taken out with the water in the *nāda*. He then called me, took me to the *nāda* and showed me that it was brimming with milk.

From Moth, my father was transferred to Garotha, another Tehsil headquarters in Jhansi District. By that time I was nearly five years old. I used to go to school in the morning around 7 a.m. My mother would cook fresh *kuchainyās* (small-sized breads) and give to me two of these along with one *laddoo* made of *nigonā* (green gram). Then she would go for a bath, leaving me to eat the breakfast. I was very fond of the *laddoo*s. While she was away, I used to steal one or two *laddoo*s and hurriedly swallow the same before my mother returned. She did not have any inkling whatsoever of the extra *laddoo*s that I had stolen and eaten. What a crafty move!

But there is yet another, and indeed more despicable, anecdote that relates to my attempt to steal. One day my mother gave me one *ānā* (a coin then in use, equivalent to 1/16th of a rupee) and asked me to go to the market and buy a grocery item that she needed urgently for cooking. I went to the shop from where we used to buy our grocery. I told the shopkeeper, who was seated right at the entrance to the shop, to get for me the item I needed and placed the one-*ānā* coin before him. Without putting the coin inside his *golaka* (cash-box), he went inside the shop to fetch the item and I quietly removed the coin and put it into my pocket. The shopkeeper returned, delivered the item to me and looked around for the coin. On not finding it there he asked me about it. I flatly told him that I had placed the coin before him and he must have put it inside the *golaka.* He said that he did not at all remember having done so, and I insisted that he had done so. The shopkeeper knew my father well enough and thus accepted my version and let me off. On returning home I narrated, with a sense of bravado, the entire story to my elder sister, "Look here, I have brought not only the item concerned but also the one-*ānā* coin," which I took out from my pocket and placed it on her hand. My sister was very much annoyed on hearing this and told the whole story to my mother, who in turn told the same to my father. Instead of rebuking or beating me, my father asked me to go back to the shop, narrate to the shopkeeper my entire misdeed in detail, apologize to him touching his feet and return the one-*ānā* coin to him. In order to ensure that I did exactly as he had asked me to do, he sent along with me his *chaparāsī* (office-peon) who had by then arrived there. I had no other option but to follow the peon, though most reluctantly. I was sobbing all the way, but there was no escape. On reaching the shop, I burst into tears and could hardly speak a word. I placed the coin in the hands of the shopkeeper, touched his feet, as directed by my father, and in broken words narrated how I had put the coin back into my pocket while he (the shopkeeper) had gone inside the shop to fetch the grocery item. I can still very vividly recall this incident.

In retrospect, it appears to me that my father was more for a corrective punishment than a corporal one. Another incident, though of a different kind, makes me think on these lines.

The house that we were living in at Garotha had a large courtyard within its premises, where we used to sleep during the summer nights. Right at dusk, the beds were laid out and after an early dinner we, the children, would retire into our beds. I occupied one bed and my elder sister another. Adjacent to the wall of the courtyard, on the exterior, there was a *neem* tree. Somehow I started looking at it and after a while I suddenly started shouting, "Oh, there is a ghost on this tree. There is a ghost. Save me." My sister, who too had not yet gone to sleep, heard me crying and told me that there was no ghost. I insisted on my having seen one and cried with greater intensity. Thereupon the sister informed our parents who were still having their dinner. My father came running to me and tried to convince me that there was nothing like a ghost; it is just the creation of one's own mind. I did see one, I told him. Then he thought of a unique way of resolving the issue. He asked the peon, who was about to leave for his home, to stay back for a while more and take me up the tree on his back. He also provided the peon with a lighted lantern and asked him to show me the various branches of the tree so that I could see for myself if there was any ghost or not. The peon did exactly as he was told to do. I was up on the tree with the peon. He asked me to show him the ghost but I couldn't, since there was really none. This kind of psychological treatment given to me by my father has taken away all kinds of fears from my mind – real or imaginary!

From Garotha, my father was again transferred to Jhansi where I studied for three years and passed the Hindi Middle School examination (equivalent to 7th Grade). But he was transferred once again, this time to Lalitpur. There I was admitted to a school at which the standard of English language was rather high and my knowledge of it was much below the required level. In order to ensure that I picked up that language well enough, my father engaged a tutor for me, who would come home every evening. I found it a little too much after the day's hard work at the school. One evening when my mother and elder sister had gone to a neighbor's house, my father had not yet returned from the office and I was all by myself, I planned to play a trick on the tutor. To make this plan of mine intelligible to the reader, I have first to explain the map of the house in which we were living. It had two adjacent rooms on the exterior. One of these was a *baiṭhaka* (a kind of Drawing Room) while the other served as a passage into the courtyard around which were located the bed-rooms. The *baiṭhaka* and the passage-room, though juxtaposed to each other, had their independent entrances which could be locked both from inside and outside. First I opened the inside latches of both these rooms. Then I went outside the house and locked the passage-room from the outside. Putting the key into my pocket, I entered the *baiṭhaka* and secured the latch from the inside. Thus, when the tutor came at the appointed time, he found the house locked. Disgusted and annoyed, he had to get back to his home. I was greatly pleased that I had succeeded in bluffing the tutor. Later, when he had left I opened the door of the *baiṭhaka* from inside, came outside the house, removed the lock from the exterior of the passage-room and re-entered the house, as if nothing had happened. When my mother and sister came back after their visit to the neighbor's house, I gleefully narrated my mischievous planning to my sister. But this time she was kind enough not to tell my parents about my misdeed. Perhaps, she remembered the punishment that I was given at Garotha when I had stolen the one-*ānā* coin.

My elder sister and I used to quarrel quite often. I would use foul tongue and she, in return, her hands to beat me up. Nevertheless, she was always obliging. I used to study pretty late into the night. We had no electricity and kerosene lantern was the only means of getting light. My sister would clean up the lantern and light it up for me. And that was not all. In the open courtyard, where I used to carry on my studies, I felt very lonely. So, I often requested her to give me company and she was affectionate enough to oblige. What a sweet and sour relationship between a sister and her younger brother!

Our stay at Lalitpur was hardly for a year, after which my father was transferred back to Jhansi. By now I was about 13-14 years old and had made quite a few friends in the neighborhood. One of them was of a leader-type and wanted the rest of us to follow him. One afternoon, during the summer vacations, we were playing in a *bagiyā* (tiny garden), frequently climbing up and down the trees. Right nearby was the house of an elderly person whose relations were very sour with the family of our leader. He started hurling abuses on the daughter of this elderly person. The language he used was very filthy. He directed us to follow him. We had no other option but to do that. The elderly gentleman was very much annoyed and asked us to behave. But our leader did not stop and I, too, continued to join the chorus. After a while, the leader called it a day and all of us dispersed.

Towards the evening, when my father was returning home from office, this elderly neighbor who was sitting on the *chabūtarā* (platform) outside his house, beckoned my father: "Ramcharan, this afternoon your son was using very filthy language against my daughter. Is that what you have taught him?" My father apologized to him and moved on to our house. As usual, to relax himself, he started smoking his *hukkā*. (The *hukkā* has two components: a metallic vertical part atop which is placed a small, hollow-stemmed earthen cup which holds the tobacco with charcoal-fire placed on it; and, attached to its lower part, about 2-feet long wooden tube through which the tobacco-smoke is sucked in.) As chance would have it, just about that time I entered the house. Without asking me any questions, my father took out the wooden pipe from the *hukkā* and started beating me. When he was satisfied that he had given me enough beating, he came out with all that the elderly neighbor had told him. I had no explanations to offer. At night, my mother massaged my beaten limbs and that was the end of the story.

Perhaps my father had realized that I was no longer a child, as at Moth, who could be dealt with gently, but a grown-up boy of 13-14 years who must be taught how to behave, and had begun to believe in the dictum 'spare the rod and spoil the child'.

10

The Lal Family

In previous chapters there have been quite a few references to my father, Shri Ram Charan Lal, which depict not only his kind heart but also his strict disciplinarian outlook. He was very firm in his views and naturally wished the members of the family to follow his example. He used to do physical exercises to keep himself fit. On nearing 80 years of age, he reduced these exercises and took to long walks. Towards the end of his 80s, he curtailed even these. When he was 90-plus, he once had a severe sun-stoke and became unconscious. He had to be admitted to the German Hospital in Jhansi. On getting telegraphic intimation from my youngest brother who was then posted in Jhansi, I rushed from Delhi and attended on my father but we could do nothing and he passed away in about a week. The entire family grieved at the loss of the guiding light (Pl. XXXIX).

In contrast to my father, my mother was a very sweet and soft person. I never saw her getting angry at anyone, be it a family member or an outsider. Her gentleness will become self-apparent from the little episode that I am going to narrate now. After joining the university at Allahabad, I returned to Jhansi in the first available vacation, in October 1939. I thought I had become an important person having been to a university. Thus, on waking up one morning I asked for a cup of tea to be served while I was still in the bed. The mother was busy preparing the other children for the school. She took nearly half-an-hour to finish the work on hand and then brought me the cup of tea. The ego in me – the thought that I should have been attended to on a priority basis – made me return the cup of tea. My poor mother, instead of chiding me for my misbehavior, sat down on the floor and started sobbing, regretting the delay. What a sweet mother in contrast to a haughty son!

Earlier, I referred to my participation in the 1942 Quit India Movement. However, because of the government warning to my father that if I did not give up my role in the Movement his services would be terminated, I had no option but to withdraw myself from it. At that time, my father was once again posted in Moth. So I spent a few months over there. During this period I became very close to my mother. She would ask me to read out to her every evening the Hindi translation of the *Bhāgavatam*. At these sessions some of the ladies of the neighborhood would also be present. I too enjoyed reading this religious text since I had never done so before. Sometimes she would ask me to read out the *Bhagavadgītā* and translate it for her in Hindi. These sessions left a great impact on me.

During those years, Moth was witnessing an upsurge of the Arya Samaj movement. The preachers, amongst other things, condemned *mūrti-pūjā* (idol-worship). Unconsciously I began to be charmed by these preachers. My mother, after taking her morning bath, used to worship the idols of her chosen gods, washing them and then besmearing them with sandal-wood paste. This was followed by reciting prayer-songs. Once, acting subconsciously under the influence of the Arya Samajists, I questioned my mother: "*Jaba Īśvara saba jagaha hai to āpa ina mūrtiyon ko kyon pūjatī hain?* (When God is omnipresent why do you worship these metal idols?)" Do you know what her spontaneous reply was? "*Baite, agara tuma yaha mānate ho ki bhagawān saba jagaha hai,to fir yaha batāo ki waha ina mūrtiyon men kyon nahin hai?* (My dear son, if you admit that God is omnipresent, tell me why he is not there in these statues?)" I was left completely speechless. What an example of unflinching faith!

In her late years, when we were staying at 127, Satya Marg, Chanakya Puri, New Delhi, she was initiated into spiritual life by one Mata ji, a God-realized person. She kept on practising what she was told to do. As a result, in due course of time, she began to have wonderful mystical experiences. Once, later on when we were in Gwalior, my wife and I requested her to tell us something about these experiences. She initially declined to do so, but when we insisted a lot, she relented and told us about the tremendous experience of light that she had been having. She stopped speaking and went, as if, into a trance. That was my mother.

When in 1976 I left Gwalior and joined the Indian Institute of Advanced Study, Shimla, I had to leave my parents with my youngest brother, Shri Prakash, who was first posted in Agra and then in Jhansi. Shimla was too cold for them. My mother passed away a year before my father. Unfortunately, I was not there when she died, since I was busy with the excavations at Śṛiṅgaverapura and got the sad message too late. Of course, I reached there for the other rites.

We were six brothers and sisters, who now are five, our youngest sister having died in an accident quite a few years ago. The eldest amongst us is a sister, Leela Devi, about whom I have already written in one of the earlier chapters. We quarreled a lot as children but lived at peace when we became somewhat sensible. She is now 92, and currently lives with her youngest son, Shailendra, who is an advocate at the High Court in Jaipur. Thank God, she enjoys reasonably good health. The brother-in-law, unfortunately, had passed away some time back.

I am next to her. Then comes a sister, Vidya Devi, who is now past 81. She and her husband, Kashi Prasad, live in Lucknow, where the latter retired from UP government service. On the spiritual plane, he is highly advanced, having been initiated by his *guru* at an early age. They have no son but as many as nine daughters. My sister calls them her *nava-durgās*, i.e., nine Durgās (Durgā being the name of a Hindu goddess). All these daughters are well educated and are married to well-to-do persons – something that my sister and brother-in-law ascribe solely to the grace of their *guru.* The two younger brothers, Om Prakash and Shri Prakash, are also retired. They live respectively in Allahabad and Jhansi, with their families. Om Prakash's son, Ajaya, and daughter-in-law, Archana, are the only ones in the entire family who are indirectly associated with my subject, archaeology, teaching ancient Indian history at Degree Colleges in and near Allahabad.

In some of the previous chapters, I have already referred to my wife, Kusum (Pl. XX). She is now 82 and has been all through my real companion in the fullest sense of the word. All wives in India look after the household, but my wife, I must say, has not only managed the household very efficiently but has also helped me in my field-work and research. I cannot recall any excavation, including the one in Egypt, where she was not with me. Likewise, in most of the writing work she has helped me in one way or another. Even the present book is the result of her goading me to write out my ups and downs. In token of the immense help my wife gave me in the field-work, I dedicated to her my first major book, *The Earliest Civilization of South Asia*, published in 1997, with the following Sanskrit verse:

> *Babhūva yā sarvasukhāni hitvā*
> *sagāminī kṣetra-viśodha karye,*
> *Samarpitam vai* ***kusuma****priyāyai*
> *purāṇagandhaih kusumam prasiktam/*
>
> Forsaking all comforts, who became a companion also on the difficult path of (archaeological) field-work,
> To such a beloved, **Kusuma**, is dedicated this kusuma (flower), saturated with the fragrance of the past.

My wife is one of the bravest persons I have seen. Over the years she has had a number of bouts with illness and bore them with courage and patience. When I was posted in Calcutta in 1954, she developed severe abdominal pain and was bed-ridden. She had to be brought to Delhi where it was discovered that she was actually suffering from tuberculosis of the cecum. The surgeon cautioned us that he was sharpening his knife and would have to use it one day. Meanwhile, he gave bi-weekly streptomycin injections and administered INH tablets orally. It took nearly three months for this treatment to control the tuberculosis, but the surgeon's knife was spared.

In 1990, my wife and I were staying in the guest house at Purana Qila, New Delhi, in connection with the preparation of the report on my excavations at Śṛiṅgaverapura. It was around 5 p.m. and we were taking our evening cup of tea. Suddenly, my wife noted that the tea was spilling out of her mouth. I looked at her face carefully and discovered that the right half was slightly twisted. We immediately rushed to the Wellingdon Hospital (now called Ram Manohar Lohia Hospital) where the doctors declared that it was a case of Bell's Palsy. She was given the necessary treatment but had to undergo a very long course of physiotherapy. Even then some vestiges of

Pl. XIX. The Lal Family at Hotel Hilton in Honolulu, Hawaii, USA, 2009.

Pl. XX. Professor B.B. Lal & Shrimati Kusum Lal, enjoying a drink in a restaurant in Honolulu, 2009.

Pl. XXI. *Gurudeva*, Professor R.D. Ranade. (Courtesy Gurudeva Ranade Trust)

Pl. XXII. Śṛiṅgaverapura: Terracotta head of Three-eyed Śiva. Circa Ist century CE. (Courtesy ASI)

Pl. XXIII. Gupteshwar (Gwalior): Mesolithic paintings in a cave.

Pl. XXIV. Bharadvāja Āśrama: A lump of clay with reed-marks, found in the sandy deposits, suggestive of wattle-and-daub huts. (Courtesy ASI)

Pl. XXV. A terracotta figure currently lodged in the Los Angeles County Museum of Arts, USA, but believed to have come from Nachāra Kherā in Haryana, India. It portrays Rāma whose name is also inscribed, in Brāhmī characters of 3rd century CE. (Courtesy LACMA)

Pl. XXVI. 'The Damsel who whisked me off to Unknown Lands.' The famous bronze figure of a 'dancing girl' from Mohenjo-daro. Mature Harappan.

Pl. XXVII. Ayodhyā: This inscribed stone slab came out from within the thick walls of the Babari Masjid when it was demolished by the Kar Sevaks. Written in characters of the 12th century CE, the inscription gives all the details about the construction of the temple.

Pl. XXVIII. Ayodhyā: Kar Sevaks carrying a huge sculpted stone slab on their shoulders, which they had rescued from the debris of the Babari Masjid and were in the process of depositing it in a safe place. This photograph was published in the December 31, 1992 issue of *India Today*.

Pl. XXIX. Delhi: Constituting a part of the Quwwatu'l-Islam (Might of Islam) Mosque, this colonnade was constructed by using pillars of Hindu and Jain temples destroyed by Qutb-ud-din Aibak. (Courtesy ASI)

Pl. XXX. Ayodhyā: A pillar of the pre-existing Hindu temple, re-fixed against a pier of the Babari Masjid. (Courtesy Indian History & Culture Society)

Pl. XXXI. Rakhigarhi: Terracotta wheel. The painted lines radiating from the central hub clearly represent the spokes of the wheel. Mature Harappan. (Courtesy ASI)

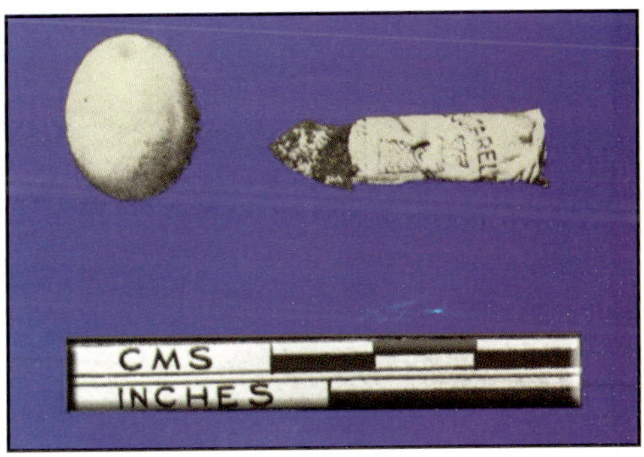

Pl. XXXII. Nubia (Egypt): A plastic bead and a cigarette-end found in the plundered graves. These give an inkling of the probable date of the plundering. (Courtesy ASI)

Pl. XXXIII. Close-up of the Rāma Setu (Adam's Bridge) between India and Sri Lanka.

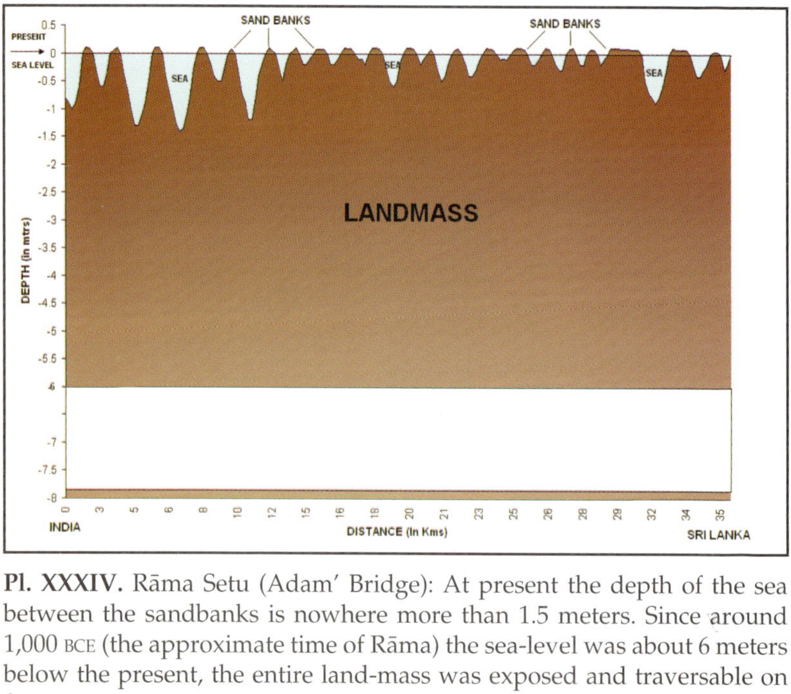

Pl. XXXIV. Rāma Setu (Adam' Bridge): At present the depth of the sea between the sandbanks is nowhere more than 1.5 meters. Since around 1,000 BCE (the approximate time of Rāma) the sea-level was about 6 meters below the present, the entire land-mass was exposed and traversable on foot.

Pl. XXXV. February 2010: Professor B.B. Lal in front of his ancestral house in Baidora, his birth-place, which he had left when he was less than 4 years old, and revisited it when he was past 88. (Courtesy Rajeev Srivastava)

Pl. XXXVI. April 2010: Professor Lal being presented the V.S. Wakankar Award.

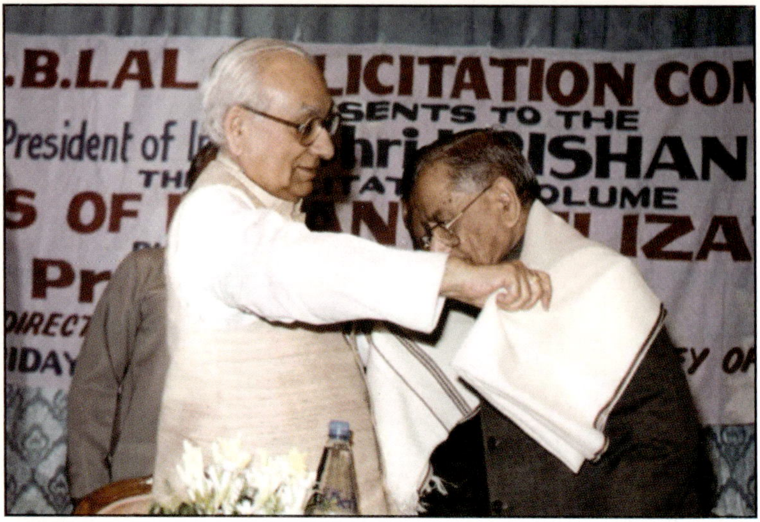

Pl. XXXVII. Year 1997: The then Vice-President of India, Shri Krishna Kant, felicitating Professor B.B. Lal.

Pl. XXXVIII. Year 2000: The then President of India, Dr. K.R. Narayanan, honoring Professor B.B. Lal with **Padma Bhushan.**

this illness may still be observed on her right eye and right upper lip.

In 2003, while she was going to the bathroom, her right foot got stuck up in the carpet on the floor and she fell down on her right arm. There was not only a great pain in it, but also a severe sensation of its 'electrification'. She had to be admitted to the Military Hospital in Delhi Cantonment and remained there for about a week. In 2005, when we were living in 79, Lodhi Estate Bungalows, she collapsed immediately on trying to get off the bed and to go to the adjacent bathroom. Again, she had to be rushed to the hospital. It was discovered that her haemoglobin was as low as 6. She had to be given plasma intravenously and other medicines by mouth. It took her a very long time to come to the normal level of haemoglobin, viz., 11-12.

Yet another of her bouts with illness was in 2006. At that time we were living in our own house in Hauz Khas Enclave. One night, around 11 p.m., we discovered that she was very restless and breathless. She was no doubt a patient of blood pressure, but we had never seen her in such a bad state. We immediately took her to Max Devki Hospital in Saket. The doctors put her straightway in the Intensive Care Unit, where she was placed on a temporary pace-maker. This was removed after two days. It was discovered that her potassium level had gone very high, resulting in this kind of physical condition.

The latest in the series is the accident which occurred in December 2008. We were in Fursatganj where my eldest son is presently located. One morning we were all set to leave by our car to Delhi via Jhansi where my youngest brother had been ailing for some time. The luggage had been put in the car and we were waiting for Kusum to come out of the bathroom and join us for breakfast. Suddenly there was a thud in the bathroom and a groaning by Kusum. She had slipped on the wet floor and broken three of her right ribs. Immediately an ambulance was called in and

Kusum was taken to an orthopedic surgeon in Raibareli. She was confined to bed for two months and all our trips had to be cancelled.

Recounting her bouts, she proudly proclaims, "I am a frequent visitor to hospitals. But mind you, I have always managed to sneak out!"

We have three sons. Unfortunately, no daughter. Our eldest son, Rajesh, retired as Air Vice Marshal from the Indian Air Force in 2006. Thereafter, he has taken up an assignment with the Indira Gandhi Rashtriya Udan Academy (IGRUA), as the Chief Flying Instructor. Located at Fursatganj, near Raibareli, U. P., this Academy trains pilots for civil aviation. The story of Rajesh's joining the Indian Air Force may be of some interest to readers. The year was 1963. We were living in 127, Satya Marg, Chanakya Puri, New Delhi. One morning when I had just returned from an official tour, Rajesh confronted me with a completed application form and requested me to sign it. I asked him what it was about. He told me that he was applying to appear at an examination for admission to the National Defence Academy (NDA). When I told him that he should have taken my prior consent for joining the NDA, he replied that he was just sending an application and if finally I did not permit him to join NDA, he wouldn't. I signed the application and it went off. He appeared at the examination and was selected. Not quite willingly, my wife and I had to allow him to join NDA. The cadets have to give their preference, namely, which of the three wings – Army, Navy or Air Force – they would like to join. Rajesh gave his preference for the Air Force, something we were not quite happy with, expressing our concern about safety. Rajesh argued in favor of his joining the Air Force, as follows. "Papa," he said, "the people in the Army have often to live away from their families, since they have to go out frequently for field-exercises. Further, in the case of a war, they are the ones who have to bear the brunt of it. The Navy people have a very boring life. They have to be on the sea for months together, leaving their families at home. As against this, the Air Force personnel are stationed at one place and after performing their assignment come back to the base." This analysis appeared to us reasonable and we allowed him to opt for the Air Force. Then came a more crucial question, namely, which Wing of the Air Force he should join: Transport, Helicopter or Fighter. He again told us: "A pilot flying a transport aircraft has to take men and materials right into the area of actual war. His airplane can be fired at by the enemy but he cannot return the fire since there is no provision for it in a transport plane. He is, thus, totally helpless. A pilot flying the helicopter is also exposed to near-similar risks, though he does have the firing power. Quite often his job can be to pick up wounded soldiers from amidst an enemy-held terrain, which is decidedly risky. As against this, a fighter-pilot takes off the plane from his base, shoots at the enemy target and immediately returns to the base." We could not argue any further and had to yield. I have narrated this episode in some detail, just to highlight that a person who has firm determination always succeeds in achieving his aim!

Rajesh's wife, Sushama, is the daughter of a very dear friend of mine, Shri M.N. Deshpande, who, alas, is no more. Shri Deshpande was my colleague in the Survey and succeeded me as its Director General. Sushama is a Fine Arts graduate and has done many paintings which have been published in my books from time to time. Her paintings also adorn the walls of our house at F7, Hauz Khas Enclave. But that is a minor point. As a human being, she is a gem, full of kindness towards one and all. Not only has she looked after my wife and me in the most affectionate manner all through the past decades, but she has also taken care of others in the family equally well. And her love extends far beyond the family. She takes good care of the children of our domestic help, teaches them and provides them with necessary teaching aids. She has also been rendering voluntary assistance to the Spastic Society of Northern India, Hauz Khas, which looks after physically disabled children.

But what I am going to state now will show her immense love even for the non-human beings. In 2006 we were living in 79, Lodhi Estate Bungalows, which had been allotted to Rajesh. One summer evening, my wife, Sushama and I came out of the house to have some fresh air. It was the month of June and the mango trees were loaded with fruits. We saw a parrot sitting on the branch of one of the trees, pecking a mango. My first reaction was to clap loudly so that the parrot may fly away and the fruits saved. But the reaction of Sushama is worth noting. She exclaimed in joy: "How beautiful is the sight, the parrot pecking the fruit and enjoying it. It is certainly worth a photograph." She immediately went inside the house, brought her camera and photographed the parrot. The bird was allowed to continue eating fruits. What an affectionate attitude!

Rajesh and Sushama have two daughters, no son. The elder daughter, Nirupama, first got her Master's degree in English Literature from Delhi University in 1999. But, like her mother, was keen to look after handicapped children. Thus, she got her second Master's degree in Special Education from Temple University, Philadelphia, USA in 2003 and is currently working with Spectrum Center Schools in Oakland, California, as Senior Clinician, which job involves training teachers and other staff who look after special needs of the children. The second daughter, Anjali, helped me a lot a few years ago when I was being treated for problems of the lumbar region at the All India Institute of Medical Sciences, New Delhi. She got her Master's degree in Social Work in 2003 from the Tata Institute of Social Sciences, Bombay. In May 2008 she was married to Shiva

Shankar who is working with Dell Global Services in Austin, Texas, USA. Over there she is pursuing studies for another Master's degree in Women and Gender Studies and after her graduation in 2010, she intends to work for a women's organization.

The second son, Vrajesh, is no less adventurous. After obtaining his B.Tech degree in Metallurgy from Indian Institute of Technology, Kanpur, he left for Los Angeles, USA and joined the University of Southern California for an MBA degree. He came out with flying colors and worked with the Dean of the Faculty for some time. However, through a series of circumstances, he switched on to garment-manufacturing and started a company, in collaboration with Maurice Breslev, a French designer of repute. Later, Vrajesh bought this company and in course of time raised it to a very big manufacturing unit named 'Just for Wraps'. Until the recent recession in USA (as elsewhere), the company was doing excellently well. My wife and I have been annual visitors to Los Angeles for the past 25 years and have thoroughly enjoyed our stay there.

Vrajesh has donated a large sum of money to his alma mater, IIT, Kanpur, whereby has been established a professorship in my name, combining Archaeology and Technology. In India, whereas the cultural aspects of archaeological data are being well taken care of, little is being done to study their technological aspects. It is to meet this need that Vrajesh has made the donation. May we hope that his wishes are fulfilled, at least partly, in the near future.

Vrajesh's wife, Bina, is yet another jewel in the Lal family. I have no words to praise her human qualities. She holds a Ph. D. in Genetics from Punjab University, Chandigarh. Some time after coming to Los Angeles, she took up an assignment at UCLA, which she later gave up. She has successfully brought up her son, Nikhil, and daughter, Ritu, both of whom are now well settled. Nikhil did his Bachelor's degree in Textile and Apparel Management from Cornell University and is now working with Macy's, a renowned Department Store of USA. Ritu has gone out of the routine and has graduated in Theater and Design from Sarah Lawrence College. She is looking forward to being an actress – of repute, God willing.

But what gives me the greatest satisfaction about this couple is that both Vrajesh and Bina are on the spiritual path and, as far as I can make out, are well advanced. They were initiated into *Kriyā Yoga,* some time after their joining the Self Realization Fellowship, a spiritual organization established by Paramahansa Yogananda who has inspired millions of disciples all over the world. Yogananda took his *mahāsamādhi* in 1952 and currently Shri Daya Mata leads the organization on the spiritual path.

Our youngest son, Rakesh, had his degree in Hotel Management and was with the Oberoi's in Dubai. But after a short spell over there, he left for Los Angeles and joined the up-coming garment factory started by his elder brother. His wife, Nishi, had her Master's degree and M. Phil. in Political Science from Jawaharlal Nehru University, New Delhi. After reaching Los Angeles, she had plans to continue her studies for a Ph.D. degree, but household needs prevented her from doing so. Both Rakesh and Nishi are highly affectionate and dutiful. They have two sons. The elder one, Niraj, is currently studying for a Bachelor's degree in Business Management at the University of Miami, while the younger, Rahul, is in High School and will hopefully turn out to be an excellent basket ball player.

It needs to be added that Rakesh as well as Nishi are excellent photographers and it is a treat to go through their albums. Further, a collection of photographs taken by them during their recent European tour has been published by a travel website and has been acclaimed as superb.

I have a few friends in Los Angeles, the nearest and dearest of them being Professor Shiva Bajpai. He used to teach History at the California State University, Northridge, but is now in part-retirement. He has been kind enough to visit and join us over a cup of tea or dinner. Once the talk turned about our family. I told Professor Bajpai, with a sense of immense satisfaction, that God has been exceptionally kind to us in giving such affectionate and well-behaved sons and daughters-in-law. They are our most valuable assets and may God shower His blessings on all of them.

Incidentally, all my daughters-in-law are excellent cooks. Besides preparing superb Indian dishes, they cook very good Italian, Thai, Chinese and Mexican food. As if not to be brow-beaten, the sons too are very good cooks. They have been hosting large parties of friends and relatives. Kusum is also a very good cook, but her field is only Indian. When young, she often threw large parties. The only black sheep in the family is myself. I cannot prepare even a cup of tea. But I really do not regret that, since I am saved of all botherations. Would you care to agree with me?

I would like to complete this family saga with an event which took place in May 2009. That month the entire family, of fifteen members, landed in Honolulu, Hawaii, USA (Pl. XIX). We stayed in Hotel Hilton, which overlooks the sea. A fantastic view, indeed! Many events were planned: sight-seeing, cruises, sea-surfing and dinners. There were also several family celebrations. On the 23rd of May was the 60th birthday of Vrajesh; on the 24th, the marriage anniversary of Anjali and Shiva Shankar; on the 25th, the marriage anniversary of Sushama and Rajesh; and on 27th, Rajesh's birthday. Each and every moment of our stay there was thoroughly enjoyed. In its wake, it was also decided that we should have such a get-together every year. The next one is planned for December 2010, in Kerala, India. Hopefully it matures.

11

Calcutta 1953-55

In 1953 I was transferred to Calcutta (now renamed as Kolkata) as Superintending Archaeologist in charge of the Eastern Circle of the Survey. Over there the main task was the conservation of centrally protected monuments. The jurisdiction was from Orissa in the south to Assam in the north. During the period of my stay over there, I did my best to look after the monuments, paying particular attention to the Sun Temple at Konark, Raja Rani and Mukteshwar temples in Bhuvaneshvar, monuments at Malda in West Bengal and monuments of the Ahom Period in Assam.

But the excavator in me was restless all the time. Thus, during the course of my tours in West Bengal I explored a number of sites, amongst which Birbhanpur, in Burdwan District, appeared to be very promising for an investigation of the Mesolithic period. Since the results are of great significance, the same are given below in some detail.

The site lay on the left bank of the Damodar River, of which two terraces were identified. Of these, the lower one was relatively recent and bereft of any implements. Thus, trenches, two in number, were laid out only on the higher terrace, both of which yielded the same kind of deposits. At the base there was highly decayed coarse-grained sandstone, generally whitish but sometimes having black streaks and somewhat pinkish granules. Over it there lay a deposit of mottled silty sand having white and red patches, representing the weathering *in situ* of the underlying sandstone. Above it was a layer comprising lateritic gravel and sandstone fragments in a silty matrix. The top of this deposit formed the land-surface on which lived the Mesolithic man, as revealed by the presence of microlithic tools. Also found were a few post-holes indicating the construction of some kind of a wind-break. The presence of a stone anvil with a cluster of debitage suggests an on-the-spot manufacture of the tools. The deposit that sealed the microlithic layer consisted of sandy earth, about 75 cm in thickness, the upper 10-15 cm of which had weathered black owing to a long-term vegetation cover. Thus, it is abundantly clear that this microlithic industry lay in a geological context.

The raw material used for the manufacture of the tools was mostly quartz, besides which crystal, chert, chalcedony and even fossil wood were also used. The tool-types included blades, lunates, points, scrapers, borers, burins, etc. The association of geometric tools such as the triangle and trapeze is not attested to. It also needs to be added that there was total absence of any kind of pottery. Thus, this assemblage may be termed as 'a non-geometric, pre-pottery microlithic industry'. On this acoount as well as on account of its geological context, this industry is evidently of a high antiquity and although we do not have any C-14 dates available, it may well be placed soon after the beginning of the Holocene, say somewhere between 10,000 and 8,000 BCE.

I would like to narrate a few instances from my personal life during my stay in Calcutta. When I joined the Eastern Circle, Shri Shasadhar Mukerjee, who was with me in Taxila, was already there as Deputy Superintending Archaeologist. He was residing in Behala, a locality in southern Calcutta, and was kind enough to arrange for me a house on rent in that area. From Behala to Chittaranjan Avenue in central Calcutta, where my office was located, was a long way off and I had to take a tramway or a bus to commute between the two places. This trip took about 30-40 minutes each way. Besides being time-consuming, the journey was very boring. An idea occurred to me: why not utilize the time to learn Bangla language? Thus, I began by picking up the Bangla script first. This I did in a most peculiar manner. The names of the destinations and places on the way were mentioned on the bodies of these vehicles, both in the Bangla script and the Roman. I also took advantage of the bi-lingual sign-boards at shops. Thus, starting with the Roman script and looking for parallels in Bangla script, I was able to familiarize myself with most of the Bangla letters. Having done so, I decided to read a book. I thought that reading one of the famous novels of the Bengali literature would be ideal. Hence, I chose to begin with *Ānanda Maṭha* written by the great novelist Bankim Chandra. I took this decision since I was told that the language used by him contained a good deal of words akin to Sanskrit, a language I was already familiar with. It was rather a very tough job. I could read only about half-a-page during my out-going and in-coming journeys, put together. But even that was satisfying as I began to enjoy the nuances of this great novel. Later on, I picked up some speed, but it took me about six months to complete this novel. I never tried reading Sharat Chandra, since his language contained a great deal of colloquial stuff which was hard for me to follow.

I did not like the Behala locality and was thus looking for a change. After about three months I was able to rent a house in Bali Ganj, a reasonably decent locality but, again, far away from my office. Tramway and bus were, again, the only options.

The incident that I am going to narrate now depicts my mental set-up those days in the most naked way. One morning, at the breakfast table there was a heated discussion between my wife and me on some topic which I cannot distinctly recall now. I was getting angry and angrier at her. And then in a huff I left the house. On reaching the bus-stand I got into a bus that was about to leave. Seated in the bus, I kept on mentally quarreling with my wife always laying the entire blame at her door. How could I be wrong? – was my typical stand. After some time, when I looked through the windows of the bus I discovered that I was in Shyam Bazar area, which was on a different route altogether. I then realized that I had not taken the right bus and had got into just some bus caring little where it was headed for. I got down from the bus and took another which included Chittaranjan Avenue on its route. In the evening when I reached home, I narrated the entire story to my wife and told her to avoid quarrelling at least in the morning. Pity that I didn't have the courage to confess to her that I was in the wrong!

While still continuing to stay in the Bali Ganj house, I purchased a second-hand car and learnt driving it. On weekends, my wife and I used to go out sightseeing or shopping. One day we went to a major shopping center in central Calcutta. After buying other items we reached a shop specializing in crockery. We selected a nice set and asked the shopkeeper to pack it up. I gave him five hundred rupees and he returned some amount, along with a receipt, which I put in my purse and drove back to our house. After opening the package and checking up the crockery, I looked into my purse to ensure that the shopkeeper had returned the right amount of money. Surprisingly, I discovered that the returned amount was in excess of what was due. Immediately my wife and I decided that we should drive back to the shop concerned and return the excess amount. We did the same and derived great satisfaction from it. Perhaps, the 'one-ānā' episode of Garotha (cf. pp. 60-61) was operating subconsciously in the mind.

Although I now had a car, the time taken in driving to the office and back was in no way less than what it was when I was commuting by bus. The traffic on the main road from Bali Ganj to Esplanade was very heavy. Thus, I rented a flat, which was hardly a mile away from the office. It was located on the Indian Mirror Street and owned by a well-known family, the Nahars of Rajasthan. My second son, Vrajesh, who was by now about five years old, was with us, the eldest, Rajesh, having been left behind with his maternal grandmother in Delhi. We got Vrajesh admitted to Loretto, an English-medium school, located on way to my office. One evening when he came back from school, we asked him as to what he had learnt that day in the school. We were on the terrace of the flat. We cannot forget the scene. Little Vrajesh, who was still dressed in his white school uniform with a red tie, went away from us to the end of the terrace and told us that that day he had learnt the word 'come' and how to act on it on being commanded to do so. Thus, when we said, 'come, Vrajesh', he walked up to us giving a demonstration of the lesson of the day. We could not but hug him in great delight. Vrajesh, I must say, was very intelligent right from his childhood. After our dinner one evening we were removing the dishes from the table. I had picked up two glasses, one in each hand. Vrajesh offered to collect the glasses and he picked all the three glasses with one hand, fitting them in between the fingers. Again, after the excavation at Birbhanpur (above, pp. 78-79) when we started returning to Calcutta, Vrajesh refused to leave the place, saying, *'Pāpā, ham Kalkattā nahīn jāyenge. Yahān to* microlith *milate hain, Kalkatte men nahīn.'* He had picked up the word 'microlith' and became very fond of collecting them from the surface.

12

From Calcutta to Agra, 1955

In 1955 I was transferred to Agra. Taj Mahal indeed was, is and will always remain, a charming monument – every inch of it. My wife and I spent hours on several moonlit nights going around it or sitting in the garden in front of it and enjoying the unique glimmer caused by the rays of the moon falling on the inlay pieces.

While in Agra Circle, I devoted most of my attention to the conservation of monuments. Thus, besides the Taj, the Fort at Agra itself and monuments at Fatehpur Sikri were duly taken care of. Away from the headquarters, the palace at Deegh and temples at Khajuraho were focused on. And now I will cite just two examples of how strict I was with my conservation staff, which doubtless made me somewhat unpopular with them – or at least with some of them.

The Senior Conservation Assistant of the Circle, Shri Ram Kishen, was in-charge of the repairs, amongst others, of the monuments at Deegh. The practice was that before the bills of the contractors were passed for payment, the work done was first checked by the Conservation Assistant concerned and then test-checked by an officer. Thus, I went to Deegh to check up the repairs done over there. Ram Kishen was with me. He took me to the areas where the work had been done. With a small pickaxe in hand, I started striking at the surface of the walls on which plastering had been done. Immediately large chunks of the plaster began to fall, and it was discovered that, instead of the prescribed mix of lime, cement and sand, a very high percentage of sand had been used. Hence the quick collapse of the plaster. On seeing this, Ram Kishen became nervous since he had already certified that the work had been executed as per the specifications provided in the estimate. One could easily guess that there was some deal between him and the contractor concerned. Ram Kishen had no option but to admit his guilt and ask for pardon. Although I could have easily taken severe penal action, I did not do so because of his immediate and public admission of the guilt. But I told him to re-do the entire work at his cost and then have it test-checked once again. He did it and I test-checked the same. Then alone the bills were passed.

Here is yet another example, though of a different kind, of my strictness. I went to Khajuraho for a check-up of the repairs to the temples. Since this work was of a specialized nature, it could not be given to a contractor. Hence, it was being done under the direct supervision of the Conservation Assistant (CA) posted over there, Shri D.D. Gupta. For this purpose masons and other technicians were employed on daily wages and their names were entered on a muster roll. I asked the CA to let me have the muster roll. On having a look at it, I noted that out of the twenty-and-odd people put on the muster roll, three were marked absent on that day and a day before. I was to have arrived the previous day but was delayed by a day. This absence-mark against the names of the three persons just for these two days led me to suspect that something was wrong somewhere. I asked the CA about their absence and he told me that they had been taken ill and hence did not come to work. On further enquiry he gave me the name of the *Vaidya* (Ayurvedic physician) under whose treatment these people were. I immediately went to the physician who told me that no such persons were under his treatment. I then asked the CA to give me the local address of these persons. They also were found to be non-existent. The truth fully revealed itself. The CA had made fictitious entries in the muster roll. I immediately charge-sheeted the CA and, after recording all the relevant evidence, including statements of all concerned, awarded him the punishment, though not very harsh.

The above-mentioned two incidents sent an unwritten message to all the Conservation Assistants in the Circle that I meant business and no hanky-panky would do.

13

From Agra to Delhi Circle, 1956

While still holding charge of Agra Circle, I came out on a tour to visit monuments in the hilly districts of Uttar Pradesh which fell under the jurisdiction of this Circle. Since Delhi was on the route, I halted there for a couple of days in order to transact some official business at the Survey's headquarters. My uncle-in-law, Shri H.L. Srivastava, had already retired from the post of Joint Director General in the Survey and was now living in a private house in Hauz Khas Colony which had just started coming up. Naturally, my wife and I who was accompanying me stayed with him. Most unfortunately, on the second night my uncle-in-law developed a severe heart problem. The doctor came, gave some treatment and asked me to get an oxygen cylinder since my uncle-in-law was getting short of breath. I went to Connaught Place to get the cylinder but before I could return, he breathed his last. Since Shrimati Srivastava was left all alone, I had to cancel my tour and give her some comfort and company. Shri A. Ghosh, who had worked for quite a few years in Central Circle, Patna, as a junior colleague of Shri

Srivastava, was the Director General of the Survey at that time. He sympathetically assessed the situation and transferred me to Delhi Circle so that the wife of his former colleague was not left in a lurch. Under these circumstances, I took charge of Delhi Circle and started my work.

After going round the Delhi monuments and giving instructions to the conservation staff concerned about the repairs to be carried out, I embarked on a tour of the monuments located in Kangra District. On my way, I inspected the work executed at certain monuments which fell under the charge of Shri Uttam Chand Sharma, the Senior Conservation Assistant of the Circle. At one of the monuments, I test-checked the strength of the concrete-covering laid on its terrace to make it water-proof and I must say that the end of the pickaxe broke down and not the concrete. This was in marked contrast to what had happened in the case of repairs carried out at Deegh by Ram Kishen of Agra Circle. Not everybody amongst the staff of the Survey was cast in the image of Ram Kishen!

I camped at Kangra from where I inspected the various monuments in the region. As usual, my wife, Kusum, was with me. The arduous travel, however, took a toll on her health and she was down with fever for a couple of days. My next place of visit was Masrur, where there were rock-cut temples. The entire journey of about fifteen kilometers each way had to be done on foot. Also involved was the steep crossing of the Banganga River on whose bank Kangra is located. Kusum was keen on coming along, even though she had not yet fully recovered. No amount of advice from me not to come worked and there she was. However, it turned out to be a blessing in disguise.

As we were moving along the route, I noticed the terraces of the Banganga as well as pebbles jutting out from these. I told Kusum that such a setting was quite suitable for the Stone Age man to live in. He would utilize these

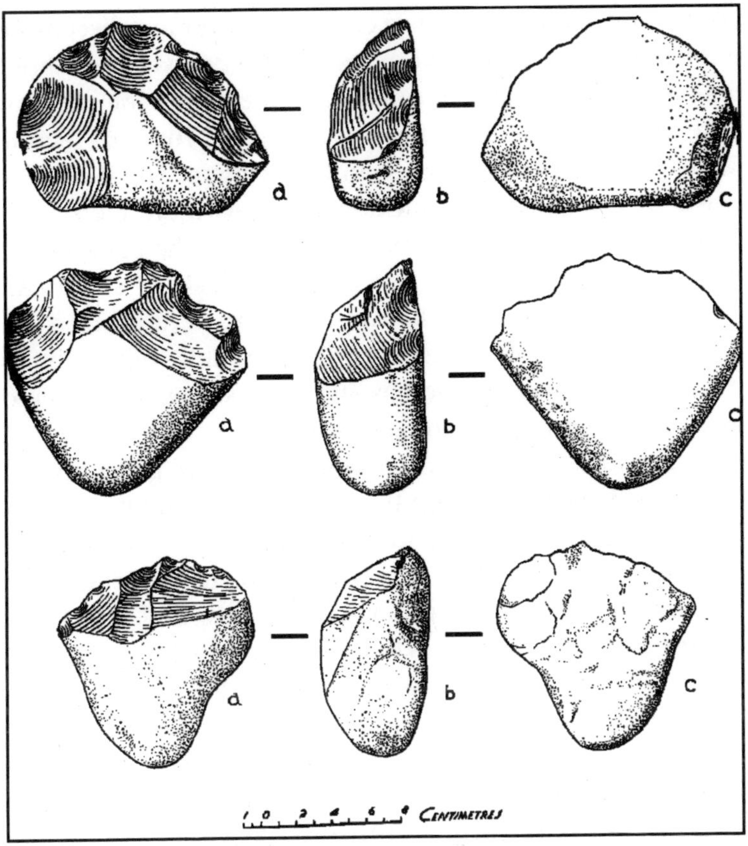

Fig. 4. Guler: 'Unifacial' choppers.

pebbles to make his tools and use them for hunting wild animals roaming about in the partially forested environment. I picked up a pebble and explained to her how a series of flakes were detached from the pebbles and they were converted into tools. And lo and behold, while I was only theorizing, Kusum picked up a flaked pebble from the ground and told me that it well responded to the description of a tool that I had been talking about. This, indeed, was a pebble-tool and hence the credit of discovering the palaeolithic site of Guler must go to Kusum.

Thereafter, she and I made a concerted effort to collect more tools and by the time we reached Masrur, we had about half-a-dozen of them in our bag. We camped the night at Masrur, spent the next day in visiting the rock-cut temple and the conservation carried out over there. The third day we returned to Kangra, picking up a few more tools.

In all, five terraces were observed on the bank of the Banganga. The bed-rock over here consists of shale and sandstone, which had tilted in antiquity because of some drastic upheaval. This was overlain by boulders and pebbles which in turn were capped by silt. The tools were recovered only from the upper three terraces.

The tools are made on pebbles which are generally flat on one side but convex on the other. Thus, only the convex side is flaked and hence the tools are known as unifacial pebble-tools (Fig. 4) – in contrast to the bifacial tools (handaxes and cleavers) met with at sites in Central and South India. It may, perhaps, be added here that the discovery of the pebble-tools at Guler and at other neighboring sites on the Beas, such as Dehra and Dhaliara, was an important addition to our knowledge, since after the Partition of India in 1947 practically all the sites of the pebble-tool palaeolithic culture, known as the 'Sohan Culture', fell within the Pakistan region.

14

January 17, 1957: My Rebirth

Do not be surprised at the title. I have no idea about life after death nor about re-birth thereafter. But the re-birth I am talking about here is my own, during this very life.

In 1957 I was working as the Director of Monuments in the Survey and the first assignment I was given was to survey the monuments in Bijapur District, Karnataka. Over there, nearly two hundred monuments were on the Central List of protection. These included some very important monuments like the Gol Gumbad, but a good many of them were not important enough to continue enjoying Central protection. In fact, because of lack of funds with the Survey in those days many of these monuments could not be duly attended to. Thus, it was decided by the Survey that it should continue to look after only those monuments which really fulfilled the then laid-down criteria of being designated as 'monuments of national importance'. The rest, being of local importance, should be handed over to the State Government.

In January of that year, I embarked on this re-survey of the monuments in Bijapur District. Shri M.N. Deshpande was the Superintending Archaeologist of the Circle, with headquarters at Aurangabad. I joined him there and in his jeep we started for Bijapur. There we camped for about three weeks. At the first weekend, on Saturday afternoon, Shri Deshpande asked me if he could go to Nimbal, a place about 25-30 kilometers from Bijapur. I asked him about the purpose of his visit to Nimbal and, rather shyly, he told me that he was going there to pay regards to his Guru, Professor R.D. Ranade. At Nimbal, too, there were a few Centrally protected monuments. So it was decided that we would assess those monument on Monday when Shri Deshpande would be free. Thus, he left for Nimbal on Saturday evening by a railway train, leaving the jeep behind for me to go to Nimbal on Monday morning.

I reached Nimbal as scheduled and we surveyed the monuments located in Nimbal village and its neighborhood. After the day's work was over, we planned to return to Bijapur. Two of Gurudeva Ranade's disciples, who were residents of Bijapur, wanted a lift. We offered the same and our journey back to Bijapur commenced. These gentlemen were seated in the back row and I was in the front. They began talking to each other and I was quietly overhearing them. One of them told the other, "Some time back an American journalist had come to India and interviewed three distinguished philosophers of the country, namely, Dr. S. Radhakrishnan, Shri J. Krishnamurti and Dr. R.D. Ranade. His main question was: 'What do you believe in'. While the other two dignitaries gave their own answers, Dr. Ranade's reply was: 'I don't believe, I perceive'." They continued their talk about Dr. Ranade, which was full of eulogies for him.

But, I was fired by Dr. Ranade's sharply focused reply, viz.: 'I don't believe, I perceive.' I decided to visit Dr. Ranade over the next weekend when Shri Deshpande was scheduled to visit him again.

Here, perhaps, it seems necessary to let the reader know who this Dr. R. (Rambhau) D. (Dattatreya) Ranade was (Pl. XXI). He was born on July 3, 1886 at Jamakhandi in Bijapur District, Karnataka. At a very early age, he was initiated into spiritual life by Bhau Saheb Maharaj, a great saint of Umadi, who, it must be stressed, was no recluse but a normal house-holder, serving as a Talukdar in the Revenue Department of the State.

Rambhau had a very brilliant academic career and was the winner of several gold medals and scholarships. Alongside his studies, he pursued his *sādhanā* (meditation) and had wonderful spiritual experiences even during those early days. In search of an explanation for these experiences, he embarked on a serious study of the life and works of saints and philosophers, both Indian and Western. He had a remarkable grip on the works of even Aristotle, Socrates, Kant, Hegel and other Western philosophers. On the Indian side, there was nothing that went beyond his ken. His first monumental work, published in 1926, was *A Constructive Survey of Upaniadic Philosophy*. This was followed by another great work, namely, *Mysticism in Maharashtra*, which appeared in 1933. These brought him international fame and in 1937 Mahāmahopādhyāya Dr. Ganganatha Jha, the then Vice-Chancellor of Allahabad University, invited him to join that University as a Professor of Philosophy. Towards the end of his career at the University, he also became its Vice-Chancellor. At the University, however, only a few close associates knew about the spiritual heights which Professor Ranade had achieved. For the rest, he was just an outstanding scholar of Philosophy.

Way back, in 1922, he had a dream-vision which directed him to Nimbal where he built a small house and would stay there during the summer vacations of the University. Later on, it assumed the form of an *āśrama* where he spent the rest of his life. He passed away on June 6, 1957.

To come back to my second visit to Nimbal. On reaching there, I put in a request that I wanted to see the learned professor, which was readily granted. When I met him I was surprised that he hugged me, as if he already knew me. After paying my regards to him, I lost no time in firing one question after another at him. I began, "Sir, I have heard from one of your disciples that an American journalist interviewed you and asked you 'what do you believe in?' and your reply was 'I don't believe, I perceive'. Is that really so?" For a while Professor Ranade tried to avoid answering my question by talking about a few other things. But when I insisted on getting a reply, he relented and confirmed what the disciple had said. Immediately I fired my next question, "Sir, 'perceive' is a transitive verb and hence there must be an object of perception." Again, he tried to avoid the question, adding that I shouldn't bother about these matters. My dogged insistence brought forth an answer in the affirmative. Thereafter I told him, "If that be so, there must be a method of perception." At this, he smiled and replied, "Read, my boy, read and you will get the answer." This did not satisfy me and I went on, "Sir, if with your frail body you can claim to perceive 'something' (as I put it), why can't I? After all, I too have a body and a mind, just as you have." Nothing but an amused smile was the reaction.

Later in the day, I was asked by a senior inmate of the *āśrama*, "Which name of God do you believe in?" "I don't believe in God, much less in any particular name," was my prompt reply. "Don't you utter some name of God when in difficulty," came a supplementary question. I shot back, "Well, there is no consistency about it. Sometimes I even say 'Ya Allah'." I don't know what reaction it produced on the enquirer.

Anyway, next morning I was told that I could be initiated, if I so wished. I was in a fix since I had never thought of getting initiated. An initiation meant getting a *nāma* (a seeded Name of God) from the guru with a view to repeating it mentally in a prescribed manner and with devotion. I consulted my wife who was there with me. She expressed all sorts of apprehensions. We called on Professor Ranade once again and I told him: "Sir, my wife is afraid that the guru might become angry if she, after getting initiated, did not continue to practise what was prescribed." To that I hurriedly added my own comments: "In my own view no guru can ever become angry with his disciple since the guru is said to be an incarnation of God and thus ought to be full of compassion." Professor Ranade smiled both at my wife's fears and at my logic. I then told him about a very specific fear of my wife. "She is worried that since *pūjā*s (rituals) are forbidden during the monthly 'periods' of ladies, so how can she continue to practice *nāma-smaraṇa* during those 'periods'." "Do you think God ceases to exist during certain 'periods'?" was his simple but very penetrating reply.

Thus, our doubts were set at rest, but we were still not very enthusiastic about getting initiated. "Anyway, let us give the thing a trial and we shall give it up if we don't feel comfortable with it," we told each other. We were thus initiated, as if we were obliging the guru. What an attitude!

Hardly a week had passed and I began getting certain spiritual experiences which, I was told by brother disciples, were of a high order. Evidently, these were due to the grace of the guru because I had not put in any worthwhile effort during that brief period. Since then I have been blessed with many more spiritual experiences – of light, sound and visions, which I cannot describe here because tradition forbids us from doing so. Anyway, these experiences are but milestones on the journey; the destination is still far off.

Putting aside these spiritual experiences, the *nāma-smaraṇa* has brought about a fundamental transformation in my life – weaning me gradually away from enemies like *kāma* (lust), *krodha* (anger), *lobha* (greed), etc. and leading me towards a life full of peace and joy. Professor Ranade is no longer to me just a Professor of Philosophy; he is now my *gurudeva* (God-and-guru-in-one) who has been showering his blessings on me at every stage of my life. **He has given me a re-birth!**

15

Vegetarian/Non-vegetarian/ Vegetarian

In India one is often asked if he/she is a vegetarian or a non-vegetarian. I don't know why? Perhaps there is an underlying belief that vegetarianism is conducive to spiritualism. I do not know how far this assumption is valid.

Anyway, I was a vegetarian for the first twenty years of my life, though my father had all along been a non-vegetarian and was even given to alcohol. After my serious illness at the time of my B.A. examination in 1941 and its persistence beyond that, I was given treatment by Baḍe Hakimji of Datia (above, pp. 17-19) who prescribed to me the *yaqinī* (a soup made from the bone marrow of goat) for speedy recovery. Most unwillingly, I agreed to make that experiment. The *yaqinī* was prepared almost everyday and I began to like it. In due course of time, I started eating meat also and became a confirmed non-vegetarian. Further on, I turned into an omnivorous creature, since while traveling in far-off countries in Europe I was confronted with beef-dishes only. When questioned about this unexpected change in my food habits, I defended my action by retorting that all animals are alike; if killing one kind is justified, why not the other?

I not only took to meat-eating but took to hunting animals as well. I borrowed my father's gun and kept it for long years until I passed it on to my younger brother, Om Prakash. However, one incident of shooting seems to be worth narrating since it brings out not only my callousness towards innocent birds but also my insensitivity towards the noble feelings of my wife. Once, in 1956, my wife, I and a few members of the Delhi Circle staff were traveling in a jeep from Delhi to Ajmer. A little before sunset, we came across a small river and decided to stop the jeep and relax for a while. The sunset view was fabulous and for a while we were engrossed in it. Meanwhile, my eyes fell on a group of birds that had descended on the river-bank to quench their thirst. The devil in me woke up and a sinister idea came to my mind. Why not shoot them down? It would make for a nice dinner. Immediately I took out my gun. Notwithstanding my wife's protests, I shot down a couple of birds, bundled them up in a bag and put them in the back of the car. On reaching the Circuit House in Ajmer, I ordered the chef there to cook the birds and bring them up for the dinner. My wife refused to come to the dining table. In fact, she was so much upset that she did not take any food at all. Indeed, a callous husband!

There is yet another incident reflecting my insensitivity in this regard. As a Director of Monuments in 1957, I was traveling in Aurangabad Circle. Besides my wife there was Dr. M.N. Deshpande, the Superintending Archaeologist of the Circle. We reached Ajanta, where Abdul Wahid was the Officer-in-charge. He invited us to dinner. Also present on the occasion was Dr. Paramasivan, Assistant Archaeological Chemist. As we sat down for dinner, lavish dishes were laid out on the table, both vegetarian and non-vegetarian. I started off, as the chief guest and so did my wife. But after a while I noticed that my wife stopped eating. I also noticed that, following the Muslim way of dining together, Wahid and his colleagues were taking out with their hands the pieces of chicken from the bowl. With the same hands they were also picking up the *chapātīs*, with the result that the latter got besmeared with the curry of the chicken. My wife, being a strict vegetarian, naturally couldn't eat those *chapātīs*. The situation was rather odd. Dr. Paramasivan offered to me a wise counsel: "When you are traveling with Mrs. Lal, you should tell the host to serve only vegetarian meal. No non-veg." And do you know what my reply was: "If she so desires she can take out the vegetarian items first, keep them separately and eat them, but I see no reason why I should give up my non-vegetarian dishes on such occasions." That was me, a hard-core non-vegetarian then. But have a look at what followed.

After a few days, we reached Bijapur to assess the centrally protected monuments over there. As mentioned in the chapter 'My Rebirth', I ran into Gurudeva Ranade and was initiated. On our return from Nimbal, we stayed in Hyderabad as Dr. Parmasivan's guests. At the breakfast table there were, besides nice *idalīs*, some cake-pastries as well. The latter contained some parts of egg. I do not know why and how I did not feel like having the cakes and avoided them. Everybody was surprised. Let me add here that no one, as a part of the initiation process at Nimbal, ever asked me or even remotely suggested that I should give up non-vegetarian food. In fact, the question whether one was a vegetarian or non-vegetarian never ever came up in the picture. Since then, however, I am a vegetarian.

16

1959: Establishment of the School of Archaeology

In 1944, on assuming charge of the Survey as its new Director General, Mortimer Wheeler set up a Training Camp at Taxila (now in Pakistan) to impart practical training to selected students from all over India in the new technique of excavation, which was quite different from what was then being practised in the country (cf. Chapter 1). I happened to be one of the trainees. Thereafter, a second training camp was set up at Arikamedu, which I was invited to join as a Site Supervisor – some sort of a functionary between the Director of the excavations (Wheeler) and the new batch of students, this time mostly drawn from the southern parts of the country.

Very little was done after the departure of Wheeler in terms of training and this lacuna was being realized more and more as time passed. Thus, in 1959 a School of Archaeology was founded under the auspices of the Survey and I was given the privilege of being its first Director. Unlike Wheeler's camps which provided training only in field-archaeology, the School was a full-fledged institution, offering courses in wide-ranging disciplines, both practical as well as theoretical. On the practical side, not only excavation and exploration techniques were included but also those of structural conservation of monuments and their chemical preservation. Practical training was also given in drawing, surveying and photography, since these were considered essential for an archaeologist. On the theoretical side were included subjects like prehistory, protohistory and historical archaeology, as well as art, architecture, epigraphy and numismatics. Of course, the idea was not to create specialists in these subjects but to generate an all-round awareness so that the person concerned may be able to meet the immediate needs while functioning as a future officer in the Survey. Various officers of the Survey and sometimes even experts from outside were requested to deliver lectures in their specialities.

The course was of two-year duration and, to begin with, about a dozen students were admitted. The candidates were required to have a Master's degree in any of the following subjects: Indian History, Sanskrit, Arabic, Persian, Pali, Prakrit and Archaeology. On successfully passing the required examination, the students were awarded a Post-graduate Diploma in Archaeology. The course was open to students even from outside the country and thus we had on the roll trainees from Nepal, Thailand, Afghanistan, etc.

The School had been performing its function very satisfactorily and in 1985 it was renamed as Institute of Archaeology. To my mind, this Institute has a much greater role to play, as recommended by the Archaeology Review Committee, set up in 2000 under my Chairmanship (pp. 191-92).

The first batch of students was given practical training in excavation at a site called Gilund, located in Rajasthan. It yielded substantial remains of a chalcolithic complex, distinguished by its black-and-red and black-slipped wares painted with linear and curvilinear designs in white pigment. Of the structural remains discovered at the site, the most remarkable one was a complex comprising a series of parallel walls. It may have been a part of a large-sized granary – something which indicated not only the affluence of inhabitants but also a kind of organized socio-administrative system.

At the time of the excavation, no Carbon-14 dates were obtained but recent work at the site under the joint direction of Vasant Shinde of the Deccan College, Pune, and Gregory L. Possehl of the University of Pennsylvania, USA, has provided C-14 dates which take the antiquity of this chalcolithic complex back to the third millennium BCE. In fact, a new microlith-bearing sub-stratum has also been brought to light.

To provide practical training in conservation, the picturesque Kashmir Valley was chosen, which contains wide-ranging standing monuments, from the early historical times to the medieval. While the former are of bricks, the latter of stone. Thus, it was possible to train the students in conserving monuments requiring different kinds of skills – which included grouting, underpinning and even restoration of selected parts, but to a very limited extent.

17

1961: International Conference on Asian Archaeology

In 1961 the Archaeological Survey of India organized an International Conference on Asian Archaeology. It was a part of the various activities that took place on the occasion of the Centenary of the Survey. Shri A. Ghosh was the Director General, who asked me, Shri M.N. Deshpande and a few other officers of the Survey to assist him in the organizational work. The Conference was the first of its kind. Distinguished archaeologists from all over the world were invited to participate in it. These included: Sir Max Mallowan, Lady Agatha Christie, Dr. Hanna Rydh, Dr. J.M. Casal, Sir Mortimer Wheeler, Professor F.E. Zeuner and many others from abroad, besides of course those from India such as Professor H.D. Sankalia, Professor B.P. Sinha, in addition to many officers of the Survey itself. On this occasion, an exhibition of sculptures and of models of some select archaeological monuments was also set up. The Conference was inaugurated by the then Prime Minister of India, Pandit Jawaharlal Nehru.

Many interesting papers were presented by the participants and one of them was by me as well. However, before coming to the nuances of this paper of mine, I would like to tell my readers the background and genesis of this paper.

Ever since the discovery of the Harappan script in early 1920s, several attempts have been made to decipher it. Unfortunately, none of these has been successful. Let that alone, for quite some time there was a dispute even about the direction of writing in this script. Some held that it was from left to right while others thought that it was the other way round. Luckily for us, Kalibangan in Rajasthan, a Harappan site excavated by me, produced some inscribed potsherds, on which there is an overlap of the signs, which, as will be shown a little later, has fully resolved this issue.

In this context, it may also interest the reader to know how the idea that an overlap of signs might resolve the issue came to my mind. Once, after the close of the office at Janpath, New Delhi, I took out my car from the garage to return home. I drew it back for some distance and then forward in the direction of the exit gate. Meanwhile, someone beckoned me. I stopped the car and came out of it. After finishing the chat with this gentleman, when I was about to re-enter the car I noticed the marks left by the tires on the ground. Since it had rained a while ago, the soil was wet and hence the tire-marks were rather deep. I observed that the marks left by the tires when the car was driven back from the garage were overrun by the subsequent ones made by the tires when the car was driven towards the exit. I further noted that at the point of intersection of these marks, the edges of the earlier marks were obliterated by the later marks and that the edges of the later marks were intact. This observation led me to a wishful thinking that if in my excavation at KaliIbangan, which was then on, I could find a few potsherds on which there was an overlap of the inscribed signs it may perhaps be possible to determine which way these were written. Luckily, the wish was fulfilled and I did get a few potsherds on which there was an overlap of the signs.

On the basis of the evidence provided by these inscribed potsherds, viz., parts of the signs on the right were cut by the adjacent signs on the left, it became absolutely clear that in each case the sign on the right was written first and then came the sign on the left (Pl. VI). In other words, the direction of writing was from right to left. The paper was greeted with great applause by one and all, and commenting on it my guru, Sir Mortimer Wheeler, publicly said that that was the kind of penetrating analysis that he had expected from his favorite student. Later on, at his instance, the paper was published in *Antiquity*, XL (157): 52-55.

As I have mentioned earlier, many scholars claim that they have succeeded in deciphering the Harappan script. In 1969 when Asko Parpola and his colleagues came with a bang that the Harappan language was Dravidian, there was a great furore, so much so that even the then Tamil Nadu Government thought it worthwhile to endorse it. On the other hand, a German scholar, Richter-Ushanas, claims to have read even the Vedic verses in these inscriptions. I have thoroughly examined most of these claims from time to time and shown that they are unacceptable. In fact, at an International Symposium on Undeciphered Languages, held in London in1973, I presented a thorough critique of these claims and the participants agreed with me. These included eminent authorities such as Sir Harold Bailey, Sir Max Mallowan and Sir Mortimer Wheeler (Pl. XLI). However, in order to let the reader know in some detail the methodology adopted for ascertaining the direction of writing in the Harappan script and the unacceptability of the various claims regarding the decipherment of the Harappan script, I would like to draw the reader's attention to a paper, 'Some Observations on the Harappan Script', which I published in 1970 in *India's Contribution to World Thought and Culture* (eds. Lokesh Chandra *et al.*, Madras: Vivekanand Rock Memorial Committee).

18

Nubia (Egypt) 1962

In order to get a much greater amount of water-supply for irrigation and for generating greater quantum of hydro-electricity for its various industrial enterprises, the Government of United Arab Republic decided in 1950s to construct a High Dam (Sadd-el-Aālī) on the Nile, a few kilometers upstream from the then dam at Aswan, thereby raising the water-level from 121 to 182 meters above the mean sea-level. The project was to result in the formation of a vast lake in the Nubian region, which at places would extend up to 25 kilometers in width. This evidently threatened a number of sites and monuments, including the world-renowned temples at Abu Simbel. Finding its own resources very limited to cope with the salvage work of these sites and monuments, the UAR Government approached UNSECO for help, which in turn issued a worldwide appeal to come forward in the rescue operations. Ever willing to participate in such noble projects, the Government of India decided to send in 1962 a team of archaeologists and other technicians, under my leadership, to carry out excavations in the Nubian region.

Before I pass on to a narration of the excavations and their contribution to the archaeology of Egypt as well as the light these threw on Indo-Egyptian relationship in antiquity, I would like to let the reader know some very interesting experiences which came our way during the course of our expedition in Egypt.

My wife and I landed in Cairo by an Air India flight, on an afternoon around the middle of January 1962. Arrangements had been made for our stay at a five-star hotel in the city, where we were taken by the Egyptian staff that had come to receive us. It was about 4 p.m. in the evening and we were served a hot cup of tea and some snacks. My wife had unfortunately developed some fever on the flight from Delhi to Cairo. Thus, we decided to stay put in the hotel room, avoiding the temptation of having a first look at the city. All that we could do was to enjoy the bright city lights through the windows of our room. Since my wife was running fever, we decided to have our dinner in the room itself.

I telephoned the Room Service section of the hotel and told the person concerned to send our dinner to the room, adding that we were vegetarians and did not eat meat. Within half-an-hour, a bearer turned up with dinner. When I opened it, I discovered that there was chicken curry instead of the vegetable curry we had ordered for. I told the bearer that I had clearly told the person who had attended the call that we were vegetarians and did not eat meat. He replied, "Sir, that is why I have brought chicken and not mutton curry." I told the bearer to take the food back and bring neither chicken nor mutton. He took the food back and turned up after fifteen minutes, this time with fish curry. I was very much annoyed and shouted at him to bring only vegetables and nothing else. Finally, he brought some lintel soup, rice and baked potatoes. We heaved a sigh of relief. The bearer who was not in the least familiar – and why should he be? – with the Indian definitions of vegetarian and non-vegetarian meals, quietly asked, "Sir, how are you able to survive without eating mutton, chicken or even fish.". I gave him the simplest possible answer: "Isn't the very fact that we are alive proof enough that people can live without mutton, chicken, etc." Though surprised at the answer, the bearer quietly bowed out of the room.

During the night, my wife developed high fever. We did not have a thermometer so we could not ascertain how high it was. At the break of the dawn, I got in touch with the hotel manager and requested him to arrange for a doctor to come over and check my wife's illness. It turned out that she was having mumps. The doctor prescribed the necessary medicines and advised her to take complete rest. But that morning we were scheduled to visit the pyramids and few other monuments around Cairo. A member of the staff of the Egyptian Department of Antiquities turned up around 9 a.m. to take us to the monuments. I told my wife to rest and assured her that I would cut short my visit and come back as early as possible. She wouldn't listen to me and insisted that she would go. My pleading was of no avail. She got ready and came down to the lobby with me and we left to see the monuments.

Would you believe that in high fever she walked up and down the monuments and even went inside a pyramid. Because of high fever and a lot of walking about, she felt very thirsty. Unfortunately, we had not picked up a bottle of water from the hotel, hence we looked out for whatever water was available on the spot. There were large jars full of water and nearby there lay a few mugs with which to drink it. We saw people picking up the mugs, taking out water from the jars, drinking the water and placing the mugs back without cleaning or even rinsing them. This process was being repeated over and over again, by every person who drank the water. My wife, thanks to her immense fondness for hygiene, refused to drink water from those jars and with those unclean mugs. The result was that she had to go on without water even though her throat was very much parched. I do not know how to comment on this kind of attitude – exercise of will power or sheer stubbornness!

Her fever subsided in a couple of days and we, along with the other members of the team, left by a railway train for Aswan. On the other side of the dam, a boat was waiting for us. It was indeed a welcome surprise – with ten cabins on the lower floor and a big drawing-cum-dining room and a kitchen on the upper. It must have been the envy of other teams – European and American – working in that region alongside us, since their boats were much smaller. Even our Ambassador Shri Azim Hussain and his wife, who came to visit us (Pl. XLIV) during the course of our field-work, were surprised to find us living in such a luxurious boat.

The team, a homogenous unit, comprised an excavation assistant, Shri K.M. Srivastava, a photographer, Shri R. Chatterji, a draftsman, Shri Amir Singh and a surveyor, Shri S.P. Jain. Shri Jain, a very practical person, offered his services to manage the kitchen. There were two Egyptian members associated with the kitchen, a cook and a helper. Jain taught them, within a few days, how to cook Indian meals and there we were enjoying *parāthā*s (a kind of shallow-fried bread) and *chholā*s (chick-pea curry) at the breakfast table before setting out for exploration or excavation. And let me not forget to mention that every evening after the day's work, Chatterji enjoyed sitting on the deck with a fishing rod in his hand, trying to catch fish from the Nile. Quite often he was greatly delighted at the catch, though sometimes the fish dodged him. My wife volunteered to register the antiquities, prepare cards for them and sort out and mark the pottery. Whenever we went out exploring the neighboring region for ancient remains, womenfolk from the villages would come out of their houses, jostling with one another, to have a look at an Indian woman draped in a *sārī* and applying on the forehead a red *bindī*. What a sight to see! Anyway, we all thoroughly enjoyed those delightful days.

We were allotted two sites by the Egyptian Government, namely, Afyeh and Tumas. Now submerged, these were located on the left bank of the Nile, roughly 250 kilometers along the river south-west of Aswan and about 80 kilometers north-east of Abu Simbel. Besides conducting excavations at these two sites, we also explored the ancient terraces of the Nile in the neighborhood. On the terrace on which Afyeh was situated, we found two kinds of Stone Age tools, rather mixed up. Typologically, one group comprised medium-sized tools made on silicrete and ferricrete sandstones, rhyolite and what looked like quartzite. These included points, borers and scrapers of various kinds and a few specimens which were reminiscent of 'pebble tools'. In the other category were relatively smaller tools, made on fine-grained stones like chert, jasper, chalcedony, etc. and comprising points, sometimes with an incipient tang, backed blades, borers, as also an example each of a burin and a lunate. It was also observed that whereas most of the specimens of the former category were rolled and worn out, those of the latter were in a fresh condition, signifying a time-difference between the two.

Moving away from the river-bank towards the adjacent hill, we came across the remnants of what may have been an earlier terrace. On it the medium-sized tools referred to above were found in a fresh condition and there were no tools of the other category. All this shows that the medium-sized tools were, indeed, earlier than those of the other category. In terms of the prevailing nomenclature, the two kinds of tools may be ascribed respectively to the Middle and Late Stone Ages. Further, since, to best of our knowledge, such kinds of tools had not been reported earlier from the Afyeh-Tumas region, our discovery may be said to have added a new chapter to the prehistory of the region.

A little to the north-east of the Afyeh village, there lay an ancient settlement. On excavation it was found to belong to what may be called a Neolithic-Chalcolithic stage of cultural evolution, since the habitation deposits yielded not only polished stone axes and backed blades, points and borers of chert but also a well-made chisel of copper. Agricultural activities were also in full swing, as is indicated by the discovery of specimens of wheat, barley, lentil, gram and pea. Saddle querns and mullers of stone were used for grinding these cereals. The houses were made of stone rubble and sometimes comprised as many as six rooms, suggestive of a large family living together. However, only two structural sub-periods were met with, accounting for a total deposit of about half-a-meter. C-14 dates obtained from the cereals place the occupation in the second quarter of the third millennium BCE.

About half-a-kilometer to the north-west of the ancient settlement just referred to, there was a group of six tumuli, which unfortunately had been plundered. But the presence in them of a few human bones and a skull suggested their funerary association. A modern-looking cap, also found in one of the tumuli, indicated that the plundering was a recent affair. However, in one of the graves, the plunderers missed picking away a seal, which on stylistic ground may be ascribed to a period between 1785 and 1580 BCE.

About a kilometer east-north-east of Afyeh was located the village of Tumas. Close to it was a cemetery of what are known in Egyptian terminology as the C-Group people. The Indian team excavated over a hundred graves there. Although many of the graves had been plundered, the evidence obtained from the intact examples threw welcome light on the structural features of these graves and the method of the disposal of the dead. First, an oblong or oval pit, measuring about 1½ to 2 meters in length, about a meter in width and 1 to 1½ in depth was dug into the ground, the longer axis being from north-west to south-east. On the floor of the pit was placed the dead body in a crouched position, the head being on the easterly side. The dead wore ornaments like necklaces, bracelets and anklets made of beads of shell, faience, steatite, etc. The funerary objects included: a quartz dish with kohl-marks, a wooden mirror-handle, a seal and lots of pottery. The last-named category comprised jars and jar-stands of red ware and all-black and black-and-red ware bowls. Some of the bowls bore on the exterior a variety of incised designs, including dancing females, filled in with a white substance – perhaps gypsum.

After the funerary objects had been placed, the grave was filled with earth over which was put up a low dome of stone-rubble. Sometimes the dome rested on a circular wall, again of stone-rubble. In this context, it is interesting to note that the last-named feature recalls some of the megalithic structures of South India. And so do the black-and-red ware bowls and red ware jar-stands. But what the implications of these similarities are yet remain to be determined, particularly since the Nubian graves are ascribable to the 2nd millennium BCE whereas the South Indian megaliths do not appear to be earlier than circa 1000 BCE.

Finally, here is some discovery of an unusual interest. From within one of the plundered graves was recovered a plastic bead while from another came the burnt end of a cigarette (Pl. XXXII). In the latter case, the paper with which the tobacco was wrapped bore the following inscription: 'Coutarelli Freres', 'Alexandrie' and 'le Caire', indicating the brand name as well as the places of manufacture. On enquiry, it was found that the production of this particular brand of cigarette had commenced in the last decade of the 19th century, whereas the manufacture of plastic beads in

Egypt started somewhere around 1940. Thus, one may very well visualize that the person concerned was smoking this particular kind of cigarette while plundering the grave and threw the stub back in it after the job was done. Likewise, the bead, too, must have dropped from the necklace/rosary of the plunderer at the time of his operations. Piecing together the evidence, it appears that the graves were plundered sometime in the first half of the 20th century. Isn't it a nice piece of a detective's job!

19

1961-69: Excavations at Kalibangan and Their Contribution to Our Knowledge of the Harappan Civilization

Located on the left bank of the now-dry Ghaggar (ancient Sarasvatī) River in Hanumangarh District of Rajasthan, Kalibangan is one of the most important sites excavated on the Indian side of the border after Independence. The work was carried out by me, B.K. Thapar and J.P. Joshi, variously during the field-seasons of 1961-69. It has made some very valuable contributions to our knowledge of the Harappan Civilization, also known as the Indus/Indus-Sarasvatī Civilization.

The ancient site consists of three mounds, the largest in the middle (named KLB-2), a smaller one on the west (KLB-1) and the smallest on the east (KLB-3) (Fig. 5). Altogether, two major cultural periods were identified: an Early Harappan (circa 3000-2700 BCE) and the other, Mature

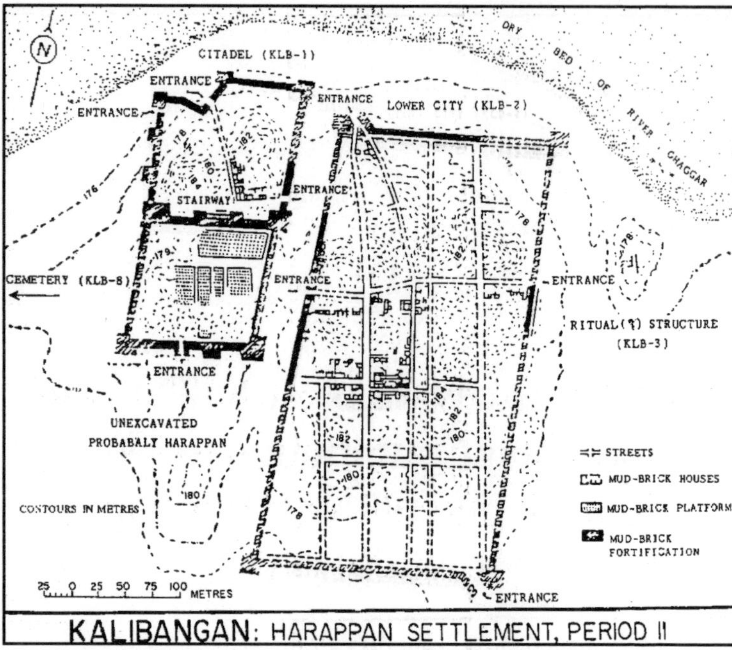

Fig. 5. Kalibangan: Harappan settlement, Period II. (Courtesy ASI)

Harappan (circa 2600-2000 BCE). Some of the more interesting features relating to these periods are as follow:

The Early Harappan settlement was enclosed by a peripheral wall, covering an area about 240-250 m north-south and 170-180 m east-west. At least one gate, opening on the river-front, was duly identified, though there may have been more. Within the fortifications there lay regular houses, oriented along the cardinal directions. The most noteworthy discovery relating to the Early Harappan times, however, was an agricultural field – the earliest one ever to have been discovered in an archaeological excavation! It had two sets of furrows, running respectively north-south and east-west and thus cutting each other at right angles (Pl. VIII). The intermediary space in between the north-south furrows was 1.9 m, whereas that in between the east-west ones was only 30 cm. It is of great interest to note that this very pattern of ploughing the fields continues even today not only in Rajasthan but also in neighboring Haryana, Panjab and even western Uttar Pradesh (Pl. IX). In the widely distanced furrows, the farmers today grow mustard plant, while in the narrowly spaced ones it is the gram (Pl. X). The reason for this kind of plantation is not far to seek. Both the above-mentioned plants are raised during the winter in which season the sun goes down to the southern hemisphere and casts longer northwards shadows than it does in the summer. Thus, if the tall mustard plants were to be grown in the east-west furrows and the gram plants in the north-south ones, the shadows of the former plants would completely cover up the latter, telling heavily on their growth. Since we have the evidence of both mustard and gram during the Harappan times, it is most likely that this very pattern of plantation was followed even then. And, if that were so, should we not take our hats off to the Early Harappans for having devised this specific pattern of ploughing the fields?

The Early Harappan pottery, though having certain individualitic features, did include elements which gave rise to the subsequent Mature Harappan pottery. Likewise, the bronze and copper objects and other small finds had their own story to tell. However, most exciting is the story of how the Early Harappan settlement came to an end. Even within the limited area that was exposed of these early levels, there were encountered shattered occupational strata and sheared walls (Pl. XIII). Evidently, this could have happened only if there was a major shaking of the ground beneath – in other words, an earthquake. Maybe the intensity was not very high and the incident took place at a time when the inmates were by and large out – for no buried skeletons were met with, but the shock was enough to make the people desert the settlement.

When, after about a century, the people returned to Kalibangan, they not only occupied the abandoned Early Harappan mound and re-fortified it, but also laid out another settlement on its east, which was much larger. We have called these two parts respectively the Citadel and the Lower Town. While the former seems to have been occupied by a priestly class and elites, there lived in the latter merchants, agriculturists and other common men. However, it is important to note that even the so-called 'Lower Town' at Kalibangan was also found to be fortified – a discovery which triggered the search for a similar disposition at other Harappan sites.

Though the southern part of KLB-2 is eroded, its overall size seems to have been approximately 360 m north-south and 240 m east-west. Of the gateways of the fortifications, at least two were clearly identified, one in the north-western part, opening on the river-side, and another on the western side providing communication with the Citadel, the northern part of which too had a gate on its eastern side.

The town within the fortifications was laid out in what is generally called the grid-pattern, though strictly speaking the result was not a perfect grid, since while most of the north-south streets ran all through the length of the township, the east-west ones were often staggered. It is interesting to note that the lanes/streets were laid out more or less in a set ratio of width, viz., 1:2:3:4, with the respective measurements being approximately 1.8 m, 3.6 m, 5.4 m and 7.2 m. Bullock-carts could easily ply through all these except the lane which was only 1.8 m wide. An important feature was noticed at the crossings of the wider streets. At the exterior corners of the houses over there, wooden fender-posts were provided in order to protect the corners from being damaged by vehicular traffic. Also, full care was taken by the civic authorities that no encroachments were made on the streets, although the site

Pl. XXXIX. Parents of Professor Lal: Shri Ramcharan Lal and Shrimati Sarayu Devi.

Pl. XL. Professor Lal with Shrimati Indira Gandhi, the then Prime Minister of India, who released the book, *Frontiers of the Indus Civilization,* edited by Professor Lal and others.

Pl. XLI. London, 1973. Participants in an International Symposium on Undeciphered Languages. Sir Mortimer Wheeler (middle row, extreme left), Professor B.B. Lal (on the left of Sir Mortimer), Sir Max Mallowan (middle row, center), Sir Harold Bailey (Chairman, front row, middle).

Pl. XLII. Professor B.B. Lal, taking down notes, in the Tank at Śṛiṅgaverapura.

Pl. XLIII. The taught and the teacher: Professor B.B. Lal and Sir Mortimer Wheeler, on the occasion of the latter's visit to the excavations at Purana Qila, New Delhi.

Pl. XLIV. Nubia (Egypt), 1961: Above, our boat on the Nile. Below, from right, Professor B.B. Lal, Shri Azim Hussain (India's Ambassador to Egypt) and his wife and Shrimati Kusum Lal. (Courtesy ASI)

witnessed as many as nine structural phases accounting for a total vertical height of about 10 m (Pl. XIV). The only kind of construction to be seen in these streets was that of narrow platforms (*chabūtarā*s) adjacent to the entrances to the houses, which seem to have been used by the occupants for a chit-chat with the neighbors, as is the case even now in the nearby villages.

The streets and lanes, mentioned earlier, divided the town into blocks, each block comprising a few houses. Though the sizes of the houses varied, depending evidently on the financial status of the respective owners, an average house appears to have consisted of a courtyard on two or three sides of which there were the living rooms. Piercing the wall on the fourth side of the courtyard, there was a large entrance. The large size of the entrance to these ancient houses may be understood by the analogy of the modern houses in the adjacent villages which too have such large entrances, through which bullock-carts are admitted into the courtyard and parked there. Maybe the same was the practice in the bygone days. Within the courtyard of these (ancient) houses have been discovered elongated troughs made of mud bricks, in a few of which there were also placed the broken lower halves of earthen jars. Once again, on the analogy of what obtains in the courtyards of houses in the adjacent villages, it may well be conjectured that, in the third millennium BCE too, the Kalibanganites provided fodder and drinking water in these troughs and pots for their cattle. Mention may also be made of a house which seems to have belonged to a well-to-do person. It had a flooring of kiln-fired terracotta tiles, decorated with a pleasing design of intersecting circles. In the upper levels of the site, a very interesting feature was noted. Over here, the floors consisted of a soling of broken, burnt terracotta nodules interspersed with charcoal, over which was laid a layer of clay. When these were discovered, we could not interpret the significance of the burnt-nodule-cum-charcoal soling. Luckily for us, some civil engineers from neighboring Hanumangarh happened to visit the excavations. And when we consulted them about this special feature, they told us that this is what they do even now. They explained that while the burnt nodules make the soling hard, the pieces of charcoal prevent the sub-floor dampness from traveling up along the walls, besides acting as a termite-killer. Should not the Kalibanganites of more than 4000 years ago be given full marks for this ingenuity?

Special interest attaches to the fact that one of the rooms was earmarked for ritualistic purposes. This is indicated by the presence in it, at successive levels, of what have been termed as 'fire-altars' in the absence of a much better term, though these are not to be confused with the Parsi fire-altars. Sunk into the floor to a depth of about 25 cm and lined with clay, these were roughly rectangular with somewhat rounded corners, and measured approximately a meter in length and 50 cm in width (Pl. XI). Within each of these altars, there invariably stood a stele, made of clay (sometimes burnt), measuring about 30-40 cm in height. It was usually circular on plan, with a diameter of about 15 cm, but could sometimes be faceted. Inside the altars there also lay a number of circular-biconvex 'cakes' of clay, apparently placed as offerings. These altars contained ash and charcoal showing their association with fire. Another noteworthy feature of these altars was their placement. These were so located that anyone using them had to face the east – something which may have had an extra significance in the ritual.

In marked contrast to the 'Lower Town', the Citadel was consciously located, as already stated, on a higher ground provided by the ruins of the earlier occupation, so as to give it an eminence. It was surrounded by a fortification-wall, which covered an area of about 240 m north-south and 120 m east-west. The complex was further subdivided into two parts by an east-west medial wall. The southern part had many platforms on which were located special structural features. Because of erosion over the millennia the evidence of the superstructures has been lost in many cases, but at least two of the platforms clearly showed religious association. On one of these, as many as seven contiguous 'fire-altars' were discovered (Pl. XII). Immediately to the west of these 'altars', the lower half of a jar was found embedded into the ground. It contained ash and charcoal, providing evidence that most probably fire was kept ready for the ritual. Close to these altars were a well and a bathing pavement with drain, indicating that anyone who performed the ritual was expected to have a bath. There is one more interesting point about these 'altars'. Their row ran north-south and immediately behind the row was a wall, also running north-south. Thus, anyone using these altars had to face the east. Incidentally, it may be stated that the taking of a bath and facing east are parts of a Hindu ritual.

On another platform in the southern half of the Citadel was discovered a pit, measuring about 1.3 m x .9 m internally and lined with kiln-fired bricks. In it were found, besides ash and charcoal, bovine bones and antlers, indicating some kind of animal sacrifice. That animal-sacrifice was a part of the Harappan rituals is indicated not only by certain scenes portrayed on the Harappan seals, but also by the engravings on a terracotta 'cake' found at Kalibangan itself. On one of its sides is depicted a human figure pulling forward an animal with a rope that had been tied around the latter's neck. On the other side is a deity which, on the basis of its posture and head-gear, seems to represent 'Síva', depicted on so many Harappan seals.

The northern part of the Citadel had an altogether different kind of planning. There were no platforms, but only residential houses, laid out on the two sides of a street that ran in a north-westerly direction up to a gateway which opened on the river front. Some of these houses were very large, indicating that their occupants must have been some important personages. It has been surmised, though without any inscriptional corroboration, that they were probably priests who supervised the rituals performed on the platforms in the southern part of the complex. There was yet another notable feature in the northern part. Between the medial wall separating the above-mentioned two parts and the houses in northern part, there was a mud-brick paved street, running east-west. If imagination is allowed to have a free run, it may well be that a ceremonial procession led by the priests marched on this paved passageway and entered the southern part by means of the stepped passage through the medial wall referred to in one of the preceding paragraphs. The idea of a 'procession' seems to find some sort of support from a seal from Mohenjo-daro which depicts, in the upper register, a deity within a pipal-leaf enclosure with a kneeling devotee in front and, in the lower register, seven wig-wearing figures, one behind the other, as if in a procession.

To the east of the Lower Town, at a distance of about 80 meters, there was yet another complex, named KLB-3. It covered an overall area of about 70 x 50 m, of which only a part was excavated. In it no residential houses were met with, but only fire-altars of which at least five examples were identified, wholly or partly. In these, the usual contents, namely, a stele, terracotta 'cakes', ash and charcoal were found.

At this point one might ask a question: While the presence of individual fire-altars in the houses in the Lower Town is easily explainable, what is the explanation for the provision of congregational fire-altars in the Citadel on the one hand and in KLB-3 on the other? A variety of guesses can be hazarded. Perhaps one of these may be that while the groups of the fire-altars perched on a high mud-brick platform in the well-fortified Citadel were to be used by the 'high-ups', those located in the low-lying area of KLB-3 were meant for the lowly ones of the population, such as those living in the unfortified area to the south of the Citadel. There could be other explanations too, but, I am afraid, all these will remain in the realm of conjecture.

The Harappans are known to have buried their dead. While during the course of the excavations at Mohenjo-daro no graves were located, the same were duly discovered at Harappa. The usual method of the disposal of the dead was to intern the body in a rectangular or oblong pit, sometimes lined with mud bricks and in certain cases also provided with an overhead tumulus, again of mud bricks. The body was laid supine in an extended position, with the head to the north. Alongside the body, a good deal of pottery, some other grave-furniture and even food were placed, perhaps in the belief that these might be of use to the departed in his/her journey to the next world. While this mode of burial (called here Type I) was also practised by the Kalibanganites, there came to light two new types (named II and III). The cemetery at Kalibangan was located at a distance of about 300 m to the west-south-west of the Citadel.

As many as twelve examples of Type I graves were excavated. In all these cases the pit was rectangular, with either sharp or rounded-off corners and large enough to take in an extended human body. Usually placed at the bottom of the pit, the body lay supine in an extended position with the head to the north. The face could be skywards or turned to the left or right. In one case (Fig. 6), the grave-pit was found lined with mud bricks which were also plastered. An interesting feature of this grave was that it contained a very large number of pots, about seventy, of which thirty-

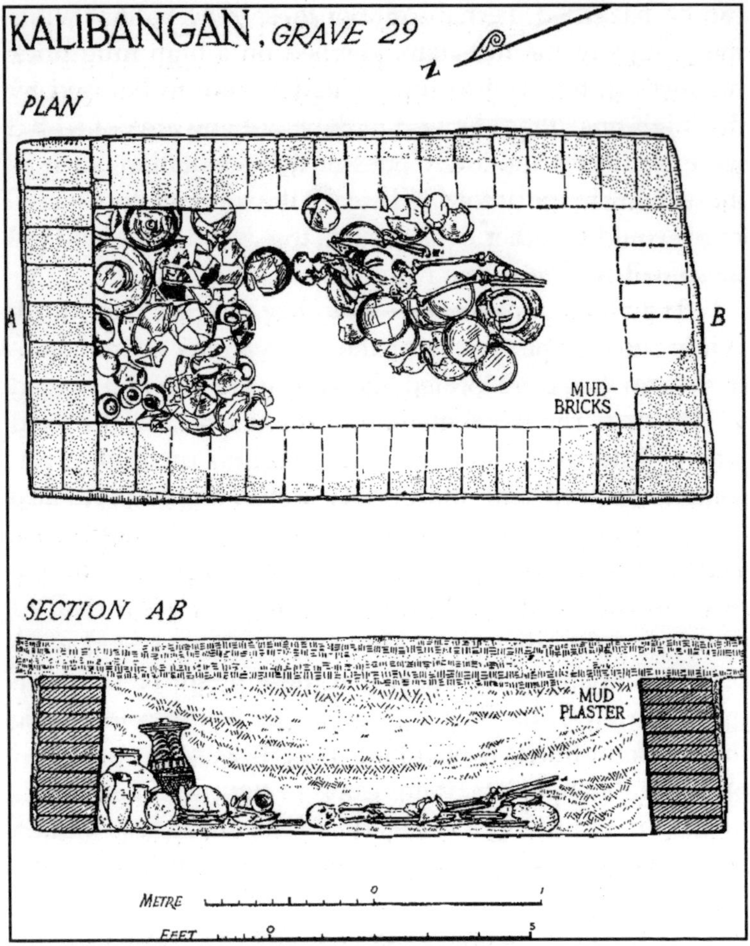

Fig. 6. Kalibangan: Grave 29. (Courtesy ASI)

seven lay to the north of the head and the rest underneath the body.

Within the same area as occupied by the above-mentioned inhumation graves (Type I), there lay graves which contained no human body – either complete or even fractional (Type II). But these did contain the usual grave furniture, such as pottery, etc. Of this type, six examples were excavated. In one case, the pit measured 4 x 2 x 1 m, the longer axis being north-south. At the bottom were placed a large number of pots spread almost all over the area. As if to complete the grave-furniture, there were three shell bangles too. Above this material were encountered a series of bands of sand and clay indicating that the pit remained open for some time, allowing this kind of deposit to accumulate. The pit was finally filled up with earth and clods thereof. In another example of this type, were met with a shell bangle, a carnelian bead and a string of steatite beads, besides, of course the usual pottery. Overlying all this stuff were the inevitable bands of sand and clay. What could indeed be the reason for such graves sans any skeletal remains? Is it that the dead body was first laid in these graves and, after certain rituals, was removed to the regular inhumation graves? Indeed, one guess is as good or bad as another.

Another kind of burial (Type III), encountered so far only at Kalibangan, is equally baffling. In this case, the grave-pits were circular or ovoid, but never rectangular. More importantly, these also did not contain the dead body. However, the siting of these pits not far away from the other two kinds of graves referred to earlier leaves no doubt that these circular pits did have something to do with the 'disposal of the dead'. As many as sixteen examples of this type were excavated but, as already mentioned, none contained a human skeleton, though in one case an unidentifiable bone-fragment was found. Nevertheless, the other appurtenances encountered in the other two kinds of graves were there. Thus, one found a large amount of pottery and other funerary objects. There was also something unusual about the pottery assemblage. Amongst the large number of pots of various types and sizes, there invariably was a large-sized jar, acting almost as central piece. It was expected that this one might provide some kind of clue – ash, charred bones, etc. in case these were post-cremation burials, but there was no such evidence. If there ever was any ash inside these jars, it got so badly mixed up with the earth that it could not be made out as a separate entity. It perhaps needs to be added that these pits did not also show up the kinds of bands of sand and clay as were encountered in the graves of Type II. Thus, the functions of Types II and III were clearly different from each other. Could the Type III have been of a somewhat symbolic nature, perhaps associated with those who died elsewhere?

The skeletal remains from the graves of Type I have thrown some interesting sidelight. The skull of a child was found to be rather unusually large, perhaps resulting from the accumulation of water in the brain cells – a hydrocephalous case? To treat the same, the Kalibangan 'surgeon' took recourse to trephination, piercing three holes on the right temporal region and branding it with some heated instrument. An example of trephination also comes from Lothal.

In yet another case, a male skeleton bore cut marks near the left knee. The size of the cut incidentally corresponds to that of the blade of an average copper axe of the Harappan period. Perhaps in the course of a quarrel the person was hit by his adversary with an axe as a result of which there may have been excessive bleeding and the person succumbed to the injury.

Like any other Harappan site, Kalibangan too yielded a rich harvest of pottery and antiquities. As regards the pottery, it may be stated that since the site was re-occupied hardly within a century of its abandonment by the Early Harappans, the Lower levels of KLB-2 contained a mix-up of Early Harappan and Mature Harappan pottery. The former, however, petered out as time passed and only the latter continued. This latter was very profuse and showed a rich variety of painted designs. The antiquities included, as usual, seals, sealings, inscribed pottery, copper objects, a variety of beads, chert blades and other tools, terracotta figurines and the ubiquitous cakes, etc.

Earlier (Chapter 17) I have already referred to two examples of inscribed pottery whereon the overlap of the signs clearly demonstrates that the direction of writing in the Harappan script was from right to left (Pl. VI).

The foregoing are some of the featutres which Kalibangan has added to our knowledge of the Harappan Civilization.

20

Not an Easy Exit

In 1971 I was invited by the University of Chicago to join its faculty as Alexander White Visiting Professor for one academic year. Since that very year I had also to deliver the Gandhi Memorial Lecture at the School of Oriental and African Studies, University of London, I combined the two. Thus, I delivered the lecture in London and thence proceeded to Chicago. Professor Pramod Chandra, whom I happened to know intimately, was already there. He offered that I and my wife, who had accompanied me, should stay with him at his new house. (His wife and his two sons were staying in their earlier house. He and his wife were not formally divorced, but had chosen to live separately.) Our deal with Pramod was that we would stay with him, but the entire care-taking of the house including the preparation of food would be done by my wife. Pramod was very happy with the meals made by Kusum and on a couple of occasions, we also invited his wife and sons to dine with us.

My stay at the university was very interesting and exciting. A room was allotted to me in the Library, and my wife and I spent a good deal of time over there. The library contained many rare books and I took the opportunity of going through as many of them as humanly possible. Would you believe that the library had all kinds of journals from India, including even such non-academic ones as *Māyā* and *Manohara Kahāniyān*. My only commitment to the university was to deliver a series of six lectures, covering the archaeology of India from the prehistoric times to the early medieval. The audience, which included the faculty members as well as students, was particularly excited by the results of my excavations at Hastināpura and their bearing on the historicity of the *Mahābhārata*. Professor Van Buitenan was so much convinced by the evidence that he referred to the same in the translation of the *Mahābhārata,* which he later published.

When I was still in Chicago, I received a newspaper-cutting from a friend of mine which stated that the Government of India had announced that its employees could take voluntary retirement on reaching the age of fifty, if they so wished. I was greatly delighted at the announcement and lost no time in sending my application for voluntary retirement as I had had already scored fifty on May 2, 1971. Having worked for nearly five years as the Director General, I had realized that carrying on research-work could not go hand-in-hand with the arduous duties of the DGA, which needed a great deal of attention for administration, conservation, public relations, etc. At the top of it, the DGA did not always have a free hand in discharging his duties, since often there was interference from the Ministry. My application, when received by the Ministry, created a great deal of furor.

A few months later when I reached Delhi, I was summoned by Shrimati Indira Gandhi, the then Prime Minister. Present in her chamber was her Principal Secretary, Shri P.N. Haksar. No sooner than I entered the chamber and took my seat, Shri Haksar started firing a volley of questions at me. He began: "*Lal Saheb, āpa baḍe achchhe Hindu mālūma hote hain.* (Lal Saheb, you appear to be a very good Hindu)." "*Isa men merī kyā galatī. Allah miyān ne jisa ghara men paidā kara diyā usī ghara kā mazahaba merā ho gayā. Agara musalmāna ke ghara men paidā hotā to Islām merā mazahaba hotā.* (There is no fault of mine. I belong to the religion of the family in which I was born. If I was born in a Muslim family, Islam would have been my religion)," was my reply. Thereupon, Shri Haksar passed on to his next observation: "A devout Hindu follows four *āśramas*. Up to the age of twenty-five he in *brahmacharya āśrama*, thereafter he enters the *gṛihastha āśrama* and continues in it up to the age of fifty. Then begins the *vāṇaprastha āśrama* which involves semi-retirement from worldly life. Thus, as a good Hindu you are asking for retirement from the post of the Director General." I took out the newspaper-cutting from my pocket and showing it to him added that it was not me as a Hindu that was asking for retirement but as an officer permitted by the government to do so. Shri Haksar became dumb-struck for a while. Meanwhile, Shrimati Indira Gandhi intervened and plainly stated that irrespective of the aforesaid government announcement, she still wanted me to continue in the post. She further added that she would issue necessary instructions so that there was no interference by the Ministry in the discharge of my duties as the DGA. She even asked the administrative department concerned that orders be issued to raise the official status of the DGA. Since it was Shrimati Gandhi's wish, at a personal level, I had no option but to give in.

With this kind of a change in the work-culture, particularly between the Directorate and the Ministry, things became easier and faster. But even then I was left with little time to carry on my research work. Most of the day was spent in meetings with colleagues within the Survey itself or with the officers of the Ministry and/or of other departments. The files had still to be carried home for study and issuance of necessary orders since these called for immediate disposal. Hence, the researcher in me was still grumbling.

Meanwhile, Professor Nurul Hasan was appointed as the Minister of State holding independent charge of the Ministry of Education and Culture. We knew each other for quite some time and had good working understanding. The day following his taking over charge of the Ministry, I went to his chamber to offer my congratulations. On reaching the entrance I said, "May I come in, Sir?" He beckoned me to get in but immediately on my taking a seat told me, in a somewhat raised voice so that the Secretary of the Ministry who was already seated there could listen to it, "Lal Saheb, the word 'Sir' is not to be used by academics. It is meant for use only in the officialdom." This crypt statement by the Minister gave the necessary signal to the Secretary and the latter knew how exactly to deal with me.

Anyway, all this was no solution to my original problem, viz., that of not finding any time for my research-work because of the heavy duties as the DGA. Thus once, after the Question Hour in the Parliament was over and I was lunching with Professor Hasan in his chamber, I told him that I wanted to make a request to him and hoped that he would accept it. Professor Hasan, as was but natural, replied that he could not commit himself unless he was told what the request was. I did not proceed any further and the matter was put on hold. However, on a similar meeting on another occasion I opened the topic once again, this time telling Professor Hasan, "Doctor Saheb (as I used to address him; he was my senior at the university by one year), you have made a grave mistake by accepting the post of a Minister. This will leave you with no time to continue the valuable research which you have hitherto been carrying out. Anyway, to compensate for your mistake", I added jocularly, "I want to get out of administration and devote myself entirely to research." He was rather taken aback since he had thought that the matter was already over after my meeting with Shrimati Indira Gandhi. He gave no reply but I added that he should give the matter due thought. After about a month, when I reminded him about the matter, he told me, "Lal Saheb, if you are so insistent, I have no option but to go by what you say."

Professor Hasan gave me a farewell dinner to which he invited my wife, my successor Shri M.N. Deshpande and his wife. It was the month of June and even at ten in the night, the hot wind was blowing. Nevertheless, Professor Hasan came out of his house, escorted my wife and me to my car and had a chat for a few minutes before getting back into the house. This is how I ultimately regained my wings to fly.

21

From Delhi to Gwalior

Since it was already in the air that I was planning to leave the Survey, offers from many universities had started pouring in. Amongst these there was an invitation from Jiwaji University, Gwalior, whose Vice-Chancellor, Professor Bhandarkar, had personally been contacting me for some time past. The university had a small School of Studies in Ancient Indian History, Culture and Archaeology, but Professor Bhandarkar wanted me to raise it up to a high standard. I gratefully accepted his offer and joined the university in July 1972.

On joining the university, I decided that I would start teaching subjects with which I had lost contact during my stay with the Survey. Thus, besides field-archaeology, I took subjects like epigraphy and numismatics. To teach these latter subjects, I had to brush up my knowledge a great deal. Quite often I had to study every morning for two to three hours, preparing lectures which had to be delivered later in the day. Though a tough job, it was indeed very rewarding: I learnt a lot of new things and, above all, thoroughly enjoyed the same. I also discovered that the students, too, took keen interest in what they were learning. All this gave me immense satisfaction.

As a part of providing training in field-archaeology, I started excavation at Jaderua, a suburb of Gwalior. The site yielded black-and-red ware and other associated pottery, besides structures of kiln-fired bricks. Although there were no C-14 dates, the other evidence suggested that the site may go back to the third century BCE, if not earlier. Thus, the excavation, at one stroke, demonstrated that the roots of Gwalior went back to a period well before the Common Era.

But there were more important discoveries in store for us. One afternoon my wife and I decided to visit the Tighara Dam, a popular picnic site located at a distance of about 15 kilometers from our residence. We were traveling in our car, and as we crossed the ridge near Gupteshwar Temple and descended into the valley, we were greatly charmed by its scenic beauty. We slowed down our car and started looking around the place. I was greatly surprised when suddenly my wife asked me to stop the car. She said that by the road-side she had just seen a few flaked pebbles which looked like tools. I stopped the car and discovered that the suspected flaked pebbles were indeed duly finished tools. There was no end to our joy and the picnic was doubly satisfying.

This chance-discovery was followed by regular exploration and subsequent excavation. A series of terraces were identified, along with their associated tools. A few trenches were also laid out on the successive terraces and tools of Early and Middle Stone Ages were found in them. The valley is surrounded by rock-shelters. Exploration of these and excavation of one of them revealed that these were inhabited by the Mesolithic man. The walls of most of these caves were painted with a variety of scenes in red ocher (Pl. XXIII). It was interesting to find some fragments of the ocher on the floor of the caves. A small museum was also set up in our Department displaying the Stone Age tools as well as the material from Jaderua. All this created a lot of interest in archaeology as a discipline and students and faculty members from other departments of the university frequently visited the museum. As a result, in the years that followed, more and more students took to archaeology.

During the period of excavations in the Gupteshwar Valley, we had set up a small camp where we used to have our lunch and mid-day rest. The food was prepared on the spot so that we could get it straight from the oven. We also had the practice of inviting visiting scholars to share the lunch with us. Once we had amongst us Professor G.M. Bongard-Levin from Moscow and it was decided to get special dishes prepared in his honor. The menu included *dāl-bātiān* (lentil soup and thick, rounded wheat-bread) and *laddoo*s. The latter were spherical in shape, about one-and-half inch in diameter, and made of powdered *bātiān* soaked in *ghee* (clarified butter). It gave us immense satisfaction to find that Professor Bongard-Levin relished the food immensely, so much so that he accepted a challenge from one of our students and defeated him by eating six of these large-sized *laddoo*s in a row.

It may be recalled that my excavation at Hastināpura and exploration at other sites associated with the Mahābhārata story yielded enough evidence to show that there was a basis for the historicity of this epic, though many details about fortifications and armies may have been exaggerations – something which an epic of this magnitude is bound to have. Anyway, the success achieved in the case of the *Mahābhārata* tempted me to find out if there was any basis for the historicity of the other great Indian epic, namely, the *Rāmāyaṇa*.

Thus, it was decided to initiate a project called 'Archaeology of the Rāmāyaṇa Sites'. Funds were obtained from the University Grants Commission, through the courtesy of its Chairman Professor Satish Chandra, and from the Archaeological Survey of India whose Director General Shri M.N. Deshpande was of immense help all through. The Project was very kindly inaugurated at Ayodhyā by Professor Nurul Hasan, the then Union Minister of Education.

22

From Gwalior to Shimla: Continuation of the Archaeology of the Rāmāyaṇa Sites Project, 1977-86

Things do not always turn out to be as one would like them to. Thus, soon after Professor Bhandarkar's term as Vice-Chancellor of Jiwaji University was over the new Vice-Chancellor, Shri Rajwade, began to trouble me. The reason? A simple one – he thought I was Bhandarkar's 'man'. Within a week of his joining the University, he issued orders that the official telephone provided by the University at my residence should be withdrawn. There was an amusing way in which he conveyed this message to me. Between our residential areas and the University campus, there used to be a railway crossing, which was barricaded whenever trains used to pass. (Now there is a flyover at this crossing.) One day it so happened that a train was about to pass and the barrier was closed. I had to stop my car. Just then Shri Rajwade also arrived in his car which had also to stop. I thought it was desirable for me to get out of my car and greet the VC. So I did. Shri Rajwade, on being greeted by me, shot back: "Professor Lal, I am sorry that the Executive Council has decided to withdraw the telephone from your residence." I quietly told him, "Sir, don't you worry. I had already anticipated this move and have, therefore, got my own telephone installed. Many thanks for the information." A visibly upset Rajwade kept mum.

While I was still at Gwalior, the then Chairperson of the India International Centre at Delhi invited me to deliver a lecture on my excavations at Hastināpura and their bearing on the historicity of the *Mahābhārata.* Prior to the lecture there was a small get-together at tea. Present on the occasion were: Professor Nurul Hasan, who was still the Minister of Education and Culture and who had been requested to preside over the lecture, Shri M.N. Deshpande, the then DG Archaeology and Professor S.C. Dube, Director of the Institute of Advanced Study, Shimla. During the course of the talks, Professor Dube complained to Professor Hasan: "*Dekhiye Mantriji, men bahut dinon se Lal Saheb ko Shimla Institute bulā rahā hoon, par woh āte hī nahīn. Zarā inhen samajhāiye to.* (For quite some time I have been inviting Professor Lal to come over to the Shimla Institute, but he doesn't. Please advise him accordingly)." I replied, "There is no provision at the Institute for undertaking any archaeological field-work. So what will I do there? I want to continue the 'Archaeology of the Rāmāyaṇa Sites Project'." Professor Hasan, who was always known to take snap decisions, at once asked the DGA to give me all the logistic support for the Project and advised Professor Dube to send me a formal letter offering a National Fellowship. And there the matter ended. I, too, lost no time and sent from Delhi itself a telegram to Shri Rajwade, offering my resignation from the University.

Perhaps at this point it may be well worthwhile to let the reader know about the background of this Project. The excavation at Hastināpura (above, pp. 42ff.) demonstrated that the *Mahābhārata* was not a figment of imagination but did have a basis in history, though all the details given in that epic may not have been true to the very letter, since after all it was a work of poetry and the poet had full freedom in composing it. Encouraged by the Hastināpura evidence, I thought of taking up another project, namely, 'Archaeology of the Rāmāyaṇa Sites'. Though conceived while I was still in the Survey, I could not undertake it since as the Director General almost all my time was taken up by administrative and other allied matters. It was only after my voluntary retirement from the Survey in 1972 that I could take up the Rāmāyaṇa Project – to begin with at the Jiwaji University, Gwalior, and later with full attention at the Indian Institute of Advanced Study, Shimla. The Survey helped me in the field-work which ran from 1977 to 1986, by deputing the staff of its Excavations Branch, which for most of the time was headed by Shri K.N. Dikshit.

Under this project, five sites were taken up for investigation: (i) Ayodhyā, the capital of the Kosala kingdom, from where Rāma hailed; (ii) Śṛiṅgaverapura, where Rāma, Sītā and Lakṣmaṇa crossed the Gaṅgā in the first lap of their exile; (iii) Bharadvāja Āśrama, where the trio stayed overnight to pay their homage to sage Bharadvāja; (iv) Chitrakūṭa, where they stayed for quite some time before proceeding further south; and (v) Nandīgrāma from where Bharata carried on the governmental affairs in the absence of Rāma (cf. map, Fig. 7).

Ayodhyā is located on the right bank of the Sarayū, in District Faizabad, Uttar Pradesh. The ancient mound over here is fairly large, covering an area of about a square

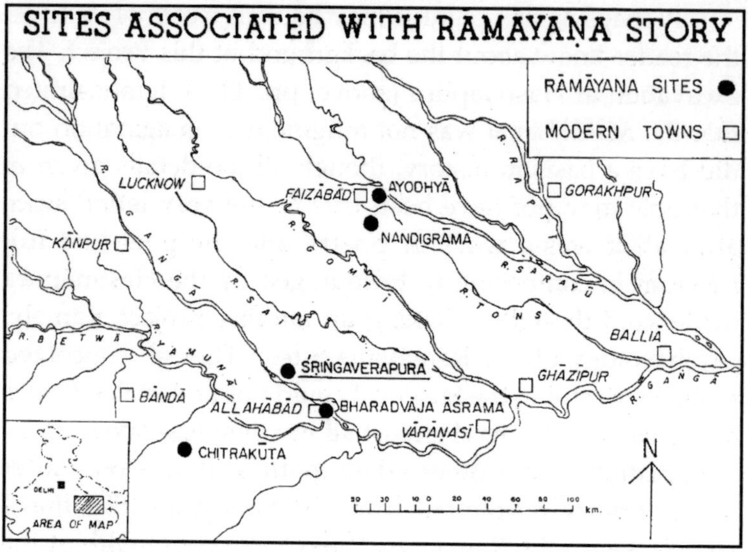

Fig. 7. Sites associated with the Rāmāyaṇa story.

kilometer and rising at places to a height of 10 meters. Excavations were carried out at fourteen different spots in order to ensure that the lowest levels were not missed just in case these existed in some areas and not in others. The areas included certain well known localities like the Janmābhūmi, Hanumānagarhī, Kauśilyā Ghāṭa, NalāTīlā, etc.

The excavations revealed that the settlement at Ayodhyā began with a phase when a very distinctive and deluxe pottery called the Northern Black Polished Ware (NBPW) had come into being. It is a highly shining ware with the surface color varying from jet black, indigo, silvery to golden. The shapes, too, were the ones that dominate the early stage of the ware, such as convex-sided dishes and bowls with corrugated profile. Tools of iron, besides of course those of copper, also characterized the NBPW levels. In due course of time, weights of fine-grained stones made their appearance, as did a system of coinage. To begin with, the structures were of mud or mud bricks, but as time passed kiln-fired bricks also came to be used.

Without any break, the settlement continued through what are known as the Śuṅga, Kushan and Gupta periods, after which some parts of Ayodhyā were deserted. However, the Janmābhūmi area was re-occupied around the 11-12th centuries CE. Over here, in the uppermost levels of a trench that lay immediately to the south of the Babari Masjid, a series of brick-cum-stone pillar-bases were discovered. Affixed to the piers of the Masjid there were stone pillars bearing Hindu motifs and sculptures (to which a detailed reference will be made in another chapter).

At **Śṛiṅgaverapura**, located in District Allahabad, U.P., there is a massive mound on the left bank of the Gaṅgā. Since the river takes a major curve hugging the site, it has cut away a sizeable portion of the mound. Nevertheless, there still remains a lot to give a fairly good picture of the various occupation strata. This site had a beginning earlier than that of Ayodhyā. In the lowest level there occurred what is known in archaeological parlance as the 'Ochre Color Ware' (OCP), datable broadly to the second millennium BCE. After a break, the site was re-occupied by people who used black-slipped and black-and-red wares. In continuation there appeared the well known Northern Black Polished Ware of the type already referred to in the case of Ayodhyā. Then came up occupations associated successively with the Śuṅga, Kushan and Gupta times. After a break, the site was re-occupied in the 12th century CE and continued to be inhabited later as well.

In Allahabad, Uttar Pradesh, there is a locality known as **Bharadvāja Āśrama**, immediately to the south of Colonelganj. It is a flat piece of land without any signs of a mound such as we have at Ayodhyā and Śṛiṅgaverapura. The local Municipality has laid out a park over it and the only indication of its ever having been associated with sage

Bharadvāja is a late medieval temple dedicated to him. The total absence of a mound was very puzzling. However, I argued within myself that if there was any truth in the association of the site with sage Bharadvāja it must yield the ancient remains.

With this kind of inquisitiveness I started excavating that flat piece of land, and hardly within 25-30 centimeters from the surface I came across structures of kiln-fired bricks. Two such structural levels were met with, one below the other. There was a lot of associated pottery, terracotta figurines, inscribed sealings – all of which are ascribable to circa fourth-fifth century CE – the Gupta Period of North Indian history. But when we dug deeper, we did not come across any structures. However, what we did meet was no less telling. There was a little over 2-meter thick deposit of sandy loam in which there occurred sporadically potsherds of the Northern Black Polished and black-slipped wares (Pl. XV). There were no regular occupational floors but some post-holes were met with. Also, there occurred lumps of clay bearing impression of reeds (Pl. XXIV). Altogether, the picture was that of a sporadic occupation with some wattle-and-daub huts.

At present the town of **Chitrakūṭa** falls partly in Uttar Pradesh and partly in Madhya Pradesh. The adjacent river is Mandākinī, on both the banks of which the ancient settlement was located. However, the mounds are overridden by so many medieval and modern temples that it was impossible to get enough space for any worthwhile excavation. Thus, we had to be content with only section-scrapping. Shards of black-slipped and NBP wares were picked up, which threw light on the antiquity of the site.

During the exile of Rāma, Bharata is said to have carried on the administrative functions not from Ayodhyā but from a place called **Nandīgrāma**. However, he did not live in that town but seems to have chosen to live in a somewhat lonely place now identified with Bharata-Kuṇḍa. There is no mound over there but not far away, there is one which may represent the ancient site. A small-scale excavation over here brought to light in the lowest levels the same culture-complex as at Ayodhyā.

A comparative analysis of the evidence from the foregoing five sites shows that the earliest time when all these were under occupation was that of the Northern Black Polished Ware. The only exception is that of Śṛiṅgaverapura where a still earlier occupation is indicated by the presence of the Ochre Color Ware. Anyway, it is the NBPW that ties these sites together. The next relevant question is: how early do these NBPW strata go in terms of absolute time? Charcoal samples collected by me, which were from the upper NBPW levels at Ayodhyā, gave a date-range from the 5th to 3rd centuries BCE. But the lower levels remained to be properly dated. This important lacuna has since been filled up by putting to test the charcoal samples collected from the lower NBPW levels by the Archaeological Survey during its renewed excavations (2002-03) in the Janmabhūmi area (short-named AYD-1). The dates provided by the laboratory of the Birbal Sahni Institute of Palaeobotany, Lucknow, are as follows:

Field-sample no., layer no. and depth in meters	B. S. Lab No.	Age of Sample based on half-life 5570+/– 30 yrs	Calibrated range in BCE
No. 1A, AYD-1	2126	2730+/– 80 BP (780 BCE)	970-810 BCE
No. 7, AYD-1, G7 Layer 16, 9.15 m	2152	2830+/– 100 BP (880 BCE)	1190-840 BCE
No. 8, AYD-1, G-7 Layer 19, 11 m	2153	2860+/– 100 BP (910 BCE)	1210-900 BCE
No. 9, AYD-1, G-7 Layer 20, 11.53 m	2154	3200+/– 130 BP (1250 BCE)	1680-1320 BCE

I do not know if Sample BS 2154 came from the lowest level. In any case, the above-mentioned C-14 dates indicate that the lower levels of the NBPW do go back to a period prior to 1000 BCE.

While no doubt the excavations at the above-mentioned five sites do establish that all these were characterized by the same kind of cultural equipment in their lower levels and were in existence around the beginning of the first millennium BCE, they have failed to provide any inscriptional evidence to show that the sites were associated with the Rāmāyaṇa story as such. In this context, however, the evidence yielded by Bharadvāja Āśrama is of utmost significance, as would be clear from the following.

It is accepted by scholars that the *Rāmāyaṇa* of Vālmīki was reduced to writing some time between the third century BCE and third century CE. During this time-bracket, whereas the other sites associated with the Rāmāyaṇa story, as indicated by the excavations, were 'living entities' (i.e. under occupation), Bharadvāja Āśrama was not. A question that now arises is: How come that this last-named site was also included in the narrative of Vālmīki when it was not a 'living entity'? One may well weave a story and include in it the names of sites that exist at that point of time or are known to have existed once, but not of places that never existed. Thus, the only possible way in which the inclusion of Bhardvāja Āśrama in the Vālmīki *Rāmāyaṇa* can be explained is that there must have existed, perhaps in the form of a ballad, a story in which this site also featured and it was this prevalent story that was reduced to writing between 3rd cent. BCE – 3rd cent. CE.

In this context, there are three very significant pieces of evidence from Bharadvāja Āśrama which call for a proper interpretation. First of all, it is the topography of the site. As already stated, it consists of a flat piece of land there being no evidence of any mound, the like of which we have at Ayodhyā or Śṛiṅgaverapura. But adjacent to it, the ground-level drops suddenly by 5-6 meters. Local people tell us that not long ago the waters of the Gaṅgā, when it was in spate during the rainy season, used to come up to this locality. A bund that has since been constructed prevents the water from coming up. In other words, all this indicates that in ancient times the Gaṅgā used to flow past the Bharadvāja Āśrama.

Secondly, the lower levels of Bharadvāja Āśrama did not yield any brick structures as did the upper. Nevertheless, shards of the Northern Black Polished Ware did occur sporadically in the thick sandy loam that lay under the brick structures (Pl. XV). Also met with were lumps of clay bearing impressions of reed (Pl. XXIV), which indicate that there were only wattle-and-daub huts in the area. This scenario fits well into the picture of an *Āśrama* (hermitage) by the side of the Gaṅgā. Surely, archaeology cannot tell us that it was the Bharadvāja Āśrama, since we have not come across any inscription from the site certifying the same.

The third point of interest is that, as already mentioned, the site was re-occupied only during the Gupta times. It is well known that it was during the Gupta period that there took place a great revival of the Brahmaṇical religion. Since oral tradition, perhaps through ballads, must have carried through the centuries the memory of the association of this site with the story of Rāma, it was but natural for the people to revive its glory by re-occupying it.

In the above context, it may also not be out of place to state that ballads based on certain noteworthy contemporary events are being composed and sung even today, though print and electronic media are in full operation. And I give here a recent example of it. It was a cold winter morning in 1954. I was traveling by the Kalka Mail from Calcutta (now Kolkata) to New Delhi. As the train halted at Allahabad, I saw thousands of people running up and down the platforms. They were desperately trying to get into the various trains. As I opened the door of my compartment to look out at what was going on, about fifty people got into it forcing me to find a shelter at the far end of my berth. Some of the people were in tears, some others were shouting and cursing the local authorities. I couldn't make out what all that was about. As the train steamed out, the commotion lessened and in due course of time these passengers alighted at their respective stations. Late in the evening, I reached my home and after a quiet dinner went to sleep. Next morning when the newspaper arrived, I saw on the front page a banner-heading stating how a major calamity had befallen the people in Allahabad, who had assembled there to participate in the *Kumbha Melā.* (This is a very important festival in which pilgrims come from far and wide to have a dip in the holy Gaṅgā.) The newspaper gave a long narrative of the event, which briefly is as follows. When the mass of humanity had gathered for the dip, a procession of *Nāgā-Sādhūs* (naked mendicants), some on foot and others seated on decorated elephants, suddenly appeared on the scene. For some unexplained reason, the elephants ran amok and overran some of the pilgrims. In the utter confusion that followed, hundreds of people lost their lives. The civil authorities did whatever they could under the very taxing circumstances. However, a tragedy of immeasurable magnitude had already taken place.

Now, whereas newspapers and electronic media had duly reported the event, within a few months it was also rendered in the form of ballads, of which three different versions are now in existence. Ballad-composers from Jhusi and Daryaganj – places right in Allahabad, and those from Śṛiṅgaverapura produced their own versions which, though different from one another in details, narrate the basics of the event. I had the occasion to listen to and tape-record the Śṛiṅgaverapura version which was sung to us one evening by one of the local workers at our excavation camp.

The point that emerges from the above is that even at present when the print and electronic media are in full operation, some people choose to record certain noteworthy events through ballads. If this is the state of affairs even today, what would have prevented the local genius of the time from composing ballads about the thrilling story of Rāma, which evidently must have drawn the attention of almost everybody. Further, as time passed, the ballad was also transmitted from generation to generation by word of mouth, it being but natural for each new singer to add some *mircha-masālā* (spicy stuff) of his own. Finally, when writing came to be used in the 3rd century BCE, the ballad assumed the form of the epic known as the *Rāmāyaṇa*.

From the foregoing archaeological evidence, it is clear that the *Rāmāyaṇa* was not the figment of imagination but did have a basis in history. This conclusion is also supported by the evidence of a purely a secular text which had no religious pretensions, namely, the *Arthaśāstra* of Kauṭilya, ascribable to the end of the 4th century BCE. Incidentally, it is interesting to note that composition-wise, this secular text is even earlier than the *Rāmāyaṇa* itself.

The *Arthaśāstra* consists of fifteen *Adhikaraṇa*s (Books); and each *Adhikaraṇa* is further divided into *Adhyāya*s (Chapters). The sixth *Adhyāya* of the first *Adhikaraṇa* is devoted to '*Indriyajaya*', i.e., 'Restraint of the Organs of Sense', with a sub-title 'The Shaking off the Aggregate of the Six Enemies'. In it Kauṭilya recommends the abandoning of the following six enemies, namely, *kāma* (lust), *krodha* (anger), *lobha* (greed), *māna* (vanity), *mada* (haughtiness) and *harṣa* (overjoy). He then proceeds to give examples how various kings and eminent personalities of the past had suffered adversely on account of having succumbed to these vices.

Proceeding further, he states: "*mānādrāvaṇah. paradārānaprayachchhan. Duryodhano rājyādaṁśam cha*", i.e., **"Rāvaṇa, unwilling under the influence of vanity to restore a stranger's wife, as well as Duryodhana to part with a portion of his kingdom."** Thus, according to Kauṭilya, Rāvaṇa perished because of having abducted the wife of a stranger, and Duryodhana for having refused to part with even a portion of his kingdom. The reference in the latter case is evidently to the story of the *Mahābhārata.* Then what about the former? Does it not refer to the *Rāmāyaṇa* story? The wife of a 'stranger' 'not restored by Rāvaṇa' is none other than Sītā. Taking the logic further, if, according to Kauṭilya, Rāvaṇa was a historical figure, the historicity of Rāma gets established *ipso facto.*

In art, too, there are some fairly early representations of the Rāmāyaṇa story. The earliest, ascribable to 2nd-1st century BCE, comes in the form of a terracotta figure from Kauśāmbi, a well known ancient site near Allahabad. It depicts a scene in which Rāvaṇa is carrying Sītā away, after having abducted her. A ferocious-looking Rāvaṇa is holding Sītā in his hands, and, greatly worried, the latter is throwing away her ornaments on the ground, in the hope that someone might come across them and thereby be able to trace her whereabouts and communicate the same to Rāma. This very scene is graphically described in the *Rāmāyaṇa* of Vālmīki (*Araṇya Kāṇda,* 54th *Sarga, Ślokas* 2 and 3).

We now pass on to a terracotta representation of Rāma himself (Pl. XXV). At present it is lodged in the Los Angeles County Museum of Art, USA, but is said to have come from Nachāra Kherā in Haryana. It has been executed in what is known as the Kushan style of art, which is very clear from the pointed lower end of the tunic that the figure wears. The right hand is in what is known as the *abhaya-mudrā.* Behind the back on this very side may also be seen the upper part of the quiver filled with arrows. However, what is most important is that the figure bears an inscription. It is located on the lower part of the tunic. (An enlarged copy of the inscription is also appended to the illustration.) Written in the Brāhmī script of circa 3rd century CE, it reads *Rāma,* thereby not leaving any doubt about its identification.

But what has been stated in the foregoing pages does not seem to satisfy the hardliners, for they say that unless there is a contemporary inscription authenticating the historicity of Rāma, his fate must continue to hang in the balance.

First of all, let these persons realize that we have not come across any inscription prior to 4th-3rd century BCE. So, how can we expect to find an inscription contemporary with Rāma who must have lived somewhere around 1000 BCE, as indicated by the Carbon-14 dates from Ayodhyā (above, p. 143)?

Secondly, if a contemporary inscription is going to be the sole adjudicator of the historicity of Rāma, then, I am afraid, we will have to treat as non-historical even the two other religious leaders of ancient India, namely, Buddha and Mahāvīra, since in their cases too there is no contemporary inscription. In the case of Buddha, the position is as follows. During the course of his tours, Emperor Ashok visited a place called Lumbini where the local inhabitants told him that Buddha's mother, while on way to her parents' place, gave birth to the child over there. On this **hearsay**, Ashok issued a pillar-edict, stating *hida budhe jate,* i.e., Buddha was born here (and consequently he reduced the quantum of taxes levied on the region). But let us not forget that there is **a clear gap of about 300 years between the supposed date of birth of Buddha and the time when Ashok visited Lumbini.** By no stretch of imagination can the Lumbini inscription be regarded as a 'contemporary' document. In the case of Mahāvira, the position is much worse. There was no Ashok to issue, as it were, a 'birth-certificate'. In fact, any inscriptional evidence relating to Mahāvīra is very much later.

Thus, the only sane thing to do is to take a holistic view of the entire available evidence, be it in the form of literature or archaeology or art. Absence of a contemporary inscription certifying Rāma's birth cannot be construed as evidence of his not having existed in flesh and blood. Thus goes the wise old saying: 'Absence of evidence is no evidence of absence.'*

* Adapted partly from my book, *Rāma: His Historicity, Mandir and Setu,* published in 2008 by Aryan Books International, New Delhi.

23

2000-year-old Unique Example of Indian Hydraulic Engineering

In the previous chapter we discussed the outcome of the 'Archaeology of the Rāmāyaṇa Sites Project' and its bearing on the historicity of Rāma. As a part of that Project, excavations were carried out at Śṛiṅgaverapura also where, besides other features, an over-200-meter long tank (Figs. 8a and b), ascribable to a period around the beginning of the Common Era, was discovered. The most remarkable points about this tank are: (i) the very concept of feeding it with the water of the Gaṅgā, without building any dam over the river; (ii) providing it with all the necessary components such as a long feeding channel which brought in the river-water, a silting chamber, a preliminary (silting) tank, a long main tank, a circular ritual tank, spill channels and finally an exit channel which drained the excess water back into the river; and (iii) constructing wells in its bed, which went deep into the sub-soil water, so that during the summer months when the tank-water began to dry up, the same could be supplemented with the underground water.

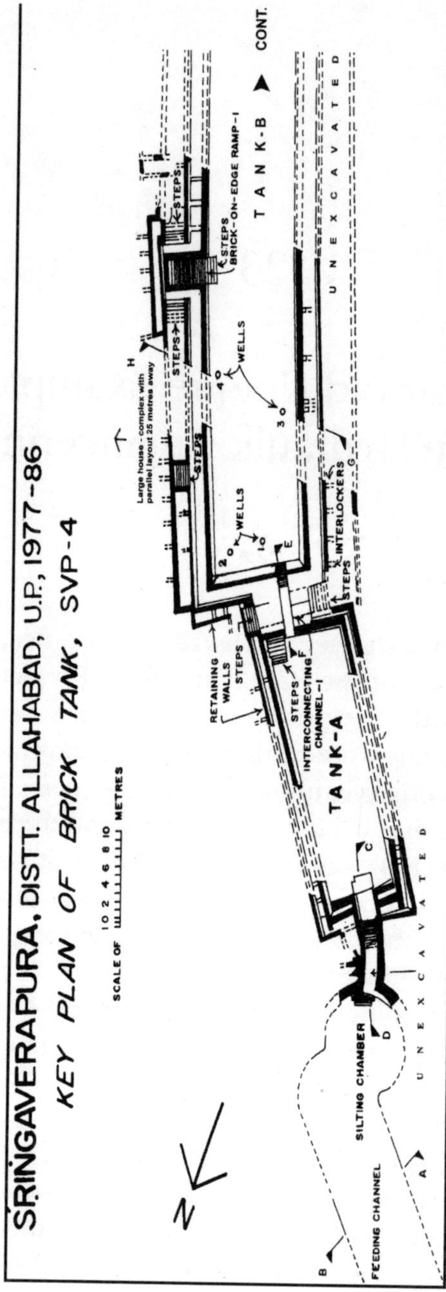
SṚIṄGAVERAPURA, DISTT. ALLAHABAD, U.P., 1977-86
KEY PLAN OF BRICK TANK, SVP-4
SCALE OF 10 2 4 6 8 10 METRES
Large house - complex with parallel layout 25 metres away
H
STEPS
BRICK-ON-EDGE RAMP-I
TANK-B
CONT.
WELLS
UNEXCAVATED
INTERLOCKERS
G
E
RETAINING WALLS
INTERCONNECTING CHANNEL-I
F
TANK-A
C
SILTING CHAMBER
D
FEEDING CHANNEL
A
B
N

Fig. 8a.

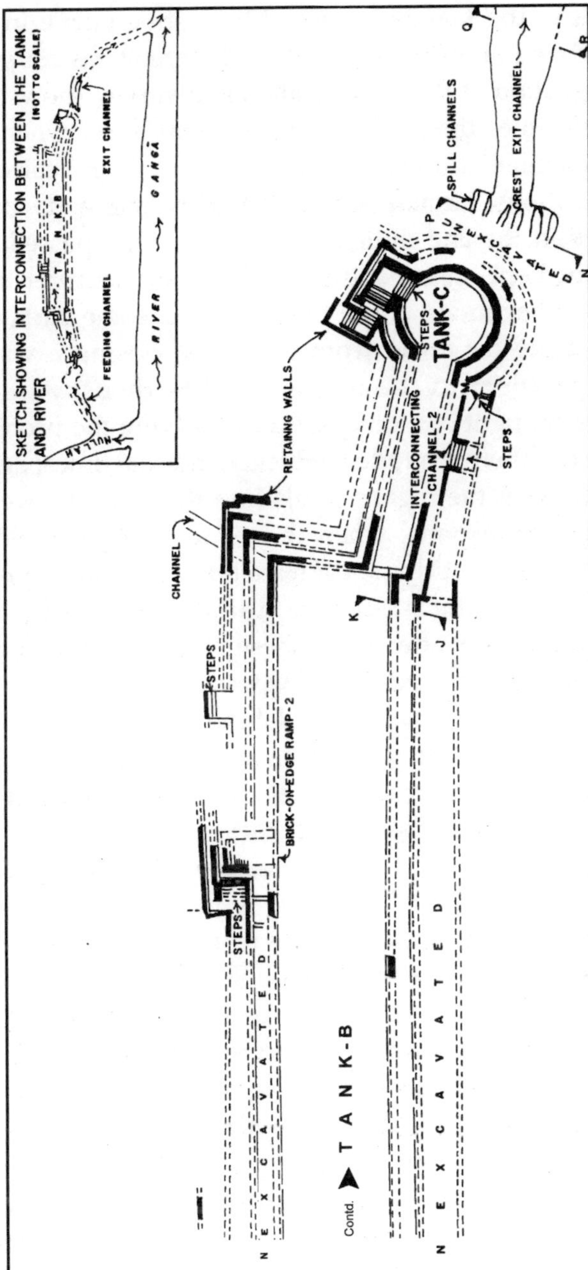

Fig. 8b. Śṛiṅgaverapura Tank (contd.). (Courtesy ASI)

Today, the Gaṅgā takes a horse-shoe curve in the neighborhood of Sṛiṅgaverapura, and thereby has cut away a major portion of the ancient site. Field-survey shows that in ancient times the river was flowing far away where an ancient channel still exists (near Basedhi). As revealed by the excavations, human occupation at the site had started way back in the 2nd millennium BCE. As time passed, the settlement kept on expanding away from the river-bank and by the beginning of the Common Era, some parts of it became quite far away from the bank, posing a water-supply problem to the township. The then hydraulic engineers thought of a unique way of solving the problem. Near the site there is a nullah which, in normal times, drains the water from the higher levels into the river. However, during the monsoons, when the river swells up and its water-level goes up by several meters, the water pushes upstream into the aforesaid nullah. Observing this phenomenon year after year, these engineers thought of harnessing this upward-going water and feeding it into a tank so that the same may be available for use by the families that were residing far away from the river-bank.

Thus, they first dug up a feeding channel, diverting the up-going river-water from the said nullah into this channel. At the end of this channel, they dug up a circular silting chamber, wherein the silt brought along with the water was made to settle down. From this chamber onwards, the entire construction was that of kiln-fired bricks. The first tank (A) was also used for siltation, whereafter the clean water passed into the main tank (B), which was over 130 meters in length. It was in this tank that wells connecting the bed with sub-soil water were provided (Pl. XVI). The water then passed on to a circular tank (C) which seems to have been associated with some rituals, as indicated by the discovery of a terracotta head of Śiva from within it (Pl. XXII). Ascribable to a period around the first century CE, it is perhaps the earliest figure of a three-eyed Śiva. Noteworthy also are the proportions of the various parts of the face.

Tank C was the last of the series, after which arrangements had to be made to let the excess water drain out. Hence, six spill channels were provided, which led the water to an exit channel through which the excess water went back into the Gaṅgā.

Hats off to these hydraulic engineers of Śṛiṅgaverapura who conceived and constructed this marvelous tank around the beginning of the Common Era.

24

My Teachers

Blessed are those who have had the right kind of teachers who, with their own model conduct, without any kind of preaching, can and do influence the lives of their students. And I must say that I have been very lucky in this respect, right from my school days.

I can recall, though somewhat vaguely, the days in Jhansi when a teacher used to come home for coaching me. I must have been a student of Grade IV at that time. I cannot recollect the face of the teacher but I do remember that he used to wear a *dhotī, kurtā, sadarī* and *topī* – all of *khādī* (hand-spun and hand-woven cloth). One day he told me and my father that from the following day he won't be able to come to teach me. When my father asked him the reason, my teacher promptly replied that he was going to join the Non-cooperation Movement of Mahatma Gandhi and offer *satyāgraha* for the freedom of the country. Looking back, it must have been around 1931 when Gandhiji gave a call for the *satyāgraha*. It was at that time that I first learnt about this unique personality who, through non-violent means, ultimately succeeded in liberating the country from the British rule. The teacher's attitude and conduct left a lasting stamp on the impressionable mind of the child in me.

Later on, I was admitted to the A.P. Mission High School in Jhansi. I have very clear memories of my class-fellows as well as the teachers over there. I would like to mention here about two of my teachers. One of them was Shri Saksena, who taught me English. He gave me full liberty to go to his residence where he would provide me extra coaching and ask me to write essays which he would correct. All this was without any fees being charged. In fact, he provided me with certain books on grammar and essay-writing for which he spent the money from his pocket.

Another teacher, Shri Agrawal, used to teach Mathematics. Not only did he teach me at his home, of course free of any charges, but he also provided me with items which were of immense help. You wouldn't believe I had no timepiece those days. Shri Agrawal happened to ask me if I had one. When I told him that I didn't, he presented me a table clock with alarm-arrangement so that I could wake up in the morning as early as I wanted. When the High School examination drew near, he bought me a very fine geometry box so that I could draw the figures accurately. I haven't ever heard of teachers going that extra-mile to help students. Have you?

At the Mission School I had two very close friends. One of them was a Muslim named Yaqub Khan and the other a Christian, Noel James Paul. They used to visit my place often and I would offer them tea and something to eat. My mother was an orthodox Hindu, though highly religious. She did not like that these friends of mine used the same utensils as did the rest of our family. Thus, I kept a separate set for these friends. I would myself wash the utensils and keep them ready for their next visit.

Yaqub was an average student but Noel was fairly brilliant. However, I saw to it that in the examinations he was left far behind me, and defeated him in the aggregate by about 60-70 marks. I was always placed first and Noel always stood second. At the eighth class final examination too, the result was the same. Our school had a provision that the student who ranked first at this examination would be awarded a ten-rupee scholarship per month. (That was a big amount those days, when milk used to sell at 10 seers per rupee.) I had expected that on joining the ninth class I would be offered that scholarship. But that was not done. The scholarship was given to Noel. I protested against this, only to be told that it would go to a Christian. What kind of justice! Anyway, Noel and I continued to be good friends.

There are two more episodes of those school days which I must record here. I had a grand-uncle staying with us. He was pretty old and a bit hard of hearing. I can recall him usually seated in the front room. Once, it so happened that nobody except he was at home. My friend Noel came to my place and enquired of him, '*Kyā Braj Basi ghar men hain?*' ('Is Braj Basi at home?'). My grand-uncle replied, '*Yahān koi Braj Basi Frij Basi nahīn rahate.*' ('Nobody by the name of Braj Basi Frij Basi lives here.) Disappointed, my friend went away. Later on, when Noel told me about this episode, I realized where exactly the trouble lay. My grand-uncle knew me only by my pet name which was 'Bachchoo', because at home the name Braj Basi was never used.

Exactly the same kind of episode was replicated some thirty years later, when we were living at 127, Satya Marg, Diplomatic Enclave, New Delhi. There it was not the case of my grand-uncle who had passed away long back, but of my wife's aunt, who was living with us. My wife's cousin came to our place one day. Again, nobody else except the aunt was at home. The cousin rang the call-bell and when our domestic help opened the door, the visitor told him that Usha had come to meet the family. The domestic help came to the aunt and told her that one Usha had come and wanted to meet the members of the family. The aunt told the domestic help to tell the visitor that no one else was at home and that she personally did not know anyone by the name of Usha. Later on, when we returned home and were told by the domestic help about the visit of one Usha, we realized that it must have been the lady whose pet name was Chukki. We told the aunt about it and she was very sorry about the misunderstanding. She always knew this lady by her pet name, Chukki, but never by the name Usha. So beware, if you visit an Indian household and happen to find only an old lady/gentleman over there, make sure that you ask for the person concerned by his/her pet name. The 'official' name may not do. Of course, you will have to gather the pet name in advance, an exercise well worth it. Isn't it?

The other episode is of a more serious kind. Those days in Jhansi we did not have a flush latrine. It was only a dry one, and a sweeper used to come and clean it every morning. One day, the sweeper was very thirsty and asked for some water to drink. I went inside the house and brought a *loṭā* (a small pitcher) full of water. I poured it and the sweeper drank it with an improvised cup made of the palms of his hands joined together. At the end I patted him on the back and enquired of him if he wanted more. He said that he was satisfied with what he had taken. In the meantime, my father had noted that I had patted the sweeper. Those days (1930s), the sweepers were treated as untouchables and my father reminded me about it, adding that it was good that no neighbour had seen me patting the sweeper. At this I could not contain myself. I told my father that I saw nothing wrong in what I had done. After all, I insisted, the sweeper was as much a human being as any one of us. Though my father did not hold very staunch orthodox views, yet he was in favor of going by the current social practice. I started arguing with my father. I told him, "Suppose this person embraces Islam tomorrow and then comes to meet you, would you not greet him with such words as these *'Āiye maulānā sahib, tashrīf lāiye.'* ('Come in please, Maulana Saheb.') My father had no answer to that.

At the University of Allahabad, too, from 1939 to 1943, I had the good fortune of being under the guardianship of some very noble teachers. I would begin with Babu Jamuna Prasad who was the Resident Tutor at the Kayastha Pathshala University College (KPUC), a constituent of the University. For all intent and purposes, the KPUC was a hostel but had its own arrangements for tutorial classes. Being a Resident Tutor, Babu Jamuna Prasad was provided residential accommodation in the central part of the first floor of the two-storeyed, U-shaped hostel building. He had no wife, but with him there lived two of his nephews. He used to run his own mess.

Right from the very beginning, he was very kindly disposed towards me, perhaps because one Radhey Bihari Lal, an ex-student of the KPUC who was stationed those days at Jhansi as a senior officer in the Indian Railways, had given me an introductory letter addressed to Babu Jamuna Prasad, in which he had also mentioned that I belonged to a family that was economically not well-off and hence I needed some financial support. Thus, the first thing Babuji did was to waive the hostel room-rent, which was Rs. 8 per month. He permitted me to join his mess, which was less costly than the other general ones. I had to pay only Rs 12 per month for two square meals per day. Further, Babuji allotted me a room next to his residential area so that he could keep an eye on me.

Having obtained a very high position at the Intermediate Examination of the U.P. Board, I was awarded a scholarship of Rs. 16 per month. But in spite of this scholarship and a rent-free hostel room, I still needed some more money to keep on going. (My father was not in a position to send me this extra money per month.) Thus, there was the need to earn some money on my own. Babuji advised me to take up some private coaching work. He knew a High Court judge who needed a private tutor for his daughter, who was preparing for her High School Examination. Babuji fixed up an appointment for me with the judge for 8:30 a.m. one of those days. He also promised to come along and introduce me to the judge. On the day concerned, we came out of the hostel building around 7:30 a.m. and started looking for a cycle rickshaw. We waited for well over 15 minutes, but there was no sign of any rickshaw. Time was running out. Hence, Babuji asked me to borrow a bicycle from one of his nephews. I was surprised at his suggestion. Anyway, I borrowed the bicycle and came to the gate where he was waiting for me. Would you believe that the elderly Babuji sat on the luggage-carrier at the back of the bicycle which I was driving? Anyway, the job was done and I was given Rs 15 per month for teaching the girl three days a week.

I have mentioned earlier (Chapter I, pp. 1-3) that I had fallen seriously ill before the B.A. Final Examination. I was confined to bed for nearly three months. During this trying period, Babuji looked after me in a manner my father would have done. He took me to the doctor, got me the medicines and saw to it that I got the right kind of food supplemented with fruits. Since the students' toilet was a bit away, he permitted me to use the commode in his toilet and saw to it that it was cleaned and kept ready for me.

But Babuji was also a great disciplinarian and did not spare me whenever I went wrong. In the final year of my M.A. I was allotted a room at the extreme end of one of the arms of the U-shaped building. Though it was a bit away from the residence of Babuji, yet well within his sight. A verandah ran in front of all the rooms. Once around 7 p.m. when I was standing on the verandah in front my room, Babuji beckoned me with his hands, *'Braj Basi, tanī yahān āwā'* ('Braj Basi, come here for a while'). I immediately went up to him. Without telling me why he called me, the very first thing he did was to twist my left ear with his right hand and ask me to get back to my room, switch off the lights and then come back to him. I remember all this very well, with the result that even today I make sure that I switch off all lights before leaving the room.

At the KPUC there were two more teachers: Mr. Bhagawat Dayal, the House Tutor, and Professor Tara Chand, the Principal. Mr. Dayal was tall, well-built, fair complexioned and having a sharp nose. He could easily be mistaken as an Englishman who had lived long enough in the hot climate of India to have turned somewhat dusky. Mr. Dayal had been in England for higher studies for quite some time and returned home with a Bar-at-Law degree. But he used to take tutorial classes in the English language. On the first day of his tutorial class, he asked the students to introduce themselves. We did that. However, one of the students, after giving out his name, added that he lived with his relations in 'Kolonelganj', pronouncing the word 'Colonelganj' like that, which should have actually been pronounced as 'Kernelganj'. Mr. Dayal had a good laugh at this and added that no Indian can pronounce the English language correctly. At this, another student said, "Sir, you do." Thereupon, Mr. Dayal retorted, "But I am not an Indian in that sense. I have lived in England for over seven years." What a mistaken identity!

Professor Tara Chand used to wear a *chūridār pāyajāmā, sherwānī* and a round black cap. The last was so typical that it began to be nicknamed as *'Tarachandī topī'*. The professor lived at a distance of about a kilometer from the KPUC and used to come there on a bicycle. He was so punctual that one could doubtless set one's watch right on seeing him arrive. It was exactly at 10 a.m. Professor Tara Chand was teaching Political Science at the University and was renowned all over the country for his excellence. He was also very much interested in Indian Philosophy. Once he was requested by a Hindi magazine to write an article for it on Shankar's philosophy. He wrote the article in English and asked me to translate it into Hindi, and the time given to me was only two days. I can well recall having worked on it continuously for over 48 hours without a wink of sleep. That is a great example of the relationship between a teacher and a taught.

On achieving Independence, India began to re-shape its administrative set-up in its own way. Pandit Jawaharlal Nehru, the first Prime Minister of the country, knew Professor Tara Chand intimately. He invited the latter to take over as Education Secretary. After some time, when the need arose, Pandit Nehru sent Professor Tara Chand to Iran as the Indian Ambassador. The Professor knew the Persian language very well and that was a very welcome asset. On retirement from that post, he settled down in Delhi, living with his son who was a high-level officer in the Government. Thereafter, Professor Tara Chand made it a point to pursue his studies and writing work, sitting in a quiet room in the building of the National Archives. On learning that he was in Delhi, one day I went to the National Archives to pay my regards to him. I touched his feet and during the course of the talk told him, "Sir, even at this age you are working so hard." The Professor very gently replied, "Braj Basi, *agar chor chorī se gayā, to kyā herā pherī se bhī?"*

("Braj Basi, if a thief is no longer fit enough to commit major thefts, nothing prevents him from carrying out petty ones.") That was his dedication to learning and its dissemination!

In the Sanskrit Department of the University there were five teachers, all of whom were very kind and helpful to me. One of them was Dr. Kshetresh Chandra Chattopadhyaya who used to teach the Vedas. He had a very good library of his own. He not only allowed me free access to it but also permitted me to borrow books from it as often and as many as I liked. In October 1944 when he came to know that I was to go to Taxila for training in Archaeology, he told me that the place was very cold, especially during the winters, and enquired of me if I had sufficient warm clothes. I told him about all that I had. On discovering that I had no overcoat, he went to the Chowk, the main down-town market, and got one prepared at his cost and gave it to me. I doubt if teachers today can be so generous. On the other hand, I am told that some of the teachers go to the extent of asking for money from students for helping them in securing a research-degree!

Earlier (p. 5), I have referred to Professor P.K. Acharya who was the Head of the Sanskrit Department at the University. He taught me ancient epigraphy, architecture, etc. He was immensely satisfied with my studies and on finding that I had obtained a first class first with a very high percentage of marks at the M.A. examination, advised me to take up the competitive examination for entering the highest civil service (ICS) of the country. When I expressed my reluctance for joining the civil services, he was rather disappointed, but was finally reconciled to it – something which he expressly mentioned in the testimonial which he gave me. The relevant part reads: " .... With his exceptionally brilliant career, he could have succeeded at any of the examinations for lucrative civil services, but he has chosen the life of a scholar." Soon after the re-opening of the

University, Professor Acharya gave me a part-time lectureship in the Department.

Finally, I must refer to Sir Mortimer Wheeler who not only was instrumental in my gate-crashing into the Archaeological Survey of India (see above pp. 8ff.), but also saw to it that I proved worthy – have I? – of the confidence he had reposed in me.

After the close of the 1946 excavations at Harappa, he asked me to write out a chapter for the Report. I prepared the chapter which ran to about 10 pages and submitted it to him for perusal. He sent for me. This scene was set in his room in the Curzon Road Barracks, which housed the office of the Survey then (1947). After having a cursory look at the text, he threw away the typed pages on the floor. I was greatly shaken. Tears started trickling down my cheeks. I could not understand what was wrong with my text. Was there any fault with the language, or was there any wrong identification of the objects discussed in my note? I could not make out anything. On seeing me in that state of shock, the boss asked me to pick up the pages from the floor and place them on his table. I did so. He then took out his pen and started pruning the text. It took him about 25-30 minutes to finish. I was standing all the while by the side of the table watching him do the job. He mercilessly cut down the text to about half the original size and then asked me to have a look at it. I did that. Then he asked me, "Have I omitted anything worthwhile that needed to be mentioned?" My answer was in the negative. He advised me, "My dear boy, brevity is the key-note of good writing. If you remember that you have to pay one (sterling) pound for publishing each word you would always be brief and precise." I do not know how far I have been able to imbibe his teaching. I have always regretted that I did not have enough training under him in the art of writing.

After leaving the Archaeological Survey of India in 1948, Wheeler joined the Government of Pakistan as its Advisor on Archaeology and hastened to publish a book, *Five Thousand Years of Pakistan*. The title of the book was prima facie deceptive. But anyway there it was. Thereafter, in 1959, appeared his book, *Early India and Pakistan*. The then editor of *Antiquity*, the renowned British journal on Archaeology, asked me to review this book for the journal. I declined to do so, since I thought that it was not proper for a student to review the book of his teacher. But the editor persisted in his request and I had ultimately to review the book, which was published in *Antiquity*, Vol. XXXIV, No. 135, September 1960, pp. 224-27. I am giving below excerpts from my review, not because it has any great merit, but just to show how unkind I was to my teacher.

> Written in a masterly style, characteristically Wheelerian, and suitable alike for the scholar and the layman, the book incorporates the latest discoveries, and shows the author's acquaintance with the latest publications in India. At the end are given ample references to allow serious student to probe deeper into the subject. The illustrations are excellent, no praise being too much for the plates in particular.
>
> A present-day Indian archaeologist is, in a way, handicapped in criticizing, or differing from, anything done or said by Sir Mortimer, for he owes, to a considerable degree, either directly or indirectly, his methods and acumen to that savant, who gave shape to Indian archaeology during four years of the last decade (1944-48) when he was in India. The present reviewer, one of the direct associates of Wheeler-in-India, has, however, ventured to overcome this handicap and the Indian's traditions reverence of his *guru* when he records the following criticism, which, he is confident, will be taken by the ever-magnimous Sir Mortimer in the spirit in which it is meant. One of the points of criticism relates to Sir

Mortimer's tendency to rush to conclusions, or throw out suggestions of far-reaching cosequence, although in reality there may not exist any basis for them. This may be illustrated by a few examples.

*****

Lastly, the reviewer would like to take up an example of Sir Mortimer's wishful thinking. On p. 170 of the book under review, he says: "It is just possible that Ashoka had Seleukid blood in his veins." One does not know what evidence Sir Mortimer has to substantiate this view, but the known facts of history show that it is almost impossible. Sir Mortimer's view evidently has its root in the *jus connubii* that was established between Seleukos Nikator and Chandragupta Maurya in *c.* 305 BC. In the first place, scholars are not agreed that this must be interpreted to mean only that a daughter of Seleukos was wedded to Chandragupta Maurya. However, even if it were accepted that Seleukos's daughter was one of the wives of Chandragupta Maurya , the question is whether Aśoka, a grandson of Chandragupta, had actually descended from this lady. This could be possible only if either of Aśoka's parents was born of that lady. Now, according to one tradition (*Aśokāvadānamālā*), Aśoka's mother was one Subhadrangi , who was the daughter of a Brahmaṇa of Champā, while, according to another tradition (*Mahāvaṁśatīkā*), her name was Dharma and she was Kshatriya by caste. Whatever be the correct name and caste of Aśoka's mother, one thing at least seems to be clear that she was not an offspring of the Greek lady. But if in spite of this one argues that , as the traditions are not unanimous about the identification of Aśoka's mother, there is still the possibility of her having been Seleukos's grand-daughter, one should pause to think of the implications of such a stand. This would mean that Bindusāra was married to his step-sister, a position absolutely unwarranted by any record or tradition and indeed unimaginable in the concerned cultural setting. The question thus finally reduces itself to whether or not Aśoka's father, Bindusāra, was born of that lady.

> Bindusara is known to have ascended the throne in *c.* 297 BC. Thus, if it is assumed that he was born of Seleukos's daughter, who was married to Chandragupta in 305 BC, the inevitable conclusion would be that at the time of ascending the throne, Bindusāra was not more than eight years old. Such a position, however, is not corroborated by any evidence – Indian, Ceylonese or Greek. On the other hand, the following circumstantial evidence suggests that Bindusāra must have been born prior to 305 BC. Aśoka is known to have acted as a Viceroy at Ujjain as well as at Taxila before ascending the throne in 273 BC. He is, therefore, likely to have been at least twenty years old at the time of his accession, which would mean that he was born not later than 293 BC. It is also well known that Aśoka was not the eldest issue of his father. This would mean that Bindusāra was already a father by 295 BC. Under the circumstances, it is difficult to imagine how Bindusāra could be born of the daughter of Seleukos, who, if at all, could have been married to Chandragupta only as late as 305 BC. To argue for the contrary would mean to conclude that Bindusāra became a father at the age of ten!
>
> The reviewer's intention in raising the above points is not to argue for or against any particular hypothesis. All that he wants is to urge that subjectivity should be kept far, far away from all archaeological interpretations, more particularly when issues of great historical significance are involved. While this precaution is necessary in the case of us all, it is certainly much more so in the case of a writer of the eminence of Sir Mortimer, whose every word carries weight with both the serious student as well as the amateur reader. Has not the leader much greater responsibility than the led?
>
> May it, however, be stated once again that the book is indeed a very welcome asset and students of Indian archaeology will always remain grateful to Sir Mortimer for this gift.

Wheeler saw this review and instead of getting angry at me – anyone else in his position would have surely been so – wrote to me on 30th August, 1960, from his British Academy office, London, as follows:

> My dear Lal,
>
> I have just read your review of my little book on Indian Archaeology, and I must write at once to thank you for it. The points which you raise are all proper subjects for discussion, and I only wish that you and I were sitting in two chairs and able to talk to one another. It would, I feel, be quite improper for me to start a discussion on paper with my Reviewer!
>
> But my purpose in writing is to tell you how proud and glad I am to think that I am in some small sense your *guru*, and that I have lived to see you do so much first-class work. The review brought it all back to me again with renewed force, and I thought that I would like you to know that you have, now as ever, my warmest and most affectionate regards.
>
> Yours very sincerely,
>
> Sd. Mortimer Wheeler

All this shows how magnanimous my boss was!

There is yet another instance of his greatness. The year was 1971. I was invited by Professor C. Von Haimendorf to deliver the Gandhi Memorial Lecture at the Institute of Oriental and African Studies, London. The lecture was on my recent excavations at Kalibangan and their contribution to our knowledge of the Harappan Civilization. Professor Haimendorf had requested Sir Mortimer to preside over the lecture. While introducing me to the august audience, Sir Mortimer referred to my training period at Taxila and mentioned the two encounters that I had with him, namely, my pointing out his misinterpretation of the stratigraphic sequence on one occasion and his faulty interrelationship of two structures on another (cf. pp. 10-11). I was entirely flabbergasted at my boss's candidness. I don't think anybody else in his position would have done that!

Up to the first half of the twentieth century there used to be a small village within the Purana Qila in Delhi. It was known as Indrapat – phonetically equivalent to Indraprastha of the *Mahābhārata* fame. Local tradition also called it 'Pāṇḍavon-kā-Kilā', i.e., a fort of the Pāṇḍavas. In 1950s, while posted as the Superintending Archaeologist of the Delhi Circle, I wished to check up if the tradition about the place did actually have any archaeological basis. Thus, I put up a small trench to the south of the building known as the library of Humayun. I took advantage of a rain-gulley and carried out the excavation in a terraced style, exposing the various pre-Mughal strata, namely, those ascribable to the Rajput, Gupta, Kushan, Śuṅga, and N.B.P. Ware periods. Below the last-named deposits were encountered stray shards of the Painted Grey Ware, so typical of all the Mahābhārata sites. Immediately to the south of the Purana Qila, there is a substantial deposit of the PGW. All this very clearly indicated that there is an archaeological basis confirming the tradition.

After his retirement from the post of the DG, ASI, Sir Mortimer Wheeler often used to visit India in various contexts. During one such visit, I requested him to come over to Purana Qila and see for himself the terraced excavation that I had carried out at the site. He visited it (Pl. XLIII) and greatly appreciated the vertical panorama of the pre-Mughal periods. Unfortunately, the view is now highly obliterated, since the excavated site has not been maintained properly.

25

Jāko Rākhe Sāinyān, Mār Sake Nā Koya

'Him, whom the Lord protects, no one can ever kill', is what the above Hindi saying emphasizes. And here I am going to narrate five different car accidents in which I was involved, yet came out every time absolutely unhurt!

It was towards the end of June in 1976. My wife and I were proceeding from New Delhi to Shimla where I had joined the Indian Institute of Advanced Study as a National Fellow and was later also asked by the government to function as its Director. We were traveling by road in our Maruti 800. I was driving the car and my wife was seated next to me. (In India we have the steering on the right as against the left-side steering concept followed in the USA.) During most of June it is very hot and often there are dust storms. But around the end of the month, the region gets its first showers. It was cloudy and during the course of our conversation I was telling my wife that if it rained it was all right but if it only drizzled, the road would become very slippery because of the thin layer of loose soil that overlay the tarred surface of the road. And lo there it was. After a while it started drizzling and the road became slippery. As a precaution against any mishap, I reduced the speed of the car. But the inevitable took place. The car slipped and could not be controlled in spite of my best efforts. This accident took place a few kilometers before Ambala. Over there the road is about 10 meters higher than the ground level on its sides. The car swerved completely to the left and fell into the ditch. It had a head-on collision with a thick tree in the ditch. The front part of the car got completely smashed and the radiator was also damaged. But neither my wife nor I had any kind of injury. We quietly stepped out of the car, she through the left door and I through the right.

We just didn't know what to do next. Luckily for us, a tractor was passing by at that time. The driver, a young man, was supportive enough and offered to help us. He happened to have a thick, long rope on his tractor. He took that out and tied it to the back bumper of our car. By pulling the rope hard with the help of the tractor, he rescued our car from the ditch and brought it up on the road. We profusely thanked him for his timely help. We also tried to offer him some reward but, generous as he was, he declined to accept any.

We got some water from a nearby place and filled the radiator. But this helped only for a while, since the radiator had started leaking. Thus, we had to refill it again and again and it was only after an hour that we reached Ambala Cantonment. Over there we went to the house of Col. Akhilesh Dube, one of the sons of my old and dear university friend S.G. Dube about whom I have already mentioned (p. 2). Akhilesh and his wife Meera (daughter of another friend of mine, Shri M.N. Deshpande) were greatly surprised yet delighted to see us, but naturally very sorry to learn of the accident. At the same time, they were also greatly relieved on learning that we suffered no injury whatsoever. We stayed there for two days during which the car was thoroughly repaired. Thereafter, we proceeded to Shimla.

The next accident took place after about six months when my wife and I were returning from Shimla to Delhi. Since this time we were going out to resume excavations at Śṛiṅgaverapura, a site near Allahabad, we were traveling in an official jeep. Sardar Hardev Singh, a very faithful young person, was driving our car. Since there was not much traffic at that time of the day, Hardev was driving the jeep rather fast. When we were about to reach Ambala, the front-left wheel of the vehicle suddenly spinned out and the vehicle rolled on its sides at least two times before it stopped, resting on its left side. The front wind-shield glass got thoroughly smashed and its pieces fell on us. There were minor bruises on the face and arms, but nobody had any fracture of the bones. Strange, isn't it?

By this time Col. Dube had been transferred out of Ambala so we had to stay in a hotel. It took a day and a half for the car to be put in order, after which we resumed our journey to Delhi. When the hotel manager enquired about the accident, I told him that there was some evil spirit residing in Ambala which was unkind to us, since we had two successive accidents near here. He immediately retorted, defending his town Ambala, "Sir, the spirit is a noble one, since he has saved you all on both the occasions." I think he was right.

Now to the third accident. Though it was much later than the previous two, it was once again on the same Delhi-Shimla route. I had been invited by the Vice-Chancellor of Punjab University, Chandigarh, to deliver the Tagore Memorial Lecture. Driving the same fateful Maruti 800, I entered the Chandigarh city and was not far away from the university campus. As I was negotiating a round-about, a bus hit my car from the left and severely damaged its hind part. However, since my wife and I were in the front seats, we were unhurt.

As is the usual attitude of the bus-drivers in India, this one too speeded off his bus and disappeared before we could even react. I was left in a lurch. I requested my wife to keep sitting in the car, while I walked off to a nearby STD booth to make a phone call to the Vice-Chancellor. I told him all about what had happened. He was kind enough to send his Personal Assistant with a car who not only took us to the University Guest House but also arranged to have the car sent to a garage for repairs. After delivering the lecture the next day, I had to stay for another day during which the repairs to the car were completed. The Vice-Chancellor, I must add, was generous enough to donate a sum of Rs. 2000 from his Discretionary Fund, to lessen my heavy expenditure on the repairs.

The venue of the next two accidents was New Delhi itself. Put together, these make rather a cock-and-bull story. The first of these occurred at the round-about near the Taj Mansingh Hotel. After leaving the Prithviraj Road, I had entered the round-about. Just then a bus, moving very fast, entered the same round-about from the Aurangzeb Road and hit my car on the front-left side. The impact was so great that my car was pushed off well on to the apron of the round-about. The bus drove off with added speed and I was a mere helpless spectator. The left-front door of the car was badly damaged, so much so that it could not be opened. Luckily, my wife, who was there on the front-left seat, sustained no injury. I was, of course, well away from the damaged portion of the car. Greatly upset, we chose to drive back home. Since the front-left door was very badly jammed, my wife could not exit through it. Thus, after I had come out of the car through the front-right door, she slipped on to my seat on the right and managed to make an exit through that door.

The next day was a Saturday and we had been invited by Shrimati Sunita Nigam, my wife's cousin, to dinner. The Nigams then lived in a Central Government flat on the Satya Marg in Chanakya Puri. We had also to buy railway tickets for a journey to Allahabad the following week. Thus, we decided to buy the tickets from the railway booking counter near Sarojini Nagar, which was on the way to Chanakya Puri. Since the front-left door of the car had been damaged the previous night, my wife had to enter the car through the driver's door on the right. Of course, it was all right for me to get into the driver's seat. After buying the tickets at the railway booking counter, we entered the main road. Just then a big, speeding car, coming from the right, hit my car and badly damaged the front-right door, with the result that I could not even come out of it to accost the driver of that car, who it appeared was drunk. Anyway, since we were very close to Chanakya Puri, we decided to move on to the cousin's house. The couple came out to receive us and the husband started opening my door, of course, as a matter of courtesy. He was surprised to find that the door wouldn't open. He immediately noticed that the door was badly damaged. My wife and I climbed over the backs of our seats, came to the hind seats, opened the left and right doors, and thus managed to come out of the car. After we had been seated and offered refreshments, I narrated the story of these two consecutive nights. Anyway, after the dinner was over, we returned to our house in Huaz Khas Enclave, slept for the night and sent the car for repairs the next day. Five accidents, all rather serious, but no repairs needed for our bodies; only for the car. My dear Maruti 800 stood me in good stead. However, later on I disposed it off and bought a new car, this time a Maruti Esteem.

26

Whisked Away by a Damsel

It may appear weird, yet it is true. One night, a damsel entered my room and whisked me off to unknown lands. Indeed, this is how it all happened.

On cozy bed, one wint'ry night,
I lay in Cashmere blanket wrapped.
And lo! the room turned white with light
As someone at the door had tapped.

'Come in,' I said. In came a lass,
With necklace dangling 'tween her breasts.
Had she transparent or no dress?
In slimness she had passed all tests.

(Pl. XXVI)

Muttering with protruding lips
Some charms, she posed her bangled hands –
The left on knee, the right on hips,
And whisked me off to unknown lands.

And there I saw the myriad rays
Of sun through mist in hurry pass

To kiss and kiss a million ways
A river bashful like a lass.

My guide, oh no, the belle looked round
And beckoned soon a cabined boat
Which to the other side was bound –
Like the boat my thoughts began to float.

The poem goes on. ... The river was none other than the Indus. We crossed over to the other side and reached Mohenjo-daro, the famous site of the Indus Civilization. The lass introduced me to her cousin and we all went round the city and the Citadel. I saw some rituals being performed as well other sights, which I thoroughly enjoyed. With the fall of the night we returned to the cousin's house where an excellent dinner had been laid out and drinks were flowing like water.

Indeed, so tasty was the food
That records own I set at naught;
To drinks I gave a latitude –
I don't know what of me they thought.

Perhaps of 'What would others think?'
I lost all count, for countless cups
Had passed 'tween friend and me of drink –
Life's levelling all downs and ups.

So drunk was she, and so was I
That consciousness loosened its grips.
She in my lap began to lie:
Something I felt so close to lips.

At last her net began to spread:
"There is no life without a wife".
So stunned was I; and then I said,
"I have not, belle, a wifeless life".

"But what of that," she stressed her point,
"And why on earth to one get tied?
Or else, we live as ladies joint."
"It can't be so," aloud I cried.

Just then sweet Kusum dinned to me,
"Get up, my love, what makes you scare?
Here is your morning cup of tea;
Your Indus talk you must prepare."

The sweet dream was shattered by the morning cup of tea offered by dear Kusum. But she is not to blame. I myself had told her before retiring for the night to wake me up early in the morning so that I could prepare myself for a lecture on 'The Indus Civilization', which I had to deliver at the School of Archaeology.

This was a poem written by me in 1964. I showed it to some of my colleagues, one of whom, Dr. B. Ch. Chhabra, liked it so much that he translated it into Sanskrit. He happened to know the then President of India, Dr. S. Radhakrishnan, and gave a copy of it to him to read. Dr. Radhakrishnan enjoyed going through it and wrote a Foreword as well. In it, amongst other things, he says:

> Relics of the past have a fascination of their own. And those of the Indus Valley Civilization have certainly a world-wide appeal. To present them in lyrical form, as Shri Braj Basi Lal has evidently done in his *Sindhu Śatakam,* is a novel idea. ....
>
> The beautiful metal figurine of a dancing girl from Mohenjo-daro has aptly been conceived as the vivacious heroine of this enchanting romance of the ancient Indus Valley. I am sure the reader will enjoy it in whatever garb it appears.

Unfortunately, the *Sindhu Śatakam* has not yet seen the light of the day. The reason: It was written just for my own satisfaction (*svāntaḥ-sukhāya*) and not with an eye on its publication. I have never regarded it as either a piece of good poetry or even a worthwhile narration of the Indus Civilization. Hence the hesitation. However, my friends are keen that I do publish it.

27

A House Well-planned, Completed Not, Alas!

It was the year 1961. I was excavating a site called Sardargarh in Ganganagar District of Rajasthan. It was a known Painted Grey Ware (PGW) site but the objective was to ascertain if it also contained any Harappan remains and, if so, what their relationship was with the Painted Grey Ware Culrure. Any interlocking?

We did not encounter any Harappan remains but came across some very interesting evidence in the post-PGW levels. We noted in one of the trenches a channel about 50 cm in width and about the same in depth. It ran east-west. There was some pottery and ordinary earth in it, but no sullage. Thus, it did not appear to be a drain. Anyway, we pursued it and found that at both the ends it turned at right angles to the south. Sharp turns at right angles further indicated that it could not have been a drain. We continued to follow its plan and discovered that the southern arm turned at right angle to the north and the northern one at right angle to the south. These did not join each other, but

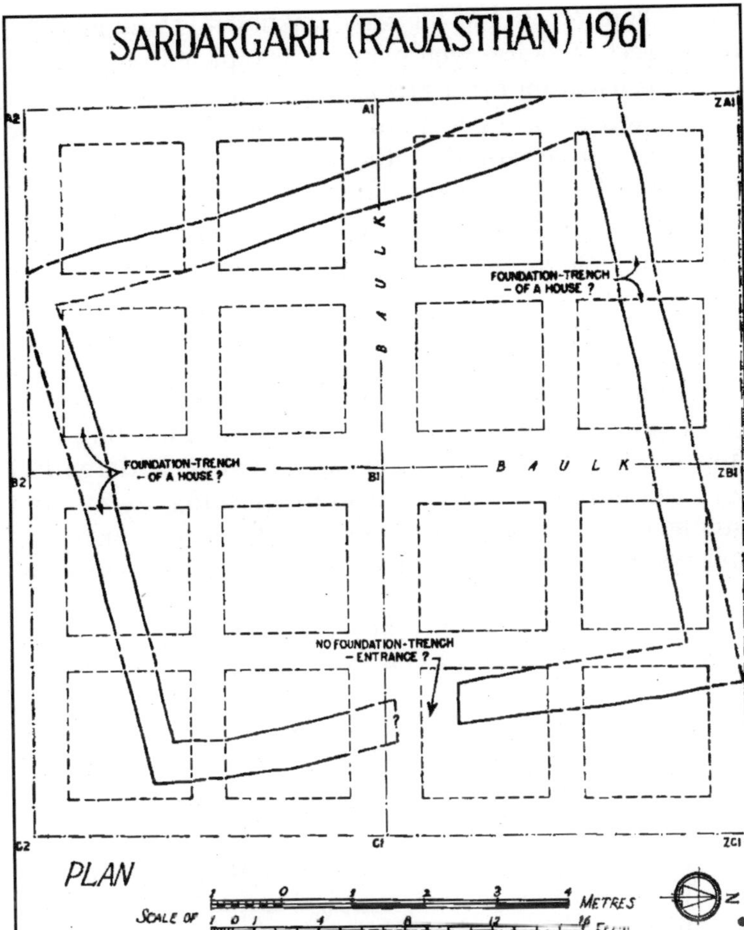

Fig. 9. Sardargarh, uncompleted house. (Courtesy ASI)

left an un-dug span a little less than a meter. All these features made it abundantly clear that it was not a drain, but a foundation trench for a house, the un-dug part representing the location where the door was meant to be (Fig. 9). The pottery recovered from within these arms was assignable to the Kushan times. Thus, it became quite clear that around that time someone wanted to build a house on the abandoned PGW mound. He had even dug the foundation trench, but for some unknown reason gave up the project: A house well-planned, completed not, alas!

It is usual for other archaeologists to visit a site under excavation in order to familiarize themselves with the outcome. Sardargarh also attracted a few scholars. One of them was Dr. B. Subbarao. Because of his exceptionally brilliant career, he was elevated to the post of a professor at a very young age and chosen to be the Head of the Department of Archaeology at the Maharaja Sayajirao University, Baroda. His book, *The Personality of India,* is indeed a pioneering piece of work.

Unfortunately, the life of this budding scholar was cut short before it could fully blossom. My last meeting with him was when he visited the excavation at Sardargarh. I was so moved by his untimely passing away that automatically a poem came out from my pen, which is as follows. It was published in the Subbarao Memorial Volume.

A HOUSE WELL-PLANNED,
COMPLETED NOT, ALAS!

A year ago in Rajasthan – so hot,
I dug at Sardargarh, on Ghaggar's left,
And found a house – without the house! But not
As Kenyon did with robber's trenches left.

Foundation-trench it was on Grey Ware mound,
With space for door. Unused, it did amass
Blown sand and things Kushan that lay around.
A house well-planned, completed not, alas!

And like the house we just have talked about
Could not come up the house called **Subbarao.**
Ere half his life, with Death he had a bout
And fell its prey – to Lord's wishes we bow.

In him has India lost – no guess is wild –
Another Bruce Foote or a Gordon Childe.

28

The Mandir-Masjid Controversy (1991-92)

As a part of the project 'Archaeology of the Rāmāyaṇa Sites', excavations were carried out in the Janmabhūmi area at Ayodhyā. Of the trenches laid out over there, one was immediately to the south of the boundary wall of the Babari Masjid. The lowest levels in this trench were characterized by an early stage of Northern Black Polished Ware, and on the basis of the Carbon-14 dates provided by the Birbal Sahni Research Institute of Palaeobotany, Lucknow, the beginning of the settlement at Ayodhyā would appear to go back to around 1000 BCE.

In this trench, hardly 50 centimetres below the surface, rows of pillar-bases were encountered. These were squarish on plan, made of brick-bats sometimes intermixed with a few stones. While most of these bases were well within the trench, a few of them lay underneath the edge of the trench towards the boundary wall of the Masjid (Pl. XVII). Associated with the pillar-base-complex there were successive floors-levels; and on the basis of the associated pottery and other antiquities, the entire complex could be dated from the twelfth to fifteenth century CE.

Attached to the piers of the Babari Masjid there were twelve stone pillars which carried not only typical Hindu motifs and mouldings but also figures of Hindu deities (Pl. XXX). Clearly, these pillars were not an integral part of the Masjid but were foreign to it. A question naturally arose whether the pillar-bases encountered in the excavation had anything to do with the above-mentioned pillars affixed to the piers of the Masjid.

The first reaction that came up from a certain category of historians was to deny the very existence of these pillar-bases. Their approach was simple: if there were no pillar-bases, the question of their relationship with the pillars affixed to the piers of the Babari Masjid became automatically redundant. These historians took recourse to publishing all sorts of unsavoury comments in the newspapers. However, when they were told that the pillar-bases were not someone's fantasy but their photographs (along with the negatives), taken at the time of the excavation, did exist in the photo-archives of the Excavations Branch of the Archaeological Survey of India, they gave up their first exercise in denial, of which more would be said later.

Then came up a brilliant brain-wave from a professor of the University of Allahabad, Dr. D. Mandal, who published a book on the issue. He drew on the photograph a black line along the right-hand edges of the pillar-bases and asserted that these constituted a 'wall'. Pl. XVIII, which is a true copy of Mandal's reconstruction, clearly shows the manipulation involved, and I don't have to offer any comments thereon.

In this context, it may also be well worth narrating an incident. Those days I was staying in the Guest House in Purana Qila, New Delhi, in connection with the preparation of the report on my excavations at Śṛiṅgaverapura. One night, after I had retired to bed, I heard a knock at the door of the guest house. When I opened the door I was surprised to see the familiar face of Professor Suraj Bhan of the University of Kurukshetra. I welcomed him and offered some coffee. He told me that he had been to Ayodhyā and had physically verified the pillar-bases but wanted to check up the field-plan on which these had been plotted. I told him that the relevant plans were in the office and I would be able show the same to him only the following morning. Annoyed, he left the guest house. Next morning what I read in the newspapers was a statement by this professor that while there did exist the pillar-bases in the Janmabhūmi area, these belonged to a cow-shed. What an ingenuous thesis to explain away the purpose of these bases which were associated with successive floors, made of a fine combination of lime and brick-jelly! In this context it needs to be added that, after a recent order of the Lucknow Branch of the Allahabad High Court, which is looking into the Mandir-Masjid dispute, the Archaeological Survey of India carried out excavation in the area which earlier lay underneath the Babari Masjid and has discovered that the series of pillar-bases continues all over the area. What kind of a cow-shed does this learned professor envisage now?

In 1991, the Museums Association of India invited me to deliver an illustrated talk on my excavations at Ayodhyā. The venue was Vijayawada and the date, 10th of February. After my lecture was over, the scholars present there asked me if there were more pillar-bases underneath the Babri Masjid and what relationship was there between the pillar-bases met with in the excavation and the pillars of a Hindu temple affixed to the piers of the Masjid. More pointedly, they wanted me to tell them if there was any temple underneath the mosque. Not being a sooth-sayer, I replied, as any archaeologist would do, that unless excavations were carried out in the area concerned, it was not possible to arrive at any conclusion. **The area covered by the floor of the Masjid was quite wide and long and it was possible to do a few probes, without in any way damaging the structure. But no one cared to listen to my suggestion.**

Curiously, events take their own course. On December 6, 1992, the Masjid was demolished by Kar Sevaks who had assembled in a large number at the site. The demolition, a sad event in itself, brought to light a great deal of archaeological material **from within the thick walls of the Masjid**. From the published reports it is gathered that there were more than 200 specimens, including many sculptured panels and architectural components, which must have once constituted parts of the demolished temple. Besides, there were three inscriptions.

Of the above-mentioned three inscriptions, the largest one **is** engraved on a stone slab, measuring 1.10 x .56 meters, and consists of 20 lines (Pl. XXVII). It has since been published by Professor Ajaya Mitra Shastri of Nagpur University in the *Puratattva,* No. 23 (1992-93), pp. 35 ff. (Professor Shastri, who unfortunately is no more, was a distinguished historian and a specialist in Epigraphy and Numismatics.) The relevant part of his paper reads as follows:

> The inscription is composed in high-flown Sanskrit verse, except for a small portion in prose, and is engraved in the chaste and classical Nāgarī script of the eleventh-twelfth century AD. It has yet to be fully deciphered, but the portions which have been fully deciphered and read are of great historical significance for our purpose here. It was evidently put up on the wall of the temple, the construction of which is recorded in the text inscribed on it. Line 15 of this inscription, for example, clearly tells us that a beautiful temple of Vishṇu-Hari, built with heaps of stone (*śilā-saṁhati-grahais*) and beautified with a golden

> spire (*hiraṇya-kalaśa-śrisundaram*) unparalleled by any other temple built by earlier kings (*pūrvvair-apy-akṛitam kṛitam nṛipatibhir*) was constructed. This wonderful temple (*aty-adbhutam*) was built in the temple-city (*vibudh-ālayanī*) of Ayodhyā situated in the Sāketamaṇdala (district, line 17) showing that Ayodhyā and Sāketa were closely connected, Sāketa being the district of which Ayodhyā was a part. Line 19 describes god Vishṇu as destroying king Bali (apparently in the Vāmana manifestation) and **the ten-headed personage (*Daśānana***

The inscription makes it abundantly clear that there did exist at the site a temple datable to circa 11th-12th century CE. The architectural pieces, sculptures and the inscribed slab that came out from within the walls of the Babri Masjid belonged to this very temple. (An inscription affixed to the Masjid stated that it was built by Mir Baki, during the reign of Babar.)

It has been contented by certain historians that these images, architectural parts and the inscribed slab were brought by the Kar Sevaks from somewhere else and surreptitiously placed there at the time of the demolition of the Masjid. This contention is absolutely baseless. Transportation of the above-mentioned material from elsewhere would have required the use of many trucks, an act which would have certainly been noticed by the innumerable representatives of the print and electronic media who were present on the spot to cover the event. On the other hand, a reputed journal, namely, *India Today*, published on p. 33 of its issue dated December 31, 1992 a photograph (here Pl. XXVIII) which shows the Kar Sevaks carrying on their shoulders a huge stone slab sculpted with a long frieze, after having picked it up from the debris. They were in the process of depositing, at a nearby safe place, the various pieces that had been recovered from within the walls of the demolished Masjid.

The above-mentioned historians have also alleged that the inscription has been forged. This is behaving like the 'Village School Master' of Oliver Goldsmith, who, 'though vanquished would argue still'. Besides Professor Ajaya Mitra Shastri, already referred to, the highest authority on epigraphical matters in the country, namely, the Director of Epigraphy, Archaeological Survey of India, Dr. K.V. Ramesh has also confirmed the same.

In this entire context, it also needs to be added that there do exist hundreds of examples, all over the country, of the destruction of temples and incorporation of their material into the mosques during the medieval times. For example, right in Delhi there is the Quwwatu'l-Islam Mosque ('Might of Islam') near the Qutb Minar, which incorporated parts of a large number of temples that had been wantonly destroyed by Qutub-ud-din Aibak after his conquest of Delhi in the last decade of the 12th century CE. Pl. XXIX shows, standing within the mosque complex, a colonnade which was constructed by using sculpted pillars of the demolished 27 Hindu and Jain temples. This was a matter of glory for the conqueror as has been recorded by him in an inscription still existing on inner lintel of the eastern entrance of the mosque. Its English translation, done by Maulvi Zafar Hasan, is as follows:

> This fort was conquered and this Jami Masjid was built in (the months of) the year 587 [AH] by the Amir, the great and glorious commander of the army (named) Qutb-ud-daulat-wa-din, the Amir-ul-umara Aibak Sultani, may God strengthen his helpers. The material of 27 temples, on (the erection of) each of which 2,000,000 Deliwals had been spent, were used in (the construction of) this mosque. May God the great and glorious have mercy on him who should pray for the faith of the founder of the good (building).

To sum up. The evidence presented in the foregoing paragraphs in respect of the existence of a Hindu temple in the Janmabhūmi area at Ayodhyā, preceding the construction of the Babri Masjid, is so eloquent that no further comments are necessary. Unfortunately, the basic problem with a ceratin category of historians and archaeologists – and others of the same ilk – is that seeing they see not and knowingly they ignore. But how long do they hope to continue with this ostrich-like attitude? Anyway, in spite of them the truth has revealed itself.*

---

* Adapted from Chapter II of my book, *Rāma: His Historicity, Mandir and Setu* (2008).

29

Review Committee on the Functioning of the Archaeological Survey of India (2000)

On May 4, 2000, the Government of India constituted a Review Committee to go into the functioning of the Archaeological Survey of India and suggest ways and means to streamline the same. The Committee comprised ten eminent persons as members, with the present writer as the Chairman.

The terms of reference of the Committee were:

(i) Restructuring the Archaeological Survey of India so as to make it more professional and effective;

(ii) Restructuring the Institute of Archaeology;

(iii) Reviewing the Recruitment Rules of Group 'A' officers of the Survey and making suitable recommendations; and

(iv) Recommending ways and means to improve the working of the technical and academic activities.

The Committee held eight sessions of varying durations, and kept on sending its recommendations to the government in instalments instead of waiting for the final outcome. This was done in order to ensure that the government started working on the recommendations as early as possible.

The first instalment, dealing with the **Revision of Recruitment Rules for the posts of the Director General, Additional Director General, and Joint Director General of the Survey,** was sent to the then Minister of Culture, Shri Anant Kumar, within a fortnight of the appointment of the Committee, since in its view the matter needed government's immediate attention. While forwarding it, the Committee added:

> As you are already aware, these posts have been lying vacant for the past nine years, and only stop-gap arrangements, by inducting non-professionals, have been made in regard to the topmost post. Expressing its anguish over such a situation, the Committee very much hopes that the Ministry, under your dynamic guidance, will take all necessary steps to fill up these posts at the earliest.

The government machinery, as we all know, moves at a snail's pace. Since 2000 a full decade passed and it was only on January 19, 2010 that an archaeologist, Dr. Gautam Sengupta, took charge as the Director General. What a long and painful wait!

The second instalment, relating to the setting up of an **autonomous Institute of Archaeology and Art**, was sent to the Minister on June 21, 2000. It contained a comprehensive plan of the proposed Institute, along with the composition of the Society and Board of Management that would govern it. The forwarding letter, sent by me, read as follows:

> Now I have the privilege of handing over to you the second instalment of our recommendations. These relate to the restructuring of the present Institute of Archaeology run by the Survey. Though it has the high-sounding title of an 'Institute', it is in no way a seat of higher learning or research. Our recommendations envisage a full-fledged National Institute of Archaeology and Art History, comprising five Schools which will deal respectively with Indian Archaeology, World Archaeology, History of Art, Conservation and Heritage Management and Archaeological Sciences. In addition, there will be four Special Centres to take care of Marine Archaeology, Museology, Tradition and Archaeology and Public Participation and Awareness, besides, of course, a Library and Documentation Wing and a Museum of Antiquities. The Institute will be a 'Deemed to be University'. The Committee has also drafted a Memorandum of Association, which is attached. I am sure that under your enlightened and dynamic guidance, the Ministry would be able to make this Institute a living reality.

After some dithering, the Ministry did ask one of its officers to look into the matter so that further necessary steps may be taken. The officer concerned is said to have worked on this project for a few months after which what happened is not known. Now that the government seems to be alive to the need of bucking up archaeology, as shown by the appointment of an archaeologist as the Director General, would it care to reopen its cupboards and once again initiate necessary steps to set up this prestigious Institute?

In the third instalment were included recommendations relating to: **(i) Clearance of arrears of reports on major excavations; (ii) Guidelines for future excavations and preparation of reports thereon; (iii) Other publications of the survey, including future planning; (iv) Central archaeological library; (v) Photographic section at the headquarters; and (vi) Drawing section at the headquarters.**

It is not intended to deal here with all the aforesaid topics. Only the first two are being taken, since these are of vital importance. Looking into the reasons for the backlog of the excavation reports, the Committee observed:

> The shifting of the excavators from one office to another, without seeing to it that the reports are completed before the shifting, has resulted in a major backlog. Thus, in many cases the officers retired without completing the reports.
>
> Even repeated requests by the excavators (who had retired) to provide the necessary facilties were totally ignored by the successive Directors General.

As a remedial measure, the Committee recommended as follows:

> (a) In the case of the retired persons –
> adequate technical and other supporting staff should be provided to assist in the preparation of the reports.
>
> Suitable contractual amount must be paid to the retired persons concerned for writing out the report. This amount would naturally vary from case to case, depending on the quantum of the work involved.
>
> In this context it must also be recalled that, on a very rough estimate, the Survey must have spent something like 30 to 40 crores of rupees on these excavations, put together. Would it not be a case of 'penny wise and pound foolish', if the Survey is not prepared to spend a paltry sum of Rs. 50 lakhs to salvage the expenditure of 30 to 40 crores which, as stated above, it has already incurred.
>
> (b) In the case of the persons still in the Survey –
> All such persons should immediately be relieved of their present posts and appointed as 'Officers on Special Duty' for clearing the arrears of reports.
>
> If the persons referred to above become eligible for promotion to a higher post, the promotion should be given

to them in situ. They must not be disturbed before the reports are completed.

While the Committee's recommendations regarding the retired persons seem to have worked reasonably well and many of the outstanding reports have since been either already published or are at an advanced stage of preparation, the same cannot be said about the reports by officers still in service. This latter is a matter which the Survey must seriously look into.

As regards future excavations and preparation of Reports thereon, the Committee recommended that –

(i) All major excavations should be done only by the Excavation Branches. Each Excavation Branch should have a Deputy Superintending Archaeologist, so that there is always a person second-in-command. Further, this second person will, in due course, be trained to undertake independent excavation.

(ii) In so far as the Circles are concerned, these should confine their excavation activity only to scientific clearance around monuments in order to expose the buried parts of the complex.

(iii) It has also been noted that sometimes officers without sufficient experience of excavation are posted as Heads of Excavation Branches. This should always be avoided.

(iv) After three years' field-work at a given site, the excavator must submit a comprehensive report, for which he/she should be given another two years in that very position. No transfer should be made during this period.

(v) The Survey should chalk out a comprehensive problem-oriented excavation and exploration programme for at least the next ten years and meticulously follow it.

One does not know how far these recommendations have been implemented.

The Fourth, Fifth and Sixth Instalments dealt respectively with: **(i) Central Archaeological Service Group 'A' and the Restructuring of the Archaeological Survey of India at the Functional Levels; (ii) Conservation and Maintenance of Monuments and Excavated Sites; and (iii) Review and Restructuring of Miscellaneous Cadres in the Archaeological Survey of India.**

Of these, only the part relating to the conservation and maintenance of monuments and sites is dealt with here, since it is of wider interest. While appreciating that some important monuments, frequented by tourists, were being well looked after by the Survey, the Committee regretted that many other monuments which too needed attention on a priority basis were not being given their due. Likewise, the Committee expressed its concern over the fact that in many cases the land appurtenant to the monuments was being encroached upon. The Committee also noted with dissatisfaction that in certain cases, large parts of the monuments had been renovated, which was quite uncalled for. Conservation is not renovation!

The Committee was very sore about the lack of conservation of excavated remains. Amongst other sites, the Committee cited the cases of Lothal and Kalibangan where the mud-brick structures posed a problem. As many as five members of the Committee visited the latter site and "all of them were in tears to see how an extremely important and well excavated site of the Harappan Civilization has been ruined", because of sheer indifference. The new Director General of the Survey, Dr. Sengupta, was kind enough to call on me soon after his taking over charge of the Survey and I drew his attention to this sorry state of affairs. I also suggested to him that a seminar-cum-workshop may be organized by the Survey to thrash out the problem of preserving mud-brick structures. If need be, experts from outside, including those accredited to UNESCO, may be invited to this workshop. Dr. Sengupta was kind enough to agree to my suggestion and I can only hope for a bright future for Kalibangan, where there already exists a site-museum. It may perhaps be recalled that this is the only site of the Harappan Civilization in the Sarasvatī Valley where one can walk through the streets and lanes with the successive walls standing on both the sides up to a total height of about 10 meters and where the fortification-walls, along with massive bastions, skirting the Citadel as well as the Lower Town, can still be seen.

In order to have a proper supervision over the works being carried out by the Circles, the Committee recommended that there ought to be **'Regional Directors'**, in between the Superintending Archaeologists in charge of the Circles and the Director General at the center. I am glad that this recommendation has since been implemented.

30

The AIT/OIT Controversy (2000-09)

The reader must be wondering what the terms *AIT* and *OIT* stand for, and rightly so. Quite away from the public eye, these are clichés used by historians and archaeologists dealing with ancient India and stand respectively for 'Aryan Invasion Theory' and 'Out of India Theory'. Whereas the former advocates that the Aryans came from outside and invaded India, the latter implies, on the other hand, that the Aryans were indigenous and went out of India to other countries. I have been involved in this controversy for nearly a decade now and have written about a dozen seminal papers in scientific journals in India and abroad and have published at least four books on this issue. In fact, my first book which touched this topic in an Appendix captioned 'It is Time to Rethink' was *The Earliest Civilization of South Asia,* published in 1997 (New Delhi: Aryan Books International). But the issue has been discussed in much greater detail in subsequent books, namely, *The Sarasvatī Flows On: The Continuity of Indian Culture* (2002), *The Homeland of the Aryans: Evidence of Ṛigvedic Flora and Fauna and Archaeology* (2005) and *How*

Deep are the Roots of Indian Civilization? Archaeology Answers (2009), all brought out by the same publisher. Towards its end, the last-named book contains a chapter, 'Did Some Vedic People Emigrate Westwards, Out of India?', which has generated a great deal of heat on the Internet. In the following few pages, I propose to place before the reader the arguments, though briefly, for and against these two theories, leaving it to him to make his own judgment.

The background of the 'Aryan Invasion' theory is as follows. In the 19th century, a German scholar, Max Muller, dated the Vedas, **on a very ad hoc basis**, to circa 1200 BCE. In 1920s, a great civilization, now called variously the Harappan/Indus/Indus-Sarasvatī Civilization, was brought to light in the north-western part of the Indian subcontinent. On the basis of its contacts with the already known Mesopotamian civilization, the Harappan Civilization was dated to the 3rd millennium BCE. Since the Vedas had been assumed to be not earlier than 1200 BCE, the Harappan Civilization was at once dubbed as non-Vedic.

In 1946, Mortimer Wheeler discovered a fortification wall around one of the mounds at Harappa. On learning that the Aryan god Indra has been referred to in the Vedas as *puraṁdara*, meaning destroyer of forts, Wheeler lost no time in propounding the theory that Aryans invaded India and destroyed the Harappan Civilization. In support of his hypothesis, he drew attention to some human skeletons found at Mohenjo-daro, another site of the Harappan Civilization, and argued that these were the people who had been massacred in the invasion.

A close examination of the context of these skeletons, however, has revealed the startling fact that these had been found at different stratigraphic levels of the site – some from the middle, some from the upper and yet others from deposits that accumulated after the site had been abandoned. Clearly, therefore, the skeletons did not represent a war-massacre, since had that been the case all these should have been found in the uppermost level after which the site was supposed to have been abandoned. Further, no arms signifying warfare nor even any other material objects relatable to any alien culture to be associated with the (imagined) invaders were found. **The hard fact is that at no site in the entire domain of the Harappan Civilization has any evidence whatsoever been found signifying any invasion – much less by the Aryans.**

According to the 'Aryan Invasion' thesis, the authors of the Harappan Civilization were a Dravidian-speaking people who were driven away to South India by the invaders. If that was really the case, one would expect to find at least a few settlements of these displaced Harappan people in South India. But, again, **the truth is that nowhere in the Dravidian-speaking States – be it Tamil Nadu, Andhra Pradesh, Karnataka or Kerala, has any site even remotely associable with the Harappan Civilization been found.**

There is yet another way of looking at the issue. All over the world, it has been observed that even when new people – invaders or immigrants – overtake a territory, settle down there and give new names to their own townships, the names of some of the rivers, mountains and towns given by the earlier people still persist. For example, in the USA, whereas New York, New Jersey, etc. are the names of towns given by the immigrant Europeans, the names given by the earlier inhabitants, now called the Red Indians, still persist – such as Chicago and Massachusetts. Likewise, the names of certain rivers, such as the Missouri and Mississippi, are pre-European. On the contrary, it has to be noted that **in the entire area occupied by the Harappans, from the Indus on the west to the upper reaches of the Yamunā on the east, there is no river, town, etc. bearing a Dravidian**

name. Why? Because the Harappans were not a Dravidian-speaking people.

Now, if there was no Aryan Invasion nor were the Harappans Dravidian-speakers, were the Harappans themselves the Sanskrit-speaking Aryans? There are four objections to a Harappan-Aryan equation. First, it has been an article of faith with most Western scholars and their Indian followers that the Vedic Aryans were 'nomads', whereas the Harappan Civilization had a major urban component. Secondly, whereas the Vedas refer to the horse, the Harappan Civilization is thought to be unfamiliar with it. Thirdly, while the Vedic vehicles had spoked wheels, the Harappan ones are supposed to be bereft of such wheels. And finally, since according to the dating of Max Muller the Vedas cannot be earlier than 1200 BCE and the Harappan Civilization belonged to the third millennium BCE, how can the two be equated, chronologically?

Nomads? The Vedic people lived a settled life and even constructed forts. In *RV* 10.101. 8 the devotee's prayer is: '**[oh gods] make strong forts as of metal, safe from assailants**. *RV* 4.30.20 refers to '**a hundred fortresses of stone'.** Sometimes these **had a hundred arms** (*RV* 7.15.14).

The Vedic people carried on trade, not merely on land but also across the sea. *RV* 9.33.6 states: 'From every side, O Soma, **for our profit, pour thou forth four seas filled with a thousand-fold riches**.' Further, the ships used in sea-trade were not petty ones but could be as large as having **a hundred oars** (*RV* 1.116.5).

Even on the political and administrative fronts, the Vedic people were highly organized. Not only did they have ***sabhās* and *samitis* which dealt with legislative and perhaps judiciary matters, but they also had a well-established hierarchy amongst the rulers, viz., *samrāṭ*, *rājan* and *rājaka*. For example, in *RV* 6. 27. 8 Abhyāvartī Chāyamāna is stated to be a *Samrāṭ* (Sovereign), whereas**

***RV* 8. 21. 8 states that, dwelling beside the Sarasvatī River, Chitra alone is the *Rājan* (king) while the rest are mere *Rājaka*s (kinglings or petty chieftains).** That these gradations were not imaginary but absolutely real is duly confirmed by the *Śatapatha Brāhmaṇa* (V.1.1.12-13), which says: 'By offering the *Rājasūya* he becomes Rājā and by the *Vājapeya* he becomes Samrāṭ, and **the office of the *Rājan* is lower and that of the *Samraj*, the higher.' Can we still call the Ṛigvedic people 'Nomads'?**

The Horse.—In his report on Mohenjo-daro, Mackay states: 'Perhaps the most interesting of the model animals is one that **I personally take to represent the horse.**' Wheeler also confirmed the view of Mackay. A lot more evidence has come to light since then. **Lothal** has yielded not only **a terracotta figure of the horse** (Pl. VII), but some **faunal remains as well.** On the faunal remains from **Surkotada,** the renowned international authority on horse-bones, Sandor Bokonyi of Hungary, states: 'The occurrence of true horse (*Equus Caballus* L.) was evidenced by the enamel pattern of the upper and lower cheek and teeth and by the size and form of the incisors and phalanges (toe bones).' In addition, there are quite a few other Harappan sites, such as Kalibangan and Rupnagar, which have yielded the faunal remains of the horse.

The Spoked Wheel.—It is absolutely wrong to say that the Harappans did not use the spoked wheel. While it would be too much to expect the remains of wooden wheels from the excavations, because of the hot and humid climate of our country which destroys all organic material in the course of time – the Harappan Civilization is nearly 5,000 years old – the terracotta models, recovered from many Harappan sites, clearly establish that the Harappans were fully familiar with the spoked wheel. On the specimens found at Kalibangan and Rakhigarhi (Pl. XXXI), the spokes of the wheel are shown by painted lines radiating from the central hub to the periphery, whereas in the case of specimens from Banawali, these are executed in low relief – a technique which continued even into the historical times.

The chronological horizon of the Vedas.—In this context, the role of the river Sarasvatī is very significant. According to certain scholars, it has to be identified with the Helmand of Afghanistan. This is totally untenable. *RV* 10.75.5 very categorically mentions that the Sarasvatī lay between the Yamunā and Sutlej. *RV* 3.23.4 states that the Dṛiṣadvatī and Āpayā were its tributaries. Further, *RV* 7.95.2 shows that the Sarasvatī flowed all the way from the mountains to the sea. In Afghanistan there are no rivers by the name of Yamunā and Sutlej, nor are there the Dṛiṣadvatī and Āpayā. Further, there is no sea in Afghanistan. So how can the Ṛigvedic Sarasvatī be placed there? **The entire evidence – positive in the case of India and negative in the case of Afghanistan – clinches the issue: The present-day Sarasvatī-Ghaggar combine, though now dry at places, does represent the Ṛigvedic Sarasvatī; the Helmand of Afghanistan does not.**

There is yet another piece of literary evidence that needs to be cited. Whereas during the Ṛigvedic times the Sarasvatī was a mighty flowing river, by the time of the *Pañchaviṁśa Brāhmaṇa* (XXV.10.16) it got dried up. Thus, on literary grounds, the *Ṛigveda* is to be dated prior to the drying up of the Sarasvatī, while the *Pañchaviṁśa Brāhmaṇa* would be posterior to this event.

To take up the archaeological evidence. On the left bank of the Sarasvatī there was the well known Harappan settlement of Kalibangan, in Rajasthan. As per the investigations carried out by a team of Italian and Indian hydrologists, the site had to be abandoned because of the drying up of this adjacent river. Further, according to the radiocarbon dates, this abandonment took place around 2000-1900 BCE. Thus, putting together the entire archaeological, radiocarbon-dating, hydrological, geological and literary evidence, the following conclusion becomes inescapable, viz., that **since during the Ṛigvedic times the Sarasvatī was a mighty flowing river and according to the archaeological-radiocarbon-dating-cum-hydrological evidence it dried up around 2000 BCE, the *Ṛigveda* has got to be earlier than 2000 BCE.** How much earlier, it would, of course, be anybody's guess. Professor N. Kazanas is of the view that the antiquity of the *Ṛigveda* may well go back to the 4th millennium BCE.

The geographical evidence provided by *RV* 10.75.5-6 shows that the entire area from the Gaṅgā on the east to the Indus on the west was occupied by the Ṛigvedic Aryans. Further, since, as just discussed, the *Ṛigveda* must be dated to a period prior to 2000 BCE, a relevant question arises: **Which archaeological culture covered this very region, i.e., from the Gaṅgā on the east to the Indus on the west, during the period prior to 2000 BCE? The inevitable answer shall have to be: the Harappan Civilization itself** (Fig. 10).

Now, if the Vedic people themselves were the authors of the Harappan Civilization, were they indigenous? To answer this question, we will first have to examine how deep are the roots of the Harappan Civilization. By now we have succeeded in identifying at least two earlier cultural stages from which the Mature Harappan Civilization had gradually evolved. These are: (i) the Early Harappan Culture which preceded the Mature stage, for example at Kalibangan. Preceding the Early Harappan stage, there was what has provisionally been termed as pre-Early Harappan, met with for example at Bhirrana. For this last-named cultural level, the Carbon-14 dates are:

Sample No. BS 2314.—Calibrated age: 1 Sigma 4770 (4536, 4506, 4504 BC) 4353 BCE

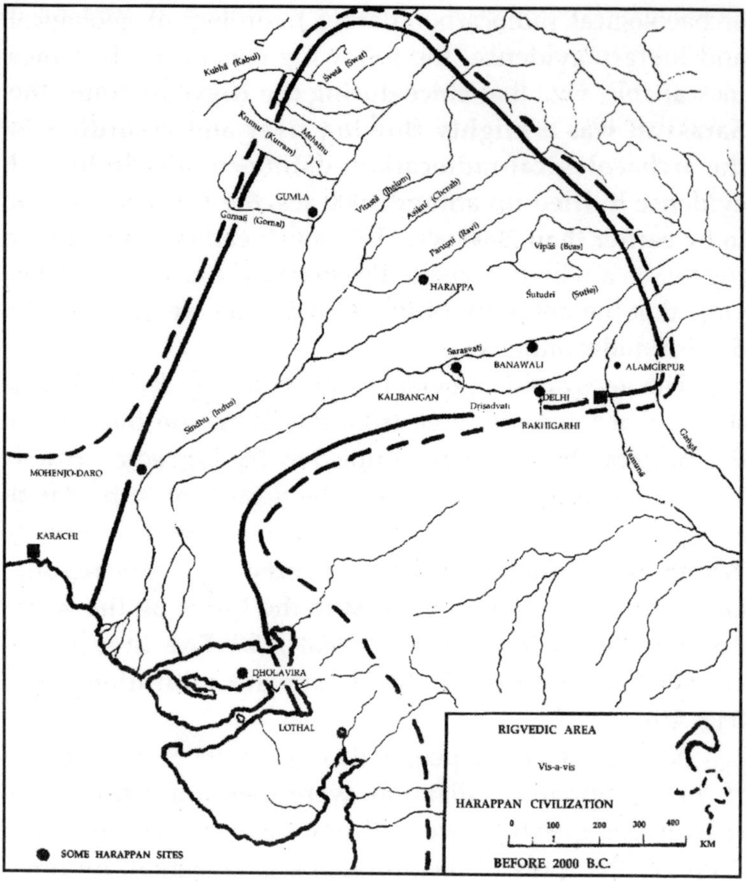

Fig. 10. Map showing a correlation between the Ṛgvedic area and the spread of the Harappan Civilization, before 2000 BCE.

Sample No. BS 2318.—Calibrated age: 1 Sigma 5336 (5041) 4721 BCE

Sample No. BS 2333.—Calibrated age: 1 Sigma 6647 (6439) 6221 BCE

Even if we temporarily ignore Sample No. BS 2333, the other two samples show that the ancestry of the Harappan Civilization in the Sarasvatī Valley goes back to circa 5,000 BCE. For all one knows, there may turn up one day even a still earlier stage.

Carbon-14 dates thus show that the Harappan Civilization was indigenous and since this civilization and the Vedic people are but two faces of the same coin, the Vedic people were *ipso facto* indigenous.

We now take up another allied question, namely, did some Vedic people emigrate out of India, to the west? As would be seen from what follows, the answer is 'Yes'. To substantiate this, we have both literary as well as archaeological evidence. The main literary text which throws light on this issue is the *Baudhāyana Śrautasūtra* (18.44), which states: '**Ayu went eastwards and his descendants are the Kuru-Pāñchālas and Kāśī-Videhas, whereas Amāvasuh migrated westwards and his descendants are the Gāndhārī, Parśu and Araṭṭa.**'

The areas mentioned in the context of the westwards emigration may be identified as follows:

Gāndhāra.—All available evidence shows that the Gāndhāra region lay in eastern Afghanistan and included an adjacent bit of the strip of present-day Pakistan, to the west of the Indus.

Paraśu.—This terms occurs not only in the *Baudhāyana Śrautasutra* but also in a completely independent document thousands of kilometers west of India. Assignable to 835 BCE, it mentions that Assyrian king Shalmaneser received tributes from 27 kings of **Parsuwas**. The region concerned is evidently **Paraśu, i.e., Persia**, which has only recently (1935) been re-named as Iran.

Araṭṭa.—A 3rd-millennium-BCE epic from Western Asia states that a king of Uruk, named Enmerkar, sent a messenger to Ensuhgiranna, the **ruler of Araṭṭa**, putting forward certain demands. In reply, the ruler of Araṭṭa told the messenger "...The queen of heaven and earth, the goddess of numerous *me*, holy Inana, **has brought to Araṭṭa, the mountain of shining *me, I whom she has let bar the entrance of the mountains as if with a great door* ...**" This would imply that Araṭṭa was located close to an opening (pass) in the mountains which the ruler of Araṭṭa could easily seal. Such a description enhances the claim of the Araraṭ region as having been Araṭṭa of the epic.

The Bogazkoy Inscribed Tablets.—These tablets, recovered from Bogazkoy in present-day Turkey, record a treaty between a Mitanni king named Matiwaza and a Hittite king, Suppiluliuma, ascribable to circa **1380** BCE. As witnesses to this treaty, some gods were invoked which included the following: *Indara* (=Vedic *Indra*), *Mitras(il)* (=Vedic *Mitra*), *Nasatia*(*nna*) (=Vedic *Nāsatya*) and *Uruvanass(il)* (=Vedic *Varuṇa*).

Further, from this region and its neighborhood more than a hundred names have come to light which have a Sanskrit stamp on them: such as: *Biridasva* (=Vedic *Vṛidhāśva*); *Urudīti*, a Hurrian king (=Skt. *Urudīti*); *Artasumara*, another Mitanni king (=Vedic *Ṛitasmara*, in addition to *Matiwaza* = *Mativaja*, already mentioned), and so on. The context of some of these names goes back to the **seventeenth century** BCE. Reference may also be made to another remarkable document, which deals with the technique of horse-training. It mentions Sanskrit numerals like *ekavartana, trivartana*, etc. meaning thereby that the horse under training should be made to make one round, three rounds and so on of the race-course.

Commenting on the Bogazkoy evidence, the renowned Indologist T. Burrow observed: "The Aryans appear in Mitanni from 1500 BC as the ruling dynasty, which means that **they must have entered the country as conquerors**." 'Conquerors from where', may not one ask? At that point of time, **there was no other country in the entire world *except India* where the above-mentioned gods were**

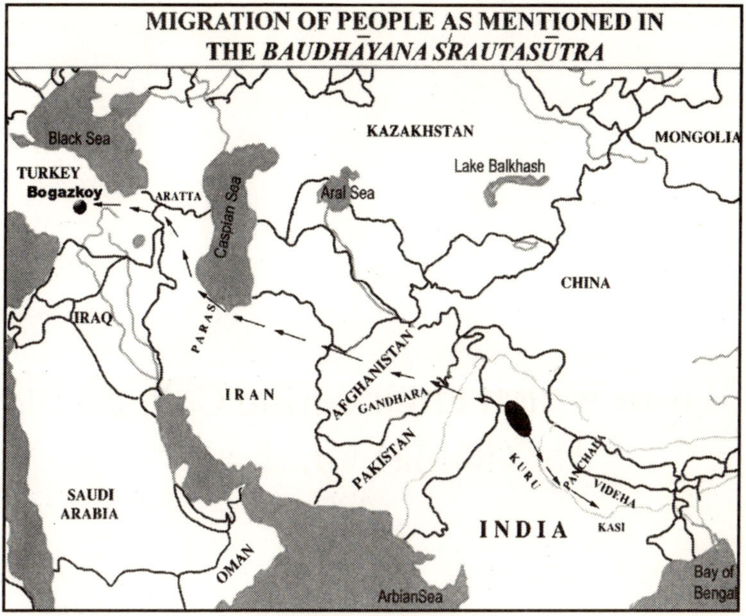

Fig. 11. Migration of the Vedic people, as mentioned in the *Baudhāyana Śrautasūtra.*

worshipped. As I have shown earlier, the ***Ṛigveda decidedly belonged to a period prior to 2000*** **BCE. Hence, there is no chronological obstacle whatsoever in visualizing a scenario in which a section of the Vedic people may have reached Turkey early in the second millennium BCE** (Fig. 11).

31

"From Which Engineering College Did He (Rāma) Graduate?"

In the Lucknow edition of the *Hindustan Times*, dated September 19, 2007, p. 7, there appeared a statement by the Chief Minister of Tamil Nadu, Thiru M. Karunanidhi, in which he raised the following two questions: "Who is this Rāma?" and "From which engineering college did he graduate?" He was addressing a public meeting in the context of the construction of a canal cutting through the Rāma Setu which stretches from the southern tip of Tamil Nadu to the northern tip of Sri Lanka. The above quote is from the Chief Minister's outburst against a section of the people who had argued that the *Setu* should not be destroyed since it was associated with Lord Rāma and hence so much revered by the Hindus.

By implication, the first of these statements seems to doubt the very historicity of Rāma. I have already dealt with this issue in an earlier chapter (22) to which the reader's attention is kindly invited. Here I would only like to let this present-day ruler of Tamil Nadu know that long back – more than 1200 years ago – one of his predecessors, namely, Nandivarman, made two very clear references to Rāma, vide his Kaśakuḍī plate inscription, dated to 752-53 CE, thereby acknowledging his historicity.

Anyway, the issue at present is whether Rāma or the members of his retinue really needed the knowledge of engineering so as to build the structure known as Rāma Setu. My answer straightway is "No". The reason, as explained in the following few paragraphs, is that in antiquity a natural reef was already exposed above the then sea-level, and thus there was no need at all to build any bridge across the sea, in order to connect India with Sri Lanka.

From Dhanushkodi, located on the sea-shore in Tamil Nadu on the Indian side, right up to Talaimannar on the Mannar island, a northern part of Sri Lanka, there runs a chain of sandbars, underlain by coral reefs and limestone shoals. The stretch is about 30 kilometers in length (Pl. XXXIII). It is this chain that is known as the Rāma Setu as well as Adam's Bridge. At present, some of these sandbars are above the sea-level and some others are submerged. But a map assignable to the 16th-17th century CE shows a land-link between India and Sri Lanka, naming it as Pont d'Adam, i.e., Adam's Bridge. Further back, in the 13th century CE the well known Venetian traveler Marco Polo visited many parts of the world and refers to this feature as 'Setabund Rameshwara' (i.e. a *Setu* = bridge, related to Rāma).

Evidence provided by inscriptions and coins, which leaves little scope for any ambiguity, also points to the existence of the Rāma Setu in ancient times. Thus, for example, the Hampi inscription of Kṛiṣṇadevarāya, dated to Śaka Era 1430 (i.e., 1508 CE) refers quite a few times to the *Setu*. Likewise, the coins issued by the Tamil kings of Nallur in Jafna, who ruled from the 13th to 17th century CE, affirm the existence of the Rāma Setu, in the same manner as does the foregoing inscription.

While the above-noted evidences of literature, tradition, cartography, epigraphy and numismatics have their own significance and value, I have tried to examine the issue in a purely scientific manner. As a first step, I got prepared a longitudinal profile of the Rāma Setu, as it exists now, right from the Indian side to its end in Sri Lanka, with the present sea-level as the datum-line. The result is presented as Pl. XXXIV, which shows that even today many of the sandbars are above the sea-level. However, what is no less important is that even in the stretches where no sandbars are seen, the depth of the sea is generally in the range of .5 and 1 meter, but in no case more than 1.5 meters.

The next step was to find out the behavior of the sea-level in antiquity. It is well known that out of the total amount of water on our planet, a part is locked up in the form of snow and the remaining flows in the sea. Further, when there is an intensely cold period, the quantum of snow becomes more and that of the water in the sea gets reduced. Geologists and palaeo-climatologists have worked out this behavior and have come to the conclusion that there have been at least four major Glacial Periods in the past, namely, Gunz, Mindel, Riss and Wurm. Each time when there was a Glacial Period, there was a corresponding lowering down of the sea-level. Likewise, with each warm period, technically named as the Inter-glacial Period, there was a rise of the sea-level.

The last glacial period is known to have ended around 10,000 years ago. Thereafter began what is known as the Holocene. With the gradual warming up of the climate, there began the melting of the snow and consequent rise of the sea-level. Scientists have worked on the quantum of this rise. While they all agree that there has been a rise in the sea-level since the beginning of the Holocene, their estimates vary. Without going into the details of the various estimates, it may suffice here to say that even the most conservative estimate holds that there has been a rise of 2 mm per year, which makes it at least 2 meters per 1,000 years.

The repercussions of this rise of the sea-level the world over are very interesting. According to a scientific study (*Microsoft Encarta 2006*): "The final melting of the ice sheets, called the Flandrian Transgression, ... caused the separation of Ireland from the mainland of Great Britain and of Great Britain from mainland Europe. Tasmania was also separated from continental Australia during this period." If such drastic has been the story of the submergence of land-connections in Europe as well as Australia, why should it be surprising if a similar phenomenon took place in respect of the land-link between the southern tip of India and the northern tip of Sri Lanka?

To take up the details of the Rāma Setu. On a projection of even the **minimum** rise of sea-level at the rate of 2 mm per year, i.e., 2 meters per 1,000 years, it would follow that around 1,000 BCE, the likely period of Rāma (see Chapter 22), the sea-level may have been at least 6 meters below the present. Such a situation would have exposed the entire land-mass from Dhanushkodi to Talaimannar, as would be absolutely clear by having a second look at Pl. XXXIV. However, even assuming, for the sake of argument, that an odd stretch here or there still contained some water, the same would have been very shallow. Hence, it would have been easily possible to fill up these short and shallow stretches by digging parts of the exposed sandbars and shoals and dumping the material into these patches, thus creating a ford in order to cross over to Sri Lanka. To achieve this, Rāma did not need to have a "graduate degree from an engineering college", as demanded by an eminent political figure of the country. Let us not lose our cool!*

---

* Based on Chapter III of my book, *Rāma: His Historicity, Mandir and Setu* (2008).

32

2010

This book is likely to go to the press by the end of July 2010 and, hopefully, may be out by the end of the year.

Today it is June 30 and by now there have taken place in the current year three events which are worth recording. A fourth one has yet to come, but I shall refer to it as well.

My youngest brother, Shri Prakash, has setlled down in Jhansi, where he had spent most of his service career, in the Indian Railways. Of late, he has been bed-ridden, has lost his speech and is also losing weight with each passing day. The disease has something to do with the nerves in the brain. He has been under the treatment of various neurologists, both in Jhansi and in Delhi, but there is no sign of any improvement. Although my wife and I had been suffering from severe pain in the knees, we decided to visit my youngest brother in Jhansi. It was a very troublesome journey since we had to be driven in wheel-chairs on the railway platforms, both in New Delhi and Jhansi. Anyway, the journey was perfomed and we were able to see my ailing brother. We stayed in Jhansi for three days and on the last day we decided to visit Baidora, my birth-place, about 20 kilometers from Jhansi. My nephew, Rajeev, drove us in his car.

For the past many years, whenever I went to Jhansi, I was keen to visit Baidora, but somehow the trip could not materialize. This time, on February 1, 2010, it finally did. I had left Baidora when I was about four years old, yet somehow I had a very clear picture in my mind of the location of our ancestral house over there. I remembered that there was a small lane in front of our house, which sloped down to join a somewhat wider street at a T-junction. At this junction, I well remembered, there were a small temple of Hanumanji, located on a low platform, and a well closeby. When we entered the village and enquired of the local people about the location of the Hanuman Mandir and the juxtaposed well, we were told that it was not far away, and we were given directions how to reach there. We hardly drove for about 200 meters and were there: everything – the ancestral house, the lane, the Mandir and the well – exactly fitting into my mental picture that I had carried with me since I was just four. Everybody in our group was surprised at the fidelity of my memory, at well past 88. Plate XXXV shows me walking in front of the ancestral house. Since none of the members of the entire family was interested in continuing to stay in Baidora, the house was sold off. Unfortunately, on the day of our visit the present owner was out of station and thus we could not have access into the house. However, though strangely, I well remember its two-storeyed plan!

The year has also seen one very unusual event in our lives. On March 9, my wife and I underwent surgery for what is commonly known as 'knee-cap replacement'. For at least a year we had been finding it very difficult to move about. Thus, both of us offered both our knees to the surgeon's knife. This, the surgeons say, was extraordinary, since they cannot recollect a couple undergoing such a surgery simultaneously. Anyway, the hospital was Orthonova and the surgeon, Dr. Pankaj Bajaj. It must be mentioned that we found Dr. Bajaj not only a very efficient surgeon but also a very kind and sympathetic human being. After we had been discharged from the hospital and were recovering at home (F7 Hauz Khas Enclave), he came all the way to our place to pay a courtesy visit – something very rare for highly placed specialists.

Since March 9 it has been a very gruelling time – in terms of physical pain. In my case, there was also low-grade fever for at least two months. The allopathic doctors could do nothing about it. Dismayed, I consulted a homeopath, Dr. Rakesh Raj, who lives in Allahabad. He is well known to my younger brother, Om Prakash, who has settled down in that city and had earlier introduced me, over the telephone, to Dr. Raj. You wouldn't believe that with his medicine the fever disappeared in a couple of days. Please do not underrate homeopathy. I had, on many earlier occasions, very good results with homeopathic medicines.

In April the same year, the Madhya Pradesh Government honored me with V.S. Wakankar Award (Pl. XXXVI). A resident of Madhya Pradesh, this great archaeologist was full of zeal and insight and was responsible for the discovery and detailed exploration of the prehistoric site of Bhim-Betka, which is now on the World Heritage List.

Another very important event, which is scheduled for November this year, is an International Conference on 'How Deep are the Roots of Indian Civilization? An Archaeological and Historical Perspective'. To it about 30 scholars from all over the world – USA, UK, Italy, Greece, Pakistan and, of course, India – have been invited. The conference is being organized by the Draupadi Trust (Chairperson Ms Neera Misra) in collaboration with the Archaeological Survey of India and the Indian Archaeological Society. Within the scope of the aforesaid conference fall two very debated topics, namely, (1) Who were the authors of the earliest civilization of the Indian subcontinent, known variously as the Harappan/Indus/Indus-Sarasvati Civilization?; and (2) Was there an Aryan Invasion, or were the Vedic Aryans indigenous? I am awaiting the fireworks. It is hoped that the proceedings of the conference will be published by the end of 2011.

33

An Assortment

There have taken place certain other events during my career which need to be chronicled, but which do not deserve to go under a separate chapter each. Hence, the same are clubbed here.

Academically, the first international recognition that came my way was in 1954 in the form of a review of my paper, 'Further Copper Hoards from the Gangetic Basin and a Review of the Problem' (*Ancient India*, No. 7, 1951, pp. 20-39), published by Professor Stuart Piggott in *Antiquity*, No. 111, 1954. It ran thus:

> The copper hoards from the Gangetic basin were discussed by the reviewer in *Antiquity*, XVIII (1944), 173. Mr. Lal not only publishes in admirable details, a mass of new material, but convincingly shows that previous conclusions on these curious assemblages of copper tools are likely to be erroneous. The reviewer tried to glimpse an Aryan ghost behind them all. Mr. Lal makes a much better case for supposing that the objects from the hoards represent a native culture more or less confined to the Gangetic basin and complementary to that of Harappa further to the west.

The year 1975 brought to me the first scholarly award. It was the presentation of S.C. Chakrabarti Medal, by the Asiatic Society of Bengal. In 1979, The Nava Nālandā Mahāvihāra, which carries on the tradition of the famous Nālandā University of yore, awarded me the title of *Vidyā Vāridhi.* Just three years later, the Mithila Viśvavidyālaya, Darbhanga, conferred on me the title of *Mahāmahopādhyāya.* The Asiatic Society, Bombay, in 1991, offered me its Honorary Fellowship for Life.

Assisted by my dear student Dr. S.P. Gupta and his student Dr. Shashi Asthana, I had chief-edited a Volume, *Frontiers of the Indus Civilization,* in memory of my teacher, Sir Mortimer Wheeler. It was released in early 1980s by the then Prime Minister of India, Shrimati Indira Gandhi (Pl. XL), who besides being an astute politician, had keen love for things academic and cultural.

The year 1994 saw two events in my life. That year I was elected President of the World Archaeological Congress, held in Delhi. The Congress was a great success, but for an unsightly demonstration made by some students in front of the opening venue of the Congress, Vigyan Bhavan. The other event was the conferment on me the honorary degree of D. Litt. by the Institute of Archaeology, St. Petersberg, Academy of Science, Russia. This latter function was held in the auditorium of the National Museum, New Delhi.

In 1997, the then Vice-President of India, Dr. Krishna Kant, felicitated me (Pl. XXXVII) and released three volumes of a publication in my honor, *Facets of Indian Civilization,* which contained essays contributed by over 130 scholars, from India and abroad. It was edited by Shri J.P. Joshi and four of his colleagues.

From Vice-Presdent to the President of India. In 2000, the then President, Dr. K.R. Narayanan, had the kindness to honour me with the ***Padma Bhushan*** award, in recognition of my humble contribution to Indian archaeology. The function was held at the Rashtrapati Bhavan, New Delhi (Pl. XXXVIII).

34

My Fellow Archaeologists

During the course of my long professional career I have had the privilege of interacting with many archaeologists, in India as well as abroad. I have greatly benefited from these interactions and would like to recall here some of them.

I will begin with my dearest student and friend Dr. S.P. Gupta. He was such a gem that no praise is enough for him. In so far as his contribution to Indian archaeology is concerned he was an all-rounder: be it Stone Age or Bronze Age archaeology or Art and Architecture or even Indian Ocean archaeology. He has published a number of books and seminal papers in various research journals in India and abroad. He was so much devoted to the cause of expanding the horizons of archaeological studies in the country that he left no stone unturned to set up a big center for the purpose on the premises of the Indian Archeological Society (IAS).

As a human being, he was larger than life. I have not come across any person who could face and fight even Death with such courage and calmness as Guptaji did. During the last couple of years of his life he was having severe bouts of asthma and his lungs were gradually shrinking. He had to be in and out of hospitals a number of times. But whenever I visited him at his residence I saw him busy at his desk, with oxygen tubes in his nostrils and a gas cylinder by his side. His last days were spent in the Intensive Care Unit (ICU) of Rockland Hospital. Just a couple of days before his breathing the last I went to the ICU and met him. He was as cheerful as ever. I showed him the typescript of my latest book, *How Deep are the Roots of Indian Civilization? Archaeology Answers*, as well as the dedicatory note in it, which is given below. Dr. Gupta smilingly looked at me and became deeply emotional. That is his last image that has etched itself on my mind.

Dedicated to
my most beloved student
Dr. S.P. Gupta
whose pursuit of knowledge
balanced judgement
unflinching devotion
self-sacrifice
and institute-building capacity
will ever remain enshrined
in the annals of Indian Archaeology

At the Indian Archaeological Society there are three more persons whom I would like to mention. They are Shri K.N. Dikshit, Dr. S.S. Biswas and Shri O.P. Tandon. They have assiduously kept the Society's flag flying after the passing away of Dr. Gupta. Dikshitji has ensured that the prestigious journal of the Society, *Purātattva*, is brought out on time for the annual meetings of the Society. In addition, he has embarked on a new venture by publishing reports on excavations carried out by various universities and institutions, for example the reports on the excavations at Śiśupālgarh, Jhūsī and Farmānā. Dr. Biswas is a museum specialist with keen interest in art. He retired as the Director General, National Museum, New Delhi. He, Dikshitji and Tandonji are working on a project to put up another building on the premises of the Society.

Shri Tandon was originally working with the Survey, but later on shifted to Banaras Hindu University (BHU) where he was the Registrar and subsequently Director of the prestigious Bharat Kala Bhavan. During my visits to that university I used to meet Shri Tandon who would invite me to a lunch or dinner. On one occasion when my wife was also with me we went to his place for a lunch and sure enough we cannot forget the dishes offered by Shrimati Tandon, which included *taḍakā-wālī-arhar-kī-dāl* (lentil with garnishing of spices fried in clarified butter). The taste still lingers in our mouth. Once, after a meeting of the Board of Management of the Society I casually referred to this Varanasi lunch with the Tandons. Shri Tandon was sharp enough to extend an invitation to me and Dr. M.N. Deshpande to yet another similar lunch, this time at his New Delhi residence All of us thoroughly enjoyed this repeat performance of the Tandon family.

One of the daughters of the Tandons, Shrimati Supriya Bali, is a physician of repute at Max Hospital in Saket, New Delhi. After my knee surgery in March 2010, I was running fever for well over a month. The surgeon could not control it. I spoke to Shri Tandon about it. He lost no time and came to my residence along with his physician daughter who examined me and prescribed medicines which were of great help. Such is the affection of the Tandon family towards us.

While reminiscing our visits to BHU, I cannot but recall the great affection that Professor Vidula Jayaswal showered on us on one occasion. She had discovered the rocky area from where the Ashokan pillars had been quarried and she wanted me to see the site. I gratefully accepted the invitation and reached Varanasi with my wife. Vidulaji arranged for a transport and we left the university guest house around 9 am, reaching the site by 11. We went around the entire area, saw a number of spots where the unwanted pillar-shafts had been abandoned and also went to the bank of the nearby river from where the selected shafts appear to have been transported by boats. All this was very satisfying – something altogether new to me. But then came the downside. It was a summer month and moving around the barren rocky area under the scorching sun not only exhausted me but also resulted in my vomiting out a number of times. I was completely flat and energy-less and almost fainted. Vidulaji decided to cut down the trip and in a couple of hours we were back in the guest house. She immediately rushed to the doctor (BHU has a renowned Medical College) and brought him to the guest house. The doctor prescribed the necessary medicines and I began to feel better. But it took me three days to recover fully. During this period Vidulaji looked after me as a mother would. Not only was she present by my bedside most of the time but brought from her home *khichari* and other light food which she cooked herself. Such an affectionate care is rather rare!

Professor Vidula Jayaswal is a great scholar in her own right. Her reports on Bhitari and other sites showcase her meticulous field-work and deftness in writing. She has all my blessings.

Belonging to BHU, there are four other professors with whom I have had close contacts. They are: Professor A.K. Narain who set up the Department of Ancient Indian History, Culture and Archaeology and Professors K.K. Sinha, Purushottam Singh and Vibha Tripathi who have continued to carry the torch. Professor Singh's recent book, *Archaeology of the Ganga Plain: Cultural-Historical Dimensions,* offers a brilliant analysis of the entire available data from the mesolithic to early historical times.

If one were to go back about half-a-century one would find almost a vacuum in our knowledge of what happened in the Gaṅgā plains between the mesolithic times and the early historical. In throwing light on this so-called 'Dark Age', many hands have contributed. They are, to name just a few: Professors V.D. Misra and J.N. Pal of Allahabad University and Dr. Rakesh Tiwari, the indefatigable Director of the U.P. State Archaeological Department. It is Dr. Tiwari's work at Lahuradewa that has put on world map the early evidence of rice in India (7th mill. BCE). In identifying cereals and other plant remains from a number of excavated sites in the Gaṅgā valley and elsewhere, the researches of Dr. S.K. Saraswat are most praiseworthy. I am personally greatly beholden to him for giving me comprehensive data on the provenance of various Ṛigvedic trees and plants, which I included in my book, *The Homeland of the Aryans: Evidence of Ṛigvedic Flora and Fauna and Archaeology*. He is a self-effacing scholar.

And one cannot forget the unrivalled king of the middle Gaṅgā valley archaeology. I mean Professor G.R. Sharma who not only was the founder of the Department of Ancient Indian History, Culture and Archaeology at Allahabad University but also its chief pilot to make it fly high on the firmament of Indian archaeology. He also set up an excellent museum in the Department, which could be the envy of any university. His publications include a wide range of subjects, from the prehistoric period to early historical times. For example, his reports on the excavations at the Stone Age sites of Koldihwa and Chopani Mando and at the towering early historical site of Kuśāmbī are indeed monumental and Indian archaeology will ever remain grateful to him for his contributions.

At a personal level, Professor G.R. Sharma's friendship is unforgettable. Though we were contemporary students at Allahabad University, from 1939 to 1942, we began getting closer to each other when he came in 1946 as a trainee to the excavations at Harappa, conducted by Dr. Mortimer Wheeler. I was then an Assistant Superintendent in the Survey and was positioned by Dr. Wheeler at Harappa to look after the operations as his aide. Our friendship kept on growing as years passed. He came to my marriage at Lucknow and was our guest whenever he came to Delhi. My wife and I well recall the morning when our youngest son, Rakesh, was born. Professor Sharma and my wife's maternal grandfather, Justice Bindhbasini Prasad, were staying with us, but the delivery took place so quietly that neither of them had any inkling of it. They were informed of it only after an hour or so. Professor Sharma, alas, is no more, but his son, Gyanendra, is now a Professor in the same Department.

No account of the archaeology of the Gaṅgā valley will be complete without reference to Professor B.P. Sinha, who once headed the Department of Ancient Indian History, Culture and Archaeology at Patna University. He was a great scholar, specializing both in history and archaeology. His excavations at Chirand and Vikramaśilā contributed a great deal to our knowledge of protohistoric and early historical Bihar. Besides being an erudite scholar, Professor Sinha was a very affectionate person and his affection was enjoyed by every one – big or small. Whenever my wife accompanied me on a trip to Patna, the Sinhas insisted on our staying with them. Shrimati Sinha is an excellent cook and for every meal she prepared new dishes. While all these were great, we cannot forget the *mālpuās* prepared by her. *Mālpuās* are a kind of leavened bread, made of refined wheat flour, fried in clarified butter and then soaked in sugar syrup. I am afraid no words, written or spoken, can convey the taste and one has to go to the ever-open guest house of the Sinhas to relish this out-of-the-world superb dish.

While speaking of the Sinhas, I think I must share with the reader an interesting episode which Shrimati Sinha herself narrated to us. She is well over eighty years of age now and this anecdote relates to some ten years back. She was admitted to a hospital for some surgery. She lay on the table and the surgeon asked her to remove all the jewelry on her person, which she did. Then the surgeon asked her to remove the set of teeth which he took for granted were false. Shrimati Sinha did nothing. The surgeon was somewhat annoyed and repeated his instructions. Shrimati Sinha again did nothing. Finally, the surgeon had to be told that the teeth were original. The surgeon was amazed since by that age people usually loose many of their original teeth and go in for false replacement.

Aligarh is yet another university which has contributed to the archaeology of the Gaṅgā basin as a whole. My excavation at Hastināpura had added a new chapter to the archaeology of this basin and this encouraged Professor R.C. Gaur of Aligarh University to undertake excavation at a site called Atranjikhera. Professor Nurul Hasan was the Head of the Department and a very good friend of mine. At that point of time I was the Director of the newly established School of Archaeology of the ASI. Professor Hasan asked me to inaugurate the excavation at Atranjikhera, which I gladly did. This site brought to light, for the first time, a black-and-red ware stratum preceding that of the Painted Grey Ware. Professor Gaur also carried out excavation at Lal Qila, yet another site in the region, and brought to light material which may have something to do with the enigmatic Ocher-Color-Ware-cum-Copper-Hoard Culture of the Gaṅgā valley.

Once Professor Gaur fell seriously ill and was brought to Delhi and admitted to the All India Institute of Medical

Sciences (AIIMS). He had become unconscious. His son was a doctor at AIIMS and perhaps the daughter too. Thus, it was easy for the Gaurs to get full attention. However, nothing worked and Professor Gaur remained in comma for more than a month. However, after coming out of the comma he lost his speech. Communication became impossible. Thus, Roman alphabets were written on a notebook and his son and daughter began to communicate with their father by placing fingers on the alphabets and thus forming the required sentence and asking him what he wanted and so on. The father also responded, though with difficulty, using the same medium of communication. It took Professor Gaur a few months to recover his speech but it was never as before. But what is most admirable is that even in this kind of physical condition Professor Gaur managed to complete his report on the excavation at Lal Qila – something we all must take inspiration from.

Aligarh has produced another good archaeologist, in the person of Professor M.D.N. Sahi. He has carried out horizontal excavation at a Painted Grey Ware site named Jakhera, obtaining a great deal of information. Whenever he comes to Delhi he is kind enough to call on me and has a great deal of discussion. He loves it.

The chief organization for archaeology in the country is the Archaeological Survey of India. After joining it in 1946 I came in contact with many eminent personalities. Earlier in the book I wrote in detail about Sir Mortimer Wheeler whose *varada-hasta* (blessed hand) was always on me. After his retirement, Dr. N.P. Chakravarti became the Director General, but my contacts with him were not all that intimate. It is Shri A. Ghosh with whom I had a long and fruitful inning. Of the DGs who held the reins of the Survey after Independence, Shri Ghosh did the utmost for it. Besides organizing conservation work at many important monuments and putting in place village-to-village archaeological survey, he set up several site museums. But his greatest contribution, to my mind, was to start a new yearly bulletin called *Indian Archaeology – a Review* which incorporates all major archaeological works done in the country, not only by the Survey but also by State Departments of Archaeology, universities and other institutions.

Shri Ghosh was a man of few words and more action. Very amiable in nature, he carried with him the goodwill of the entire Survey. This was clearly in evidence when on the occasion of International Conference on Asian Archaeology organized by the Survey in 1961 to mark its Centenary all the officers and staff gave him their whole-hearted support. The Conference was inaugurated by the then Prime Minister Pandit Jawaharlal Nehru. Academically, it was a great success.

I had the privilege of succeeding Shri Ghosh and in turn I was succeeded by my dear friend Dr. M.N. Deshpande. Thereafter came in Shri B.K. Thapar, Shrimati Debala Mitra, Dr. Nagaraj Rao, Shri J.P. Joshi and Shri M.C. Joshi who made valuable contributions in one way or another. But the most regrettable part of the Survey's history was when officers of the Indian Administrative Service sneaked into it. Thank God, the 'Dark Age' is over with the appointment of an archaeologist, Dr. Gautam Sengupta, as its new Director General. He is very enthusiastic and I very much hope that under his leadership the Survey will regain its old glory.

Dr. Deshpande passed away in August 2008. I had a variety of relationship with him. He and I were co-trainees at Taxila, under Dr. Mortimer Wheeler in 1944. Somehow we were drawn towards each other and became friends. He got me a Marathi primer and began teaching me the language. I did not make much headway, but I remember a verse from it: *Chandobā, chandobā, bhāglāsa kā, nimboḷiche jhāḍāwāḷa basalāsa kā*? (O dear moon, are you tired and, therefore, resting on the branches of the Neem tree?) Later on, both of us were selected as officers in the Survey, I in the first batch and he in the second. Thus, I became senior to him. When I became the Director General in 1968, he became my Joint. I must say that all through he gave me his unflinching support. He was an expert at conservation of monuments. The Gol Gumbad at Bijapur had lost its acoustics and it goes to his credit to have restored it. Likewise, his work at the rock-cut caves at Ajanta and Ellora deserves special mention.

In an earlier chapter, I described in some detail how he was instrumental in my meeting Gurudeva Ranade. (He had been initiated by Gurudeva earlier.) On a book which I presented to him on one of his birthdays, I inscribed: *Gurū śiṣya doū khaḍe, kāke lāgūn pāya, balihārī wā śiṣya kī jina guruvara diyo milāya* (The Guru and his disciple are both in front of me. I bow to the disciple who showed me the way to the Guru.) The above-mentioned script of mine is based on the well known verse: *Gurū Govinda doū khaḍe kāke lāgūn pāya, balihārī wā gurū kī jina govinda diyo dikhāya.*

Way back, Dr. Deshpande and I lived in the same locality, viz., Satya Marg, Chanakyapuri, New Delhi. Shrimati and Dr. Deshpande, my wife and I used to have weekly meditation meetings, either at their place or at ours. Shrimati Deshpande was an excellent singer and treated us with nice *bhajanas* (devotional songs). One day Shrimati Deshpande telephoned to say that she wanted to meet us. We wondered what it was all about. Anyway, she came and put forward to my wife a proposal for the marriage of her daughter, Sushama, with our son, Rajesh. We were completely taken by surprise. It was a knotty problem. The Deshpandes were Maharashtrian Brahmins and we Kayasthas of UP. Never before in our family had an inter-caste and interstate marriage taken place. We, thus, told

Shrimati Deshpande that we would give the matter a thought. It took me a couple of years to persuade the elders in my family to agree to the proposal. Finally, the marriage was performed on May 25, 1975 at Gwalior where I was working as a professor at the Jiwaji University.

In the context of the Survey, I would like to mention the name of Dr. B.R. Mani, at present a Joint Director General. He is an all-rounder – an excavator specializing both in protohistory and historical archaeology, as well as a good administrator. He has many publications to his credit. We wish him a bright furure.

One of the officers of the Survey who retired without reaching the acme is Dr. S.R. Rao. His excavation at Lothal has given to the world the earliest dockyard, dating back to the third millennium BCE. While he was posted in Agra my family visited the place and stayed with him. The Raos had a couple of white rabbits with whom my sons fondly played. They used to remember Dr. Rao as *khargosh-wāle-*uncle. *Khargosh* is the Hindi word for rabbit.

Yet another ex-officer of the Survey with whom I have been intimate is Dr. R.S. Bisht. His site, Dholavira in Gujarat, with its massive remains and breath-taking water reservoirs, is doubtless one of the greatest sites that Harappan Civilization bequeathed to us. I greatly admire Bisht's attempts to correlate the archaeological evidence of Harappan sites with that of the Vedas. Though neither associated with the Survey nor an archaeologist by profession, Dr. Bhagwan Singh is yet another scholar who has worked on this correlation. His book, *The Vedic Harappans,* stands testimony to it.

While each year keeps on bringing to light new sites of the Harappan Civilization, the position on the decipherment of the Harappan script stands where it was when the civilization itself was discovered. However, some positive contribution has been made by the two concordances published respectively by Dr. I. Mahadevan and Professor Asko Parpola. The former is one of those rare bureaucrats who take interest in academic pursuits, and deserves our praise. Shri B.M. Pande, formerly of the Survey, has published an excellent paper on Harappan inscribed copper tablets. It is such objective papers that might ultimately help.

There are two more former officers of the Survey who closely interacted with me. As mentioned earlier in the book, in 2000 Government of India constituted a Review Committee on the Functioning of the Archaeological Survey of India, with me as its Chairman. Dr. R.C. Agrawal was the Convener and Secretary of the Committee. I have no words to thank him for the unflinching support he gave me all through my work. Later he moved on to the National Museum as a Professor at its Institute and is currently the Principal Director of Architectural Heritage Division of Indian National Trust for Art and Cultural Heritage.

The other officer is Dr. K.M. Srivastava who, as mentioned earlier, helped me immensely in my excavations in Nubia, Egypt, in 1961. His own work at Piprahwa in Basti Dstrict of Uttar Pradesh has conclusively settled the debate about the identification of Kapilvastu, the seat of the Sakya clan which gave to the world the great messenger of peace, Lord Buddha. This identification is fully supported by the discovery, by Dr. Srivastava, of more than forty seals from a monastery at the site, bearing inscriptions: *Devaputravihare Kapilvastu Bhikkusanghas* or *Mahākapilvastu Bhikshu Sanghas* in Brahmi script of 1st-2nd century CE. At one point of time Dr. Srivastava was the Chairman of the Indian Archaeological Society. Alas, he is no more.

Deccan College Postgraduate and Research Institute, Pune, has contributed in a very big way to Indian archaeology. And it must at once be stated that one cannot think of the Deccan College without the late Professor H.D.

Sankalia who had such a big hand in building it up. He realized that a study of excavated antiquities alone was not enough to get a comprehensive picture of the past. What was needed was to have a holistic picture with emphasis on man's environment. It is with this end in view that he set up at the Deccan College branches dealing variously with archaeo-zoology, archaeo-botany, archaeo-anthropology, archaeo-chemistry, archaeo-metallurgy, etc. Today the Deccan College is indeed a leading research institute in archaeology. Professor Sankalia's own contribution to Indian archaeology is immense. His excavation-reports on various protohistoric sites are monumental and no less memorable is the guidance he gave to a number of Ph. D. scholars.

I have had very good personal relations with Professor Sankalia. In 1951, he and I were together at the Institute of Archaeology, London. His wife was also with him. Since I was alone and the Sankalias were running their own establishment, they often invited me to a lunch or dinner. In Pune too they gave me the privilege of being their guest. The nice yet simple Gujarati dishes that Shrimati Sankalia prepared were extremely delicious. Shrimati Sankalia was a great devotee of Lord Krishna and often went into trance. She made me sit in front of the Krishna image in her house and once told me how the Lord would speak to her.

Two of Professor Sankalia's successors, Professor M.K. Dhavalikar and Professor V.N. Misra, also have been close to me. The former's work on the chalcolithic cultures of central India has added new dimensions to our knowledge. He has published many books on the protohistory of India, but *Environment and Culture: A historical Perspective* is remarkable for its new approach. Though he and I do not see eye to eye on the issue of 'Aryan presence' vis-à-vis the Harappan Civilization, I have always believed that every body has a right to write what he/she thinks is right.

Professor Misra is an eminent archaeologist and, like Professor Sankalia, has guided a number of Ph. D. scholars. His own work on Stone and Bronze Ages has been very significant: the excavation at Balathal stands testimony to it. One of his recent books, *Rajasthan: Prehistoric and Early Historic Foundations*, is a model of its kind for in-depth studies of a given region. The personal affection that Professor Misra has towards me is my most cherished asset. He has also been gracious enough to review two of my recent books in *Man and Environment*. The reviews are undeservedly flattering.

While the various specialists referred to earlier in the context the Deccan College have done excellent work in recreating the ancient environmental scenario at a number of excavated sites, here is one who has given them a firm (or very nearly so) chronological horizon. It is Professor D.P. Agrawal. He began his work on C-14 dating at Tata Institute of Fundamental Research, Bombay and later continued it at Physical Research Laboratory, Ahmedabad. Besides, he has carried out very useful research on ancient Indian metallurgy and has written many valuable books on the subject. He was my student at the School of Archaeology and even at that time I could foresee his dedication and research capabilities.

I would like to record my warm relations with Dr. Michel Danino. He is a free-lancer, extremely devoted to Indian Archaeology. French by origin but drawn towards Shri Aurobindo and the Mother, he moved down to Pondicherry and stayed at the *Āśrama* for a long time. He has now built his own house in Coimbatore and lives there with his friend, Nicole. Both of them are very sweet and humble and do the favor of calling on us whenever they visit New Delhi. Dr. Danino has written many books, in French and English, relating to 'The Invasion that Never Was' (viz. The Aryan Invasion) as well as the Sarasvatī which played a vital role during the Vedic-Harappan period.

There is a person who has recently come my way and is very kindly disposed towards me. She is not an archaeologist but one deeply interested in the subject. This is Ms Neera Misra. She belongs to Kampil, ancient Kāmpilya, from where hailed Draupadī, the unrivalled heroine of the Mahābhārata story. Ms Misra has established a Trust named after Draupadi and is its Chairperson.

A few years ago Shobhit University of Meerut had organized an international conference on ancient Indian history, archaeology and culture and I was requested by its Vice-Chancellor to deliver the Inaugural Address. I was not in good health and declined the invitation. However, he persisted and most likely at his suggestion Ms Misra took me in her car to Meerut. Since then she has been meeting me often. In November 2010 she organized an international conference on 'How Deep are the Roots of Indian Civilization: An Archaeological and Historical Perspective'. It was attended by many eminent scholars from India and abroad and was a thumping success.

As a person, Ms Misra is indeed great. While the conference was on, her father passed away. She most courageously and quietly withstood this tragedy, did not tell anybody about it and continued with her organizational work at the conference. If I were in her place, I would have perhaps broken down and even asked someone else to carry on the work on my behalf.

It has been my good luck to have had close contacts with many scholars outside India. In the immediate neighborhood, Pakistan, there were many persons who were my colleagues in the Survey during the pre-Partition days. Though I kept in touch with some of them, my relations with Professor Ahmad Hasan Dani were more intimate. The friendship goes back to 1944 when he and I were trainees under Dr. Wheeler at Taxila. Professor Dani, it needs to be specially mentioned, was a very good scholar of Sanskrit and wrote an illuminating treatise on the development of early Brāhmī script. He was equally adept in Persian. In recognition of his scholarship, Government of Pakistan conferred on him high awards.

Even after Partition we used to meet at international conferences, held in India or Pakistan or even in a third country. About two decades ago one such conference was held in Islamabad, under the auspices of UNESCO. From India, Shri B.K. Thapar and I were invited. After the conference was over, Professor Dani offered to take us to Taxila. On going around Bhir Mound all the half-a-century old memories were revived. On our way back to Islamabad, Professor Dani pointed out in the distance to an area where Pakistani nuclear missiles had been piled up and jocularly added, 'Beware these are waiting for you'. Alas, Professor Dani is no more.

In European countries I have many good friends, but here I would refer to just a few. The towering personality, both academically and physically, of Professor Maurizio Tosi from Italy is the first that comes to my mind. He became my friend nearly a quarter of a century ago and since then we have met on a number of occasions and discussed matters of mutual interest. His work in the Arabian and Central Asian countries has thrown very valuable light on Harappan contacts with these regions. He is the one who attempted to recreate the seafaring scenario between the Persian Gulf and India. My wife and I have had the pleasure of inviting Professor Tosi to our residence and were immensely satisfied on seeing how he really enjoyed Indian food, in particular *kachori*s and stuffed brinjals. In 2007 he kindly invited me to deliver the Inaugural Address at the 19th International Conference on South Asian Archaeology, held at the University of Bologna, Ravenna, Italy. The

Address, 'Let not the 19th Century Paradigms continue to Haunt Us', made great impact, as I learnt from the feed-backs.

I have great admiration for Professor N.D. Kazanas of Greece, who is a renowned Sanskrit scholar and has published many important papers refuting the 'Aryan Invasion Theory'. He has taken head-on Professor Michel Witzel of Harvard University, USA, and has demonstrated how the latter had gone wrong in his theories. I understand that the learned Professor is planning to launch a journal on Vedic studies.

Earlier in the book I referred to Dr. J.M. Casal and his wife, of Paris, who were dear friends of ours. During our visits to Paris my wife and I used to stay with them and greatly enjoyed their hospitality. These visits gave me an opportunity to brush up my little knowledge of the French language. I also well recall that one evening we took the Casals out to a dinner at a very posh Indian restaurant in the heart of Paris. We were treated to live Indian music and dance and the Casals appeared to have very much enjoyed that evening.

On the occasion of a dinner hosted by Dr. Casal I came in touch with Dr. J.-F. Jarrige. He is now a leading figure in the world of archaeology: his excavations at Mehrgarh in Pakistan have opened up new vistas, taking the beginning of settlement in that region back to the 7th millennium BCE.

Way back in 1951 when I was at the Institute of Archaeology, London, I met the recently married couple Dr. Raymond Allchin and Bridget. They were very nice to me and we developed good friendship. However, as one steeped in Indian traditions, I was surprised to find that the Allchins were not living with Raymond's mother who, incidentally, had a fairly big house in London. They would, however, pay a visit to her almost every week-end. That was my first exposure to Western way of life. Later in 1971, when I was Alexander White Visiting Professor at University of Chicago, I came across another facet of Western way of life. Amongst my students there were a boy and a girl. They had been living together and I thought they were husband and wife. Thus, once when they were invited to tea at our place, I introduced them to my wife as Mr. and Mrs. So and So. The visitors rebuffed me by saying that while no doubt they lived together and enjoyed sexual relationship, they were not husband and wife.

To begin with, Dr. Raymond Allchin was appointed a Lecturer at the University of Cambridge and later rose to higher positions. He and his wife started coming to India and carrying out field-work at neolithic and chalcolithic sites in the country. In 1982 they published an excellent book, *The Rise of Civilization in India and Pakistan.* There are many other valuable books to their credit. However, it gives me immense pleasure to mention that Dr. Allchin also produced annotated translations in English of two Hindi books by the renowned saint-poet Tulasidas, viz. *Kavitāvalī* and *Vinaya-patrikā.*

While in Delhi, the Allchins often stayed with us and, likewise, we too enjoyed their hospitality during our visit to Cambridge. Unfortunately, Dr. Allchin is no more amongst us but his contribution to Indian Archaeology will always be remembered.

Another person who has been with Cambridge University after the retirement of Dr. Allchin is Professor Dilip K. Chakrabarti. I well recall my fist encounter with him. He was a student of M.A. Final at the University of Calcutta and the then Head of the Department invited me to be one of the examiners for the viva-voce of the students. I must say that I was surprised at the wide knowledge of young Chakrabarti. He had gone much beyond what was normally expected of him.

Chakrabarti has done a lot of field-work in India and has written many books and seminal papers. His latest book, *The Oxford Companion to Indian Archaeology*, is indeed monumental. For it, Professor Chakrabarti has been crowned with Gurdeva Ranade Award of the Indian Archaeological Society.

During the past half-a-century about a dozen scholars from USA have taken keen interest in the archaeology of the Indo-Pakistan subcontinent and here I shall refer to those with whom I have had close interaction. I begin with Professor Walter A. Fairservis who unfortunately is no more. His field-surveys in the western hilly tracts of Pakistan produced a great deal of material throwing light on various local pre-Harappan cultures. In particular, his excavation at Kile Ghul Mohammad revealed a neolithic-chalcolithic stage which was decidedly anterior to Harappan Culture. These survey-reports are highly valuable and his book, *The Roots of Ancient India,* was decidedly a very bold attempt at synthesizing the then available data relating to the protohistory of the subcontinent. Towards the end of his career he made bold attempts to decipher the Harappan script and published a book which, I am afraid, cut no ice.

My personal relations with Walter were very sweet and saucy. My wife and I well recall an occasion some five decades ago when we invited him and his then student Gregory L. Possehl to a dinner at our residence in New Delhi. After the meals and dessert, we served coffee and placed before the guests a plate full of dry fruits – almonds and cashew nuts. The poor guests tried hard on the fruits but could not crack them. I requested them to stop doing that and told them that the fruits were wooden imitation of the real. (Jaipur specializes in producing such nuts.) We, of course, apologized to the guests for playing the mischief on them, but, kind as ever, they took it light-heartedly. Thank God!

On the other hand, the hospitality offered by Walter and his wife during our visit to their place, some two hours' drive from New York, was most remarkable. They hosted a dinner in our honor and invited quite a few friends. Afterwards, they took us to a theatrical show in which their daughter played a vital role. Professor Fairservis was not a mere archaeologist, like me, but had varied interests. He was fond of riding horses and had a large stable for them.

In marked contrast to 'His Master's Voice' on the Indus script is that of his pupil, Professor Gregory L. Possehl, now located in Pennsylvania. In his book, *Indus Age; The Writing System,* he has admirably pieced together the available data and has added in unequivocal terms that none of the decipherers has succeeded in his attempt. His another book, *Indus Age: The beginnings,* is a very good compendium on the antecedents of the Harappan Civilization. He has two more books on the anvil, namely, *Indus Age: The Mature Harappan* and *Indus Age: The transformation.* (I do not know if any of these has since seen the light of the day.) In any case, today Professor Possehl stands out as a towering figure amongst American archaeologists who have worked on the Indus Civilization.

Professor Possehl and I have very good personal relations. During his visits to Delhi he has often been kind enough to visit our place for a lunch or dinner, forgiving us for the mischief we played on him and Professor Fairservis some fifty years ago (referred to earlier). I am sure he has also forgiven me for the adverse comments made in my book, *The Homeland of the Aryans: Evidence of Ṛigvedic Flora and Fauna and Archaeology.* In it, citing concrete evidence from the *Ṛigveda* itself, I countered his theory that the Ṛigvedic Aryans hailed from a cold-climate region.

At the other end of USA, in Berkley there used to be a very renowned scholar deeply steeped in the archaeology of the Indo-Pakistan subcontinent: Professor George F.

Dales. He carried out excellent field-work in south-western Pakistan and published many valuable papers. The most memorable of these, to my mind, is 'The Mythical Massacre at Mohenjo-daro'. Published in 1964, it completely torpedoed the 'Aryan Invasion' theory so emphatically advanced by Wheeler in 1947 in the report on his excavations at Harappa.

Dales and I were good friends and I must record one of my visits to Berkley. He and Mrs. Dales had invited me to a dinner at their place. I had thought that I would get some American dishes, but what turned up at the table was excellent Indian food – as good as I had ever before. When I asked George about the secret of the achievement, he pointed towards Dr. Mark Kenoyer, who was sharing the table with us. I was told that young Mark was in India for a very long time and took keen interest in Indian cuisine.

Today Mark is a Professor and one of the leading authorities in USA on the Indus Civilization. He has many important publications to his credit. His prolonged work at Harappa, in collaboration with Professors Richard H. Meadow and Rita P. Wright, has added new dimensions to our knowledge of the Harappan Civilization. In the lowest levels at the site he has discovered a phase (the Ravi Phase) which well antedated the Harappan and contributed towards the evolution of that civilization.

Professor Jim G. Shaffer of Case Western University is yet another outstanding archeologist in USA connected with Harappan studies. He is firmly of the view that there was no Aryan invasion and has published many seminal papers on this topic.

Though not an archaeologist in the narrow sense of the term, Dr. Pratapaditya Pal deserves mention here. He is an eminent art-historian and has published many valuable books on ancient Indian, Nepalese and Tibetan art. For a long time he was the Senior Curator of South

Asian Section of the Los Angeles County Museum of Art. He is also the General Editor of *Marg*, a renowned journal of Art, published in India. He has settled down in Los Angeles and I have the pleasure of meeting him and his family during my visits to that city.

Finally, I must refer to Dr. Monica L. Smith of University of California, Los Angeles. She and I came in touch with each other a few years ago when she began her excavation at Śiśupālgarh, a site which I had excavated way back in 1948. Her work at the 'Pillared Hall', located in the central part of the township has added new dimensions to our knowledge of the site. She is very nice and gentle and makes it a point to visit us after every field season and show on her computer the latest discoveries. She and her colleague, Professor R.K. Mohanty of Deccan College, Pune, have published a very good report on these excavations.

Our friendship is coming closer day by day. Thus, whenever my wife and I are on our annual visit to Los Angeles we make it a point to invite the Monica family – she, her husband and bright young son – to a dinner. In November 2010 she shared with us the Diwali festival at the place of our youngest son and daughter-in-law, Rakesh and Nishi. Present on the occasion were our middle son and his wife, Vrajesh and Bina, and many others including the family of my dear friend Professor Shiva Bajpai.

35

Looking Ahead

What has been done is but a part
Of what remains – things all apart.
Let not a praise then make us burst,
Complacency the spade nor rust.

The above is drawn from what I had written long back and I feel it is as valid today as ever before. Though we may take some delight in what we have achieved so far, the journey is still a long one and the goal far off. Hence no complacency, please.

At this point of time, I am thinking not in terms of the Archaeological Survey of India alone but of archaeology in the country as a whole. Thus, the first step that I believe ought to be taken is to have a brain-storming session, at least a week long, in which all those who have a stake in the matter should participate. These would obviously include not only the DGA, ASI and his senior officers but also Directors of the Achaeological Departments of all the States. Also to be invited to the discussions should be other distinguished archaeologists of the country, serving or retired, as well academics from Universities. I know this is a tall order but I do feel that there is no escape from it if a worthwhile review of the present situation is to be had and an in-detail planning for at least two decades is to be made.

Since the Survey is the largest of all the above-mentioed institutions, it is only appropriate that an initiative in the matter is taken by the Survey. It would no doubt involve a lot of hard work but I am sure the new enthusiastic Director General will be willing to take up this responsibility. The expenditure involved in this exercise will be insignificant compared to the results that are likely to be achieved. And with the Prime Minister himself holding charge of the Ministry of Culture, availability of funds for the purpose should pose no problem.

It is suggested that the topics, amongst others, that might be discussed at this brain-storming meeting could be:

(i) How to make the common man aware of his heritage. This is intended not only to make him knowledgable about the heritage, but also to kindle in him a sense of shared responsibility about the protection and preservation of the heritage. To achieve this objective, reasonably-priced yet well brought-out booklets be published in all Indian languages. Efforts should also be made to enlist the support of well-eastablished distributors so that the books reach their destinations. Schools and colleges should be targeted, because it is there that the future activists are born.

(ii) To achieve the former objective, exhibitions should also be arranged, dealing with the heritage, including new discoveries made through upcoming excavations. It would also be rewarding to organize traveling exhibitions, using the railways as well as fleets of buses, depending on the local situation. All this no doubt needs dedication on the part of the Center as well as the States. Support should also be elicited from the

Central and State Departments of Tourism, for they also stand to gain considerably from this dissemination of knowledge.

(iii) Wheras the standing monuments have been receiving a fair amount of attention in terms of preservation and upkeep, the excavated sites have not. Some of these sites, for example Kalibangan in Rajasthan, Lothal and Dholavira in Gujarat, are of world-wide importance, but their upkeep is far from satisfactory. At Dholavira, the structures are made of stones and, therefore, can withstand the vagaries of climate, but the structures at Lothal and Kalibangan, being of mud bricks are fast deteriorating. It is, therefore, necessary to hold an international workshop-seminar to discuss and devise ways and means to tackle this most important problem.

(iv) Due to the fast-growing residential complexes, many of the standing monuments and excavated sites are being encroached upon. For example, an excellent and well-planned site of the early historical times, namely, Śiśupālgarh in Orissa, is in danger of being completely overrun by modern buildings. In such cases, the land should be acquired, even if it means a good deal of expenditure. We must be well aware of the saying, "A stich in time saves nine". If the needful is not done now, I am sure, future generations will blame us for our apathy.

(v) All major excavated sites should not only be suitably conserved and preserved, but should be made visitor-friendly. Thus, exhaustive explanatory write-ups in Hindi, English and the local language should be provided in different parts of the site, as necessary. Further, each such site should also have a sizeable site-museum, wherein the excavated antiquities are suitably displayed and their significance highlighted by means of accompanying notes. Side by side, their contextual position should also be brought out by means of photographs of the site.

(vi) All the excavation-records relating to these sites as well as antiquities not displayed should be duly taken care of. In fact, as far as possible antiquities from the reserve collection should be made to rotate with some of those on the display. Further, and this is a very important point, digital documentation should be made of all the antiquities, photographs, drawings as well as other documents. These should be made available to bonafide researchers for study.

(vii) It is learnt with great regret that some of the glass photo-negatives which had been prepared more than half-a-century ago are fast decaying because of their pathetic storage. This is a serious matter and should be meticulously looked into. Even the recent non-glass negatives, in certain cases, are also suffering from the same malady. Immediate steps ought to be taken for their safe upkeep. In fact, it should be examined if and how these negatives can be copied through digital cameras, which may provide a much-needed standby.

36

Epilogue

The moving finger types, and moves on and on.
I am only a typist, the dictation-giver is
Someone Else.
However, the Ego thinks that it is the dictation-giver
since it holds that it makes the mind and intellect move.
But can these faculties function without the back-up of
the Life Force?
Surely not.
Indeed, isn't it the Life Force – call it Atman, God or by whichever
name you please –
that imparts Light and Sound to these functionaries?
And thence emanates the enlightened sound
which transforms itself into words.
They flow out unhindered
and the moving finger just types.
Through the Sadguru's Grace have I realized this great truth
that I am only the typist, the dictation-giver is
Someone Else.
Tathāstu!

Index

Chakravarti, Dr. N.P.: Wheeler's successor as D G, ASI 30, 226

Chakrabarti, Professor Dilip K.: Recently retired from Cambridge University, England; has published many valuable books including *The Oxford Companion to Indian Archaeology*, for which he was crowned with Gurudeva Ranade Award of the Indian Archaeological Society 236-37

Chandra, Professor Pramod: Professor, University of Chicago; my friend 128

Chandra, Professor Satish: Chairman UGC, gave funds for field-work 136

Chattopadhyaya, Prof. K.C. 164

Chitrakūṭa: Located on the bank of the Mandākinī, partly in Uttar Pradesh and partly in Madhya Pradesh. Occupation goes back to the earliest NBPW times 139, 142

Christie, Lady Agatha: Present at the International Conference on Asian Archaeology 103

Dales, Professor George F.: Was Professor of South Asian Archaeology at the University of California, Berkley, USA; carried out important field-work in Pakistan; amongst his various publications, the most seminal was 'The Mythical Massacre at Mohenjodaro' 238-39

Dani, Professor Ahmad Hasan.: Co-trainee with me at Taxila in 1944; well versed in Sanskrit and wrote an important book on the development of the early Brāhmī script; was decorated with honors by the Government of Pakistan 233-34

Danino, Dr. Michel.: French by birth, he has made India his home. A distinguished scholar who has written many books relating to Indian Archaeology and Culture, both in French and English, the latest being *The Lost River: On the trail of the Sarasvatī* 232

Deshpande, Dr. M.N.: My colleague in the Survey and a very close friend of mine; he was instrumental in my meeting Gurudeva Ranade; my successor as Director General ASI; helped me with funds for the 'Rāmāyaṇa Project' 73, 91-92, 98, 103, 132, 136, 138, 172, 221, 227

Dhavalikar, Professor M.K.: Has done a great deal of field-work on the chalcolithic cultures of

Notes

Notes

Notes

Notes